D0081713

# Theories of International Trade

*Theories of International Trade* utilizes the intertemporal open economy model as a case study to illuminate the phenomenon of recurrence and the problem of recurring doctrines in economic thought and analysis.

Klug examines the emergence of the intertemporal open economy model in the period between the 1920s and 1940s, and its rediscovery in the late 1970s and 1980s. The first part of the volume rigorously examines recurrence by presenting possible explanations for the phenomenon. In the second half of the book, the explanations developed are applied to the case of the intertemporal open economy model, dealing first with its modern development in the 1970s and 1980s, and then grounding the modern development of the model by means of illustrating how it originally developed over the period between the 1920s and 1940s.

This book will be of compelling interest to scholars in the history of economic thought, and to international economists in general.

**Adam Klug** was educated at Oxford and the LSE, and developed the theme of his book in his PhD thesis at Tel Aviv University. Before his untimely death in 2000, he was at the Department of Economics, Ben Gurion University, Beer Sheba, Israel. **Warren Young** is an Associate Professor of Economics at Bar Ilan University, Ramat Gan, Israel. **Michael D. Bordo** is Professor of Economics, Rutgers University, USA.

# Routledge explorations in economic history

1 **Economic Ideas and Government Policy**
Contributions to contemporary economic history
*Sir Alec Cairncross*

2 **The Organization of Labour Markets**
Modernity, culture and governance in Germany, Sweden, Britain and Japan
*Bo Stråth*

3 **Currency Convertibility**
The gold standard and beyond
*Edited by Jorge Braga de Macedo, Barry Eichengreen and Jaime Reis*

4 **Britain's Place in the World**
A historical enquiry into import controls 1945–1960
*Alan S. Milward and George Brennan*

5 **France and the International Economy**
From Vichy to the Treaty of Rome
*Frances M.B. Lynch*

6 **Monetary Standards and Exchange Rates**
*M.C. Marcuzzo, L. Officer and A. Rosselli*

7 **Production Efficiency in Domesday England, 1086**
*John McDonald*

8 **Free Trade and its Reception 1815–1960**
Freedom and trade: Volume I
*Edited by Andrew Marrison*

9  **Conceiving Companies**
Joint-stock politics in Victorian England
*Timothy L. Alborn*

10  **The British Industrial Decline Reconsidered**
*Edited by Jean-Pierre Dormois and Michael Dintenfass*

11  **The Conservatives and Industrial Efficiency, 1951–1964**
Thirteen wasted years?
*Nick Tiratsoo and Jim Tomlinson*

12  **Pacific Centuries**
Pacific and Pacific Rim economic history since the 16th century
*Edited by Dennis O. Flynn, Lionel Frost and A.J.H. Latham*

13  **The Premodern Chinese Economy**
Structural equilibrium and capitalist sterility
*Gang Deng*

14  **The Role of Banks in Monitoring Firms**
The case of the Crédit Mobilier
*Elisabeth Paulet*

15  **Management of the National Debt in the United Kingdom, 1900–1932**
*Jeremy Wormell*

16  **An Economic History of Sweden**
*Lars Magnusson*

17  **Freedom and Growth**
The rise of states and markets in Europe, 1300–1750
*S.R. Epstein*

18  **The Mediterranean Response to Globalization Before 1950**
*Sevket Pamuk and Jeffrey G. Williamson*

19  **Production and Consumption in English Households 1600–1750**
*Mark Overton, Jane Whittle, Darron Dean and Andrew Hann*

20  **Governance, The State, Regulation and Industrial Relations**
*Ian Clark*

21  **Early Modern Capitalism**
Economic and social change in Europe 1400–1800
*Edited by Maarten Prak*

22  **An Economic History of London, 1800–1914**
    *Michael Ball and David Sunderland*

23  **The Origins of National Financial Systems**
    Alexander Gerschenkron reconsidered
    *Edited by Douglas J. Forsyth and Daniel Verdier*

24  **The Russian Revolutionary Economy, 1890–1940**
    Ideas, debates and alternatives
    *Vincent Barnett*

25  **Land Rights, Ethno Nationality and Sovereignty in History**
    *Edited by Stanley L. Engerman and Jacob Metzer*

26  **An Economic History of Film**
    *Edited by John Sedgwick and Mike Pokorny*

27  **The Foreign Exchange Market of London**
    Development since 1900
    *John Atkin*

28  **Rethinking Economic Change in India**
    Labour and livelihood
    *Tirthankar Roy*

29  **The Mechanics of Modernity in Europe and East Asia**
    The institutional origins of social change and stagnation
    *Erik Ringmar*

30  **International Economic Integration in Historical Perspective**
    *Dennis M.P. McCarthy*

31  **Theories of International Trade**
    *Adam Klug*
    *Edited by Warren Young and Michael D. Bordo*

# Theories of International Trade

**Adam Klug**
**Edited by Warren Young and**
**Michael D. Bordo**
with the assistance of Daniel Schiffman

Routledge
Taylor & Francis Group

LONDON AND NEW YORK

First published 2006
by Routledge
2 Park Square, Milton Park, Abingdon, Oxon OX14 4RN

Simultaneously published in the USA and Canada
by Routledge
270 Madison Ave, New York, NY 10016

*Routledge is an imprint of the Taylor & Francis Group, an informa business*

© 2006 Deberah Davis-Klug and David Klug

Typeset in Times by Wearset Ltd, Boldon, Tyne and Wear
Printed and bound in Great Britain by TJ Digital, Padstow, Cornwall

*British Library Cataloguing in Publication Data*
A catalogue record for this book is available from the British Library

*Library of Congress Cataloging in Publication Data*
A catalog record for this book has been requested

ISBN10: 0-415-33607-4 (hbk)
ISBN10: 0-203-34004-3 (ebk)

ISBN13: 978-0-415-33607-9 (hbk)
ISBN13: 978-0-203-34004-2 (ebk)

# Contents

*Note on the author*                                                  viii
*Foreword by June Flanders*                                             ix
*Editorial introduction by Warren Young and Michael Bordo*           xiii

1   Introduction                                                        1

2   The problem of recurring doctrines in economics                    13

3   A survey and reconstruction of the modern
    intertemporal approach to international
    macroeconomics                                                     39

4   The research tradition in intertemporal international
    trade theories                                                     77

    *Notes*                                                           138
    *Bibliography*                                                    146
    *Index*                                                           161

# Note on the author

Adam Klug was born in London in 1954, grew up in Cambridge, won a scholarship to Oxford University from which he graduated in 1976 with a first class degree in History and Economics, followed by a Master's degree in Econometrics at the London School of Economics. After emigrating to Israel and working for two years in the Ministry of Energy, he enrolled for a PhD degree in Economics at Tel Aviv University. His PhD thesis entitled 'Precedents in the Theory of International Trade', done under the supervision of June Flanders, dealt in its first part with 'the problem of recurring doctrines in economics'. This drew on examples from the research tradition in intertemporal trade, and other numerous instances found throughout economics. He expanded it to take into account the models of Bachelard and Laudan for change in scientific theories. Klug's work now appears here for the first time in published form, with references brought up to date by the editors, Michael Bordo and Warren Young.

The second part of Klug's PhD thesis dealt with German buybacks of American loans made in the 1920s. This was later published in 1993 as a classic study in the monograph series Princeton Studies in International Finance under the aegis of Peter Kenen, with whom he spent two years as a postdoctoral fellow. There followed two years at Rutgers University, working with Michael Bordo and Eugene White.

In 1994 Klug returned to Israel to join the newly expanding Department of Economics at Ben Gurion University. There he tackled a number of diverse problems in economic history and political economy, such as sterling and the Suez crisis, German voting patterns on tariffs, and the role of economic elites. He died in 2000 after a brave three-year struggle with pancreatic cancer, while continuing to work productively on several papers which have been published posthumously.

# Foreword

One of the Sages of Israel, Rabbi Chanina, in the Babylonian Talmud, said: 'I have learned much from my teachers, more from my fellows, and most of all from my students.' I share this view. Working with Adam Klug as he crafted his dissertation was a trip down familiar and unfamiliar roads and side roads. Adam Klug came to me in the mid-1980s to do a thesis in international economics. There followed a period of tatonnement, of searching, struggling and coping, culminating in a thesis in November 1989, of which the present volume constitutes roughly half.

At the time that he was looking for a topic, intertemporal international economics was coming into fashion, not least at Tel Aviv University. Economists who felt the need to explain everything rationally were coping with the phenomenon of the heavy international borrowing by developing countries. The occasional excesses of such borrowing and the resulting crises were very much in the lay news, as well as in the forefront of concern in academic and financial circles. Much of the blame for the crises was laid, at least in some circles, at the foot of the bankers of the North who, floating in pools of liquidity produced by huge oil revenues, were haranguing and cajoling representatives of governments and agencies of developing countries, almost forcing credits on them. Subsequent inflation and skyrocketing of interest rates made repayment, and even servicing, well-nigh impossible for some debtor countries. At the same time, economists began to look for explanations and an understanding that was less ad hoc than this, and started to develop models of rational and efficient borrowing, which was soon labelled 'intertemporal international trade'.

Having come to economics with a First in History from Oxford, Adam began to dig into the background of concern with international borrowing and to ask whether the issue was as new a phenomenon as it appeared. Of course it was not – the large capital movements from England to the Americas in the nineteenth and early twentieth centuries were not only well known and well documented, they also formed the basis of some highly regarded and extremely fruitful study at Harvard by Frank Taussig and his students – including Jacob Viner, Harry Dexter White and John Williams. These studies, carried out in the interwar period, were concerned primarily with the mechanism of adjustment, raising the question of how the capital transfers were effected by current account imbalances in the opposite direction. (I am not aware of any studies of how the transfer of the repayment was effected.) They took as given the proposition that British capital could be more fruitfully invested abroad than at home, and that the borrowing countries, or, more accurately, companies, such as the railroads, were happy to float their bonds in the London market without thinking particularly about the overall structure and time path of the balance of payments. They viewed the issues essentially as special cases of the transfer problem and the theory of what was then called 'the balance of payments adjustment mechanism'. It never seems to have occurred to them at the time to question the rationality of either the borrowers or the lenders in that episode; although Keynes questioned it in his 1931 testimony to the Macmillan Committee. There, he deplored the openness of the British financial markets to foreign firms, diverting funds from domestic investment. Keynes's criticism was aimed at a foreign investment bias while British growth was retarded by lack of access to credit markets; and this, while Britain was experiencing widespread unemployment.

But at roughly the same time, Adam discovered that there was a literature which, at a very formal level, dealt with the issue of the rationality of incurring foreign debt; debt which had, of course, to be repaid with interest. Is it rational for a poor country (or agent) to incur debt now in the (knowledge) hope that it can be repaid out of the resulting increase in output? Does the current account ever have to be in balance? Setting formal conditions for the existence and amount of such intertemporal balancing of payments was the major thrust of neglected work by Mosak (1944) and others.

The question then becomes, why was this literature neglected at the time – and later? And why did the same questions re-emerge 50 years later? This is a special case of general issues of recurrence – in general, and specifically in economics. And Adam went down that winding path to produce a brilliant chapter on recurrence. In the 1930s, international capital movements were driven primarily by speculative movements, political and economic flights of funds, and the generally chaotic nature of international payments, exacerbated by banking crises, competitive devaluation, and, of course, massive unemployment. (See Nurkse's definitive study in *International Currency Experience*.) The approach of Mosak *et al.* would have yielded, at that time, very little of what Adam calls 'externally interesting theorems which are economically meaningful'.

And in the quarter century following the end of the Second World War, that is, in the Bretton Woods period, it seemed natural for the United States to be lending, investing and donating resources abroad for both civilian and military purposes (it was the richest kid on the block), while maintaining a current account surplus (its massive production engine was producing goods which everybody wanted, while the rest of the world had little to offer in return; exports plus imports constituted less than 10 per cent of GNP). Furthermore, the dollar was de facto the major international currency, and supplying dollars to the rest of the world implied a large short-term capital inflow. It was only later, in the 1970s and 1980s, when the current account began to move into deficit, that expectations regarding the non-sustainability of the current system brought it to an abrupt close. (At that point, the dollar went off gold, but the world did not go off the dollar. But that is another story.)

This was not an environment conducive to consideration of long-term patterns of trade by profit- and utility-maximizing individuals with complete knowledge and perfect foresight. Again 'externally interesting theorems which are economically meaningful' were not looked for in an Arrow–Debreu context. (When I was a graduate student, *after* the inter-war period, my professors were asking whether there was any way that private foreign investment could ever again exist!)

By the 1980s the world was ready for a recurrence, a rebirth of the theory. The fashion of establishing the microeconomic basis of macroeconomics, the compulsion to concentrate attention on the utility-maximizing individual made it conceptually appealing and gave it respectability. The crises in a number of debt-ridden countries gave it immediate, 'external' (empirical) clout. The proliferation of data and computational power gave it a mass of empirical material to manipulate and to study. And there it was, as is spelled out and described in this book.

A final few words, musings, about recurrence. In physics, Hawking considers himself the successor to Einstein, who is the successor to Newton. Physicists do indeed stand, as Newton is alleged to have been the first to remark, on the shoulders of giants. Kuhnian revolutionary theory to the contrary notwithstanding, Hawking thinks of himself as containing Einstein who engulfed Newton and 'portrayed modern cosmology as a comprehensive system that did not replace his predecessors' models, but instead accommodated them as special cases' (Patricia Fara (2003) *Newton: The Making of Genius*, London: Picador, 269).

In economics, this is much less true. In his introductory chapter, Adam cites Schumpeter as saying that economists need to study their history; physicists don't because they haven't abandoned it (a former colleague in economics, then married to a chemist, used to complain that economists don't need to study the history of economics, just as the chemists didn't study the history of chemistry). But economists (and mathematicians) do study their history. Ours is not a discipline that builds, that cumulates. Fashions come – and go – and come again. (It is only a slight exaggeration to say that in every generation we reinvent the wheel.) Thus, we need to explain recurrence: the price-specie-mechanism was enunciated by Isaac Gervaise in 1720, repeated by Hume (1752) and metamorphosized into the monetary approach to the balance of payments in 1976. This is the formalization and 'rhetoric' (quoting Klug citing McCloskey) that produced in 1974 Barro's subjectively original version of Ricardo's speculation about the equivalence of borrowing and taxation (an equivalence, by the way, which Ricardo, in a rare burst of 'realism', alleged was not in practice 'likely to be observed').

As for Adam Klug, I would not venture to predict what his fertile mind might have produced, had his life not been cut short.

Professor M. June Flanders
The Eitan Berglas School of Economics, Tel Aviv University

# Editorial introduction

This book, which is based in part on Adam Klug's doctoral dissertation, supervised by June Flanders, deals with the phenomenon of recurrence and the problem of recurring doctrines in economic thought and analysis, by focusing on the case study of the intertemporal open economy model, and how it was developed in the period between the 1920s and 1940s, and rediscovered in the late 1970s and 1980s. The phenomenon of recurrence is bound up with what can be termed 'the idea of a precursor', and the existence of a 'precursor' would imply that some form of 'recurrence' has taken place. However, as the historian of science Ted Porter has noted, the idea of a precursor could be regarded as a mistaken category, and thus the study of precursors *on their own account*, or for that matter, recurrence per se, should not be of serious interest, as Roy Weintraub recently put it, to historians of economic thought. Adam Klug seemed to intuitively understand this early on, and thus he attempted to explain *why* the phenomenon of recurrence occurs.

Klug's analytical approach is two-fold. In the first part of the book (Chapters 1 and 2), he dealt with recurrence by presenting possible explanations for the phenomenon, as against a 'laundry list' of examples; in the second part (Chapters 3 and 4), he applied these explanations to the case of the intertemporal open economy model, dealing first with its modern development in the 1970 and 1980s, and then grounding the modern development of the model with how it originally developed over the period between the 1920s and 1940s.

With regard to the phenomenon of 'recurrence', it is interesting to note that it is not only 'economic theories and concepts', as Klug put it, that are involved. In a recent paper, Reinert (2000) showed that the question of the use of mathematics in economics is also an example of a 'recurrent' phenomenon. He cited a book published in 1770 by the German economist Meyen whose title asked the question: 'why is it that economics so far has gained so few advantages from physics and mathematics?'; in the book, posing similar arguments to those of Nassau Senior (1836) and Jevons (1871) advocating the use of mathematics as the language of economics.

Moreover, the debate regarding the utilization of mathematics in economics is also an example of the recurrence phenomenon. This can be seen by reference to the debate started by Novick in the November 1954 issue of *Review of Economics and Statistics*, which involved Samuelson, Klein, Duesenberry, Chipman, Tinbergen, Champernowne, Solow, Dorfman and Koopmans, and continued on into 1955, with the input of Wilson and Stigler, among others. Over four decades later, Blaug (1998) renewed the debate when he wrote:

> Modern economics is 'sick'. Economics has increasingly become an intellectual game played for its own sake and not for its practical consequences. Economists have gradually converted the subject into a sort of social mathematics in which analytical rigor as understood in math departments is everything and empirical relevance (as understood in physics departments) is nothing. If a topic cannot be tackled by formal modeling, it is simply consigned to the intellectual underworld. To pick up a copy of *American Economic Review* or *Economic Journal*, not to mention *Econometrica* or *Review of Economic Studies*, these days is to wonder whether one has landed on a strange planet in which tedium is the deliberate objective of professional publication. Economics was condemned a century ago as 'the dismal science', but the dismal science of yesterday was a lot less dismal than the soporific scholasticism of today.

Whether Klug would have agreed with Blaug on this is a moot point, as, Klug's focus was not upon 'diversity' but upon the 'unity' of 'economic theories and concepts'. He wrote 'I would argue ... that the recurring nature of economic doctrines suggests the existence not of diversity, but of unity, an inner continuity which suggests that there exists a "deep structure" ... which binds economic theories and concepts together'; 'theories and concepts' which may 'resurface' or are 'rediscovered'. In fact, by hypothesizing such a 'deep structure', Klug was reacting against the prevailing conventional wisdom amongst non-economists regarding economics as an 'incomplete science' (e.g. Leshan and Margenau 1982).

Moreover, Klug was taking a position similar to that of Debreu, who wrote (1986: 1268):

> In close relationship with its axiomatization, economic theory became concerned with more fundamental questions and also more abstract. The problem of existence of a general economic equilibrium is representative of those trends. The model proposed by Walras in 1874–77 sought to explain the observed state of an economy as an equilibrium resulting from the interaction of a large number of small agents through markets for commodities. Over the century that followed its publication, that model came to be a common intellectual framework for many economists, theorists as well as practitioners.

This eventually made it compelling for mathematical economists to specify assumptions that guarantee the existence of the central concept of Walrasian theory. Only through such a specification, in particular, could the explanatory power of the model be fully appraised. The early proofs of existence of Wald in 1935–36 were followed by a pause of nearly two decades, and then by the contemporary phase of developments beginning in 1954 with the articles of Arrow and Debreu, and of Lionel McKenzie.

In the reformulation that the theory of general economic equilibrium underwent, it reached a high level of abstraction. From that new viewpoint a deeper understanding both of the mathematical form and of the economic content of the model was gained. Its role as a benchmark was also perceived more clearly, a role which prompted extensions to incomplete markets for contingent commodities, externalities, indivisibilities, increasing returns, public goods, temporary equilibrium…

In an unanticipated, yet not unprecedented, way greater abstraction brought Walrasian theory closer to concrete applications. When different areas of the field of computable general equilibrium were opened to research … the algorithms of Scarf included in their lineage proofs of existence of a general economic equilibrium by means of fixed point theorems.

A few years later, Debreu went even further when he wrote (1991: 3):

The greater logical sense of solidity of more recent analyses has contributed to the rapid contemporary construction of economic theory. It has enabled researchers to build on the work of their predecessors and to accelerate the cumulative process in which they are participating.

He went on to say (1991: 3, 6):

But a Grand Unified Theory will remain out of the reach of economics, which will keep appealing to a large collection of individual theories. Each one of them deals with a certain range of phenomena that it attempts to understand and to explain. When it has acquired axiomatic form, its explicit assumptions delimit its domain of applicability and make illegitimate overstepping of its boundary flagrant. Some of those theories take a comprehensive view of an economic system bring insights into the solutions of several global problems … The bond that ties economists together in the study of a common subject has not been tested only by differences in methodologies. It is also been tried by differences in ideologies. In their endeavors to make their field into a science, economists must renounce a favorite mode of thinking-wishful thinking; they must be impartial spectators of a play in which they are the actors. While they attempt to keep that inhuman stance, they are pressed to give immediate answers to societal questions of immense complexity and thereby to abandon the exacting slowness of the step-by-step scientific approach. Divisions according to methodologies and ideologies, criticism from outside and from inside, and intellectual fashions that sweep our discipline make each one of its steady developments remarkable.

On the basis of the views which he expressed in this book, Klug's position is clearly closer to that of Debreu, than to that of Blaug, as expressed above.

In Chapter 2, Klug provides three possible explanations for recurrence, based upon the works of Laudan (1977, 1981a, 1981b, 1984, 1986), Fleck (1935 [1976]), Schumpeter (1954) and Bachelard (1951) respectively. He noted that, according to Laudan 'theories recur ostensibly in conjunction with continuous debate over conceptual problems. In fact, this reflects a dialectic of research traditions.' He was willing to consider Laudan's explanation, despite the many critiques of Laudan's approach (Doppelt 1981; Krips 1981; McMullin 1979; Musgrave 1981; Newton-Smith 1981). He interpreted the position of Fleck and Schumpeter to be that 'theories recur because a thought style reappears'. Indeed, as Schumpeter wrote, when discussing the development of monetary theory (1954: 706, 712):

the advance of economics has been and is being impaired by ... recurrent losses of previous accumulation of knowledge. We know of course that history repeats itself. But it is amazing and perhaps a little sad to observe that economists, swayed by the prevailing humors of the hour, also repeat themselves and that, blissfully ignorant of their predecessors, they believe in each case that they are making unheard of discoveries and building up a brand-new monetary science. However, there are some things to be gleaned from a history of analysis.

In Chapter 2, Klug presented Bachelard's position to be that 'theories recur because of the continuity of certain basic scientific concepts, often linked to a reaction against some particularly monolithic body of ideas which has outlived its usefulness'. Indeed, Klug was possibly the first to apply the ideas of Bachelard (1951), as they relate to recurrence, unity and 'deep structure', to the development of economic thought. Later writers, such as McAllister (1996) and Miller (1996) have dealt with the notions of connectedness, universality (unity, unified theories) and consistency, and their treatment *complements* that of Bachelard, but their ideas have been applied only recently to economics (e.g. Lee and Lloyd 2002).

In Chapter 3, Klug surveys the literature on the intertemporal approach to international economics as it developed in the 1970s and

1980s. As background he covers the literature as it existed circa the mid 1960s. The prevalent approach then was the Mundell–Fleming model, which integrated the balance of payments into the prevailing Keynesian IS–LM model, by explicitly accounting for an open capital account, provided new insights into the debate over fixed versus flexible exchange rates, and of the role of monetary and fiscal policy in an open economy. Mundell–Fleming also opened up important avenues for further research because it did not consider the intertemporal influence of capital flows on capital accumulation, nor the intertemporal allocation of resources, and it assumed that the current account had to always be balanced.

Klug illustrates how the application of intertemporal economics by Frenkel, Razin, Helpman, Obstfeld and others in the 1970s and 1980s, based on Irving Fisher's *Theory of Interest* (1930), Milton Friedman's (1957) permanent income hypothesis, the theory of capital, and the then revolutionary theory of rational expectations, led to the conclusion that the current account need only be balanced over time. This result, as well as others nicely described in the chapter, completely revolutionized the approach taken to many of the perennial problems of international economics, such as the transfer problem and changes in the terms of trade.

Since the late 1980s, the intertemporal approach that Klug skilfully surveyed has solidified its hold on the economics profession and on the way policy-makers at the IMF and other institutions view international economic relations. The essence of this new approach is well exposited in Obstfeld and Rogoff's *Foundations of International Macroeconomics* (1996). This book integrates the many contributions Klug surveyed in Chapter 3.

An important development that has evolved since Adam Klug's tragic and premature death, is the introduction of imperfect competition into the intertemporal approach. The literature of the 1980s was in large part based on the assumption of perfect competition and the law of one price. An extensive body of empirical research since then has cast doubt on the assumption that international arbitrage quickly integrated both goods and asset markets. Based on such evidence, Obstfeld and Rogoff and others have been emphasizing the roles of price rigidities and price discrimination across national markets. This new thrust of research, although well within the paradigm spelled out by Klug, is propelling the intertemporal approach in directions not completely foreseen two decades ago.

Chapter 4 is a major contribution to the history of economic thought. In this chapter, Klug carefully documents the doctrinal antecedents of the intertemporal approach in the works of Mosak, Hayek, Iversen and others. He convincingly explains how these developments were subsequently ignored by Samuelson, Hicks and Modigliani – writers whose work set the pace for the postwar, largely static approach to international economics.

The book in our view should be of compelling interest to both scholars in the history of economic thought and to international economists in general who should be aware of the historical antecedents of the models which they teach and apply.

Warren Young<br>Michael Bordo

# 1    Introduction

> I came to believe that almost all differences of opinion when analysed,
> were differences of method ... He who can throw most light upon the
> subject of method, will do most to forward that alliance among the most
> advanced intellects and characters of the age, which has been the object of
> all my endeavours.
>
> J.S. Mill, *Earlier Letters* (1963: 78–9)

In his magisterial *History of Economic Analysis*, Schumpeter stated that:
'Filiation of Scientific Ideas – the process by which men's efforts to understand economic phenomena, produce, improve and pull down analytic
structures ... has met with more inhibitions in our field than it has in
almost all others' (Schumpeter 1954: 6). One of the characteristics of this
slow rate of progress was the fact that, according to Schumpeter: 'Much
more than in physics have results been lost on the way or remained in
abeyance for centuries. We shall meet with some instances that are little
short of appalling.'

It is for this reason that Schumpeter regarded the study of the history of
economic thought as a relevant activity for the economist:

> Stimulating suggestions and useful if disconcerting lessons are much
> more likely to come to the economist who studies the history of his
> science than to the physicist who can, in general, rely on the fact
> that almost nothing worth while has been lost in the work of his
> predecessors.

Schumpeter did not in fact develop most of his work on this premise. He
pointed out many fascinating examples of forgotten and obscure anticipa-
tion of important ideas, such as Sir Thomas More on oligopoly or Laun-
hardt's original proof of Hotelling's theorem on marginal cost pricing
(Schumpeter 1954: 308, 948). Nevertheless, Schumpeter did not catalogue
and classify this phenomenon exactly, nor did he attempt to arrive at a systematic understanding of it. I therefore intend to make a study of this

phenomenon in economics, which I call the 'prevalence of recurring doctrines'. I shall be concerned later in this book to dispel any doubts the reader may have concerning the importance and pervasiveness of this phenomenon in the history of economics, but with the exception of one chapter, I shall not deal with this problem at a high level of generality. The economic field has simply become so vast that one must concentrate on a limited, esoteric aspect in order to exhibit the detail required in a single work. In addition, when working in this area one wants not only to interpret the evolution of economic ideas but to make some kind of contribution to the sum of our historical knowledge. Instead, I have focused on intertemporal theories of the balance of payments and exchange rates. These doctrines are of considerable potential and practical importance since they deal with world issues of pressing concern. On the other hand, they are quite typical of the formal nature of much recent macroeconomics, and therefore many conclusions apply to more than just this narrow subject. It turns out, however, that the earlier versions of these doctrines which appeared in the 1920s and 1930s have been almost completely forgotten.

I would now like to give the reader a feeling for the ostensible novelty of work in international macroeconomics that took place in the 1980s, and for the even more surprising manifestations of similar ideas in the 1920s, 1930s and 1940s.

## The 'new' intertemporal international macroeconomics

In the 1980s, a 'new' approach came to dominate theoretical research on the open economy. This literature appeared to represent a complete break with the past of the subject. In fact, I shall devote much of this book to arguing that much of the 'new' approach of the 1980s had a history and even a prehistory. Yet to anyone brought up on the material which postdates the *General Theory*, the work of the 1980s will appear strikingly novel. The reason for this is the insistence that all explanations of fluctuations of the current account or exchange rates should be consistent with optimizing behaviour on the part of individual economic agents, where this behaviour is of the type to be found in microeconomic theory. At first blush this appears to be nothing more than an application of what has been termed the 'microfoundations of macroeconomics' to the problems of an open economy. In fact, as I shall be at pains to point out later, what was involved was not merely the 'opening up' of a particular class of macroeconomic models, but a fundamental change in the way economists thought about the concepts which were the object of their analyses. The phenomenon, whose behaviour is itself to be explained by the theory, the balance of payments itself, had a different significance under this approach. As will become apparent later in the exposition, the balance of payments is now held to record acts of intertemporal trade between countries, i.e. exchanges of present for future commodities. Since rational far-sighted individuals, behaving in the manner dictated by capital theory, would wish to continue such trades over time, there is, according to this approach, no theoretical reason for policy-makers to worry about the existence of current account deficits. Thus it has been stated that:

> As for the question of whether one should worry about the current account situation, it is clear that there is Pareto optimal intergenerational allocation of resources when an optimizing private sector is left to itself in a competitive framework with perfect foresight, provided that there are tradable assets. The role of government is simply to transfer income across generations according to social norms.
>
> (Razin 1982: 391)

This, of course, follows from the fact that 'in these models, a large current account deficit is not necessarily a "problem", it is a reaction of the market, given the availability of international financial markets, to an underlying disturbance to the economy' (Stockman 1988: 54).

It is no exaggeration to say that these ideas appear to constitute a complete change with regard to the analysis of balance of payments or exchange rates which was prevalent throughout the history of economics. As documented extensively by Flanders (1989) there was from about 1800 until at least the early 1960s only one underlying model of the open economy – the most simple model of the monetary approach to the balance of payments (for example Dornbusch 1973: Sec. 1). This model has, of course, been drastically altered in many ways, such as elaborating the money supply process to take account of fractional reserve banking (Taussig and the Harvard School – see Flanders 1989: Ch. 7), introducing price rigidity (the early Keynesians), adding a nontraded goods sector (Hawtrey 1928, among many others), or allowing portfolio capital movements of various types. Yet, none of these elaborations had anything new to say about the determinants of the underlying behaviour which ultimately cause the adjustments which take place in the external sector. No notice was ever taken of the idea, expressed by the great poet William Blake, that a theory should be determined at some fundamental 'molecular' level: 'Art and science cannot exist but in minutely organized particulars.' No attempt was apparently made to open up the black box called 'the balance of payments adjustment mechanism' and look at the cogs and wheels inside. Furthermore, an equilibrium condition, namely current account balance, was always imposed on the external sector in these accounts, although, as stated above, there is nothing in individual optimizing behaviour which justifies this procedure.

Yet the adoption of a reductionist research programme – so called because of the emphasis on individual behaviour, and the consequent emphasis on intertemporal preferences as determinants of behaviour in the external sector – is not the only major change of emphasis which has occurred. The attitude towards government intervention is also a basic change, in particular because discretionary policy in the external sector is an old tradition which predates the Keynesian Revolution. It is true that those of the classical economists who saw themselves as successors of Ricardo and the Currency School in particular believed that under ideal conditions the mechanism of adjustment was automatic and imposed no costs on the economy. To the extent that frictions occurred, they believed that these could be overcome by a suitable design of the monetary system which, once in place, would allow events to take their natural and desirable course with no intervention by the authorities. As described in Fetter's great work of scholarship (Fetter 1965) this attempt at creating an automatic currency system, embodied in Peel's Act of 1844, was unsuccessful. As a result of this failure, the doctrines of Bagehot's Lombard Street (1872) were eventually accepted, and the monetary authorities have since then practised a degree of discretionary policy in the external sector, in order to restore trade or current account equilibrium. The paradigmatic example of such intervention is the use, by central banks, of their discount rates to control payments imbalances during the classical gold standard period (1880–1914). Later, the scope for intervention was extended. Conversely, under the impact of the Great Depression, it was suggested that governments could also use external instruments to affect employment (an early example being Joan Robinson 1936), and finally in the 1960s it was argued that internal and external balance should be pursued simultaneously, and that the appropriate instruments (i.e. fiscal and monetary policy), would vary according to circumstances. (A classic reference is Mundell 1962.)

While the monetary approach to the balance of payments, popular in the 1970s, was sceptical about the scope for policy intervention or the real effects of devaluations (Dornbusch 1973: Sec. 1), even it did not mark a fundamental departure from the tradition sketched above. In comparing this with other approaches, Frenkel and Johnson wrote that 'the monetary approach should, in principle, give an answer no different to that provided by a correct analysis in terms of the other accounts' (Frenkel and Johnson 1976: 22). What occurred was a change in emphasis from the current account to the monetary flows to be found 'below the line in the capital account' (Frenkel and Johnson 1976: 23). Even the most sophisticated versions of the monetary approach did not depart from all of the previous literature, in the sense that ultimately the economy was required to be in a long-run equilibrium where the current account was balanced (Frenkel and Mussa 1985: 690–1). Not surprisingly then, the monetary approach, when augmented by some type of sticky wage or price mechanism in the goods sector, replicated many of the positive conclusions and policy recommendations of the 'Neo-Keynesian' era (see, for example, Dornbusch 1980: Ch. 9). We can conclude then that most analyses of the balance of payments, from the classical economists to the monetary approach of the 1970s, were essentially of a piece. The first reason for this is that they all used a concept of equilibrium which required trade or current account balance. This may refer to the short run, as in the elasticities approach or in income–expenditure models, or to the long-run dynamics only, as in some of the more sophisticated versions of the Mundell–Fleming model (which was the workhorse of international macroeconomics in the 1960s), but this definition of equilibrium was nevertheless always an integral part of the analysis. This, as I have stated above, is emphatically not the case with the 'new' intertemporal approach of the 1980s. The second reason for this apparent break with the past is that while some form of intervention, at the very least by the central bank, was advocated between the time of the Currency/Banking School controversy in the 1840s and the monetary approach in the 1970s, such discretion was trenchantly criticized in the 1980s by many writers using an optimizing approach.[1] Of course, this literature does not completely rule out the need for government intervention, but to the extent that it does, it is for a completely different reason from those previously envisaged. The reason given is the lack of complete futures markets in the economy. The last characteristic of this literature is, of course, as stressed above, its uncompromising methodological individualism, a term originated by Hayek and Popper, which means in this context that economic processes should be explained by being deduced from the principles governing the behaviour of the participating individual economic actors, given that within the situation they find themselves in, they are subject to certain constraints.[2] It is from the application of this reductionist principle that all else follows. However, as I have stressed above, this has not necessarily meant the mere replication of the result to be found in other areas of economics with strong microfoundations but also the discovery of new insights into the determinants of the balance of payments.

## The unknown antecedents

Everything I have said so far suggests that the work I have been surveying was something completely new, sui generis in the history of economics. This was certainly the view of the New Palgrave's entry on 'International Finance', which states that work based on microeconomic foundations and rational economic behaviour began in the 1980s (Obstfeld 1987). It is hardly surprising that the contributor made this statement, since previous accounts of the historical development of the subject, from Viner's classic (Viner 1937), through Kenen's survey (Kenen 1985) of work covering the 1930s to the 1980s suggest nothing else. The main contention of this book will be that this is not so; in fact, I shall try to show that the theory of the 1980s had been substantially anticipated by previous writers, mainly in the interwar years. A number of economists wrote in the modern vein – Frank

A. Fetter, Carl Iversen, Friedrich von Hayek, Pierre-Louis Reynaud, Ragnar Nurkse, Jacob Mosak and Oskar Lange. Of these, only Hayek has a strong influence on today's economics, and only he, Lange, Nurkse and Fetter are remembered.[3] However, along with the others, nothing they wrote along the lines of an intertemporal theory of the balance of payments has found its way into any recent citations or apparently provided any inspiration for the thinking of today's economists. This type of phenomenon, which, as stated by Schumpeter above, is not at all uncommon in the history of economics, has profound implications for any attempt to construct grand models of the development of the subject, or to import such schema from the history of science. It is these issues which I ultimately wish to approach by means of this particular case study.

Hegel wrote that 'the narration of a number of philosophical opinions as they have arisen and manifested themselves in time is dry and destitute of interest' (Hegel 1912: 307). I believe that this is as true for the history of economics as Hegel held it to be for philosophy. I therefore use a number of tools of intellectual inquiry, and consciously adopt more than one intellectual orientation, in order to make my interpretation as fertile as possible.

## Exegesis and explanation

There are, in effect, two goals which a study of this kind attempts to achieve. These are a clear exegesis of the doctrines concerned, and an accurate explanation of why they were held by particular economists at a particular time. For example, when studying the famous and notoriously difficult chapter of Ricardo's Principles, 'On Machinery', one should do two things: first, attempt to elucidate what Ricardo was trying to do, perhaps by means of a heuristic model, as in Barkai (1986); second, set out the machinery question in its historical context, linking it in particular to the economic problems of the time (as in Berg 1980). (To my mind, this is an exemplary work of its kind, which forcefully reminds the reader just how new and terrifying the industrial machinery was at the time of the Industrial Revolution.)

In this example, it turns out that economic theory is useful for the performance of exegesis, since it points out logical flaws or hidden assumptions in the work of an economist, while social and economic history are necessary adjuncts of explanation since they highlight particular areas of emphasis in a writer's work which may otherwise seem anachronistic, and explain why he came to hold particular views. Thus, on the one hand, Ricardo's arithmetical examples have been clarified, and on the other, his emphasis on particular aspects of the problem has been explained by the historical context in which he worked.

Researchers in the history of economic thought may attempt either exegesis or explanation. As pointed out by Laudan in his *Progress and its*

*Problems* (Laudan 1977), intellectual history has concentrated largely on exegesis, and I do not think that the history of economics has been an exception to this rule. In this book, both an exegesis of rediscovered texts and an explanation as to why these doctrines have reappeared are attempted.

## Explanations in the history of economic thought

Epistemology identifies various modes of explanation, such as causal explanation in the sciences, functional explanation in sociology and historical explanation, which is in a class of its own. It is not clear, however, what type of explanation is appropriate in the history of economic thought, since all of them appear to be relevant; economics has tried to offer scientific deductive explanations of phenomena, yet in order to explain its development, we must explain the actions of individuals in the past who are organized in a profession which has a social dimension like other professions. It therefore seems that any mode of explanation, causal (i.e. scientific), functional (i.e. sociological), or historical could constitute the correct methodological approach. Some of the other fields on the fringes of economics have adopted clear-cut methodological positions; for example, the 'counterfactual' methods of the New Economic History are obvious and conscious examples of causal explanation, while the 'evolutionary theory of the firm' invented by Nelson and Winter is an attempt at applying the functional explanations of sociology and biology to economics.[4] In the history of economic thought, on the other hand, no dominant mode of explanation is apparent, nor has any rationale been worked out as to what mode of explanation is appropriate. In fact, while practitioners in the field have made methodological analyses of economic theory as a whole, they have left their own subject curiously immune from such scrutiny. Perhaps one has no choice but to be eclectic, given the interdisciplinary nature of the subject. My response is to use various explanatory methodologies. Each in turn may help to illuminate the problem of recurrence in general, and the recurrence of intertemporal theories of the balance of payments in particular.

## Types of exegesis in the history of economic thought

It might be thought that exegesis is a less problematic concept than explanation from the cognitive point of view. This is true as long as exegesis is regarded as consisting merely of '*explication des textes*' and placing them in the correct chronological order. There are, however, a number of ideal types of exegesis in the history of ideas, and their relevance to a particular study depends on the specific questions we are asking about a given text. In a brilliant essay, the philosopher Richard Rorty (1984) has classified some of the types or genres, as he calls them, which are to be found in the history of philosophy. They are, I think, equally relevant to the history of economics, and can be used to describe clearly and succinctly much of this thesis. The first such category is that of 'rational reconstructions' of the arguments of deceased scholars, in the hope of treating these thinkers as contemporaries, as colleagues with whom one can exchange views. Attempts at constructing models of pre-analytic systems of thought clearly fall into this category. Such rational reconstructions correct past mistakes and highlight anticipations of recent doctrines. I should point out that the term as used here is subtly different from its use by Popper, Lakatos and their followers.[5] For them, the object of the rational reconstruction is to recover a synthetic 'problem situation' faced by a researcher. This consists of his objectives and those logical interrelations between them which are manipulated by his rational actions. This type of procedure has often led to the accusation that Popperians rewrite history to suit their philosophical views. Whatever the truth of these criticisms by Feyerabend (1975: Sec. 16) and others, Rorty's version of the concept of rational reconstruction, since it explicitly recognizes the way in which past texts are rewritten by the historian of ideas, is immune from them. Of greater importance, however, are 'historical reconstructions', which describe the views of the dead in their own terms. Such reconstructions permit a dialogue between, say, Malthus and Ricardo or Marshall and Wicksteed, but they must obey a constraint formulated once by the political philosopher Quentin Skinner: 'No agent can eventually be said to have meant or done something which he could never be brought to accept as a correct description of what he had meant or done' (Skinner 1969: 28).

Skinner stresses that such accounts must be written in such a way that they exclude the clearly absurd possibility that a scholar's views were themselves dependent on the use of criteria of description and classification not available to the scholar himself. Models for such an account in our field would be Patinkin's painstaking account of the development of Keynes's thought, using as a reference point not later 'Keynesian' models, but Keynes's own notes and letters, and Rymes's reconstruction of Keynes's lectures (see Rymes 1989). There exists a much more general genre which Rorty calls *geisgeschichte*. This is composed of works which reinterpret the past in terms of the present as rational reconstructions do, but do so on a broader scale.

*Geisgeschichte* asks why certain questions, usually those currently fashionable, became central to a particular discipline. To answer this question, it reorganizes the canon of great works from the past. *Geisgeschichte* history is not all that common in economics, but the works of Leijonhufuud are a familiar example of the genre.

Our last category is 'intellectual history' – broad interdisciplinary works written by generalists. In this area, the history of ideas deals as much with 'minor figures' who happened to be influential at the time as much as with the great figures of the past – with Bastiat and Schmoller as well as Say and Menger. In addition, intellectual history is concerned with individuals on the fringes of a profession who mediated between it and the world of affairs. People such as Horsley Palmer, Oliver Sprague or Karl Helferich impelled or impeded economic change and reform, and indeed did much of the practical work that economists are popularly supposed to do.[6] To paraphrase Rorty, if one wants to understand what it was to be a member of the Political Economy Club in early nineteenth-century London or the Kiel School of Social Democratic economists in Weimar Germany, if one wants to know what sort of issues and dilemmas confronted those who wanted to belong to the more economically educated part of the network of decision-making in those times and places, these are the sort of people one has to know about. An example of this kind of work, which I have selected because it is related to the research I have attempted on American economic foreign policy in the 1920s, is Barber's study (Barber 1985) of the attempts by Hoover and his advisers to formulate a policy for the reconstruction of the international and American economies, both before and during his administration. Reading this book gives one a feeling for how the possibilities open to the formulators of Hoover's economic policy changed and merged together with the views of academic economists, to provide an essential continuity with the New Deal and the even later phenomenon of Keynesian policies. Intellectual history is, by its very nature, rich and diffuse and is quite different from the type of history of economic analysis, encouraged by Schumpeter, which confines itself to those aspects of economic ideas 'which will eventually produce scientific models' (Schumpeter 1954: 7).

Each chapter of this book explores the same theme – the recurrence of economic doctrines and its illustration by the example of intertemporal theories of the balance of payments – using a particular type of exegesis and a specific mode of explanation. This approach may seem irredeemably eclectic to a purist who believes that the object of any inquiry is to get at 'the Truth'. I can only reply that this may well be valid in other areas of research such as the natural sciences or even pure economics, but the history of an idea must be viewed as an irregular polygon – when we view it from a different position its appearance will change. It is only possible to build up a picture of the whole from a number of different methodological positions.

It remains to demonstrate how these categories of exegesis and explanation unfold, chapter by chapter, throughout the book. Hopefully, by the end a full factual and poetic account of a recurring doctrine in economics will have been given.

## The problem of recurrence

The very idea that historical events may repeat themselves is anathema to many writers and thinkers. For idealist philosophers such as Croce and

Oakeshott, history is not an explanation in any scientific sense, but only exegesis writ large.[7] Thus, Oakeshott wrote that the historians' idea of explanation is 'the exhibition of a world of events intrinsically related to one another in which no lacuna is overlooked. No generalization is permitted, only more complete detail' (Oakeshott 1933: 154). From this it follows that: 'History never repeats itself because to do so would involve a contradiction of its character. And the institution of comparisons and the elaboration of analogies are activities which the historian must avoid if he is to remain an historian' (Oakeshott 1933: 150).

Such views seem to have been adopted by many historians, especially those writing within a specifically Anglo-Saxon tradition. If one were to accept this view, it would limit the history of ideas in particular to the narrow exegesis of texts and their arrangement in a correct chronological order. It would be illegitimate to search for any rhythm which governs their development and even more dubious to attempt to find satisfactory generalizations about the relationship between an economic theory and a recurring economic event. An alternative view of these matters, however, is that there exist generalizations which justify historical statements about the connections between events, although they cannot be precisely formulated. Furthermore, while it is sometimes said that there are no universal generalizations which historians can employ in the explanation of particular events, they may hypothesize connections between events over a limited historical period. The concept that laws of explanation can be applied in an approximate form can explain the development of ideas over time and the milieu from which they spring (Hempel 1959). I therefore take this view to be an invitation to use hypothetico-deductive methods in an attenuated form. I do this in the sense that I shall use historical material to test predictions derived from the philosophy of science. In this, I take my cue from Schumpeter, who argued that despite the problem of uneven development, the process of constructing new analytic structures in economics did not differ 'fundamentally' from analogous processes in other fields of knowledge (Schumpeter 1954: 6).

Thus, at one level I am trying to find what type of explanation is necessary to explain the phenomenon of recurrence. On the other hand, there is also a necessary exercise in *geisgeschichte* to be performed, which involves reassessing the way we conceive of the history of economics. Thus, Chapter 2 demonstrates the pervasive importance of the recurrence of economic doctrines throughout the development of economics by means of numerous examples, which are to be found throughout the history of the subject. To do this, it is necessary to be quite precise about what is meant in talking about 'the recurrence of doctrines'. This means introducing definitional order and system into observations of the type made by Schumpeter. I therefore define recurrence both in relation to theories and that amorphous conceptual entity which Kuhn called paradigms. Recurrence is shown to undermine the applicability of the Kuhnian and

Lakatosian models of scientific change to economics. Some alternative hypotheses, drawn from sources as diverse as Bachelard, Laudan and Fleck are presented and their potential applicability to economics is discussed. This chapter can be regarded as an attempt to demonstrate that the process of the obliteration and resurrection of economic theories is a central problem in the history of economics.

Despite the historical turn in post-Kuhnian philosophy of science, it follows that only those parts of that body of work which have some bearing on this issue are of potential use to the historian of economic ideas. Such criticisms apply particularly to attempts to use the concepts of Lakatos to explain the development of economics.

## The structuralist alternative

The exegetical genre which was described above as rational reconstruction has as its ideal the creation of a dialogue between thinkers whose material is separated by time and method. Thus, it is necessary to create a common language which permits discourse between them; in political philosophy, this would permit Marsilius of Padua to converse with Rawls if they were ever able to meet and, in economics, it would allow Torrens to dispute with Samuelson. Such an ideal cannot be attempted without constructing an organizing principle which can serve as a linguistic interpreter between different epochs and also around which comparisons and analogies between different writers can be drawn.

In economics, the rapid development, expansion and mathematization of the subject since the Second World War makes the need for 'translating devices' of this type particularly important since the economics of the past, especially that which had a literary form, can be regarded as having been written in a different language from that of today.

In order to enable the dialogue between earlier and later theories of intertemporal trade to take place, I have made use of an approach which highlights the cognitive identity common to economies at any time and place. The 'structuralist' approach to the philosophy of science identified with the German philosopher Wolfgang Stegmueller does this, in that it concentrates on the logical structure which is common to all economic theories and connects their different components ('structuralism' as used here has nothing to do with the structuralism of Levi-Strauss and his followers). In Chapter 3, I reconstruct the modern theory using a simplified form of this methodology, and in so doing, reveal its clear and consistent structure. This reconstruction makes it possible to investigate later to what extent the literature of the interwar years shared a common analytical structure. This discussion therefore sets the scene for a later appraisal of the relevance of Laudan's approach to economics.

Three main conclusions result from this exercise, and these can serve as a yardstick with which to determine to what extent earlier writers held a theory of a similar kind. First, I find that the modern theory depends on the concept of balance of payments equilibrium, as opposed to current account balance, a difference which I have discussed above. Second, this theory can be shown to be closely related to the real theory of international trade which is based, of course, on the concept of comparative advantage. The pure theory of international trade is worked out in the context of static general equilibrium; I show that intertemporal trade theories can be interpreted as the same theory worked out within the context of intertemporal general equilibrium. Third, when international payments problems are discussed in a monetary setting, as they should be, one finds that these theories depend on the existence of some kind of incomplete market structure. International monetary arrangements of the simplest kind can easily be interpreted as reflecting some kind of institutional restriction or imperfection of this type.

## Historical and rational reconstructions

Chapter 4 constitutes an historical reconstruction of the forgotten past of intertemporal trade theories. The most comprehensive attempt to incorporate the behaviour of the balance of payments into intertemporal equilibrium theory was made by Jacob Mosak in his book *General Equilibrium Theory and International Trade* (Mosak 1944). Much was written before this, however, by economists who were members of, or influenced by, the Austrian School. This chapter examines the thought of these writers and shows that many of these theories are of more than historical interest, for many of their insights are relevant to modern international macro-economies. This chapter offers an historical reconstruction of their actual views and a broader rational reconstruction of them, in that it also compares and contrasts the structure and propositions of their theories with those current today. The exposition leads up to a test of some of the hypotheses on 'the recurrence of doctrines' arrived at in Chapter 2. Much of what I have written may appear to indicate an extreme and even cumbersome methodological self-consciousness. In fact, I have tried to spare the reader most of these issues in what follows. The history of ideas, however, demands that one sets out overtly what genre of history is being written and what kind of explanation is being selected from the gallery of available types.

# 2 The problem of recurring doctrines in economics

On voit alors la nécessité éducative
de formuler une histoire récurrente
Bachelard (1951)

The idea that many doctrines have recurred throughout the history of economics seems to me to be accepted within the economics profession. This phenomenon is interpreted as implying that: 'Ideas will be proposed which are ignored at the time but at some later date are accepted as important to science' (Stigler 1983: 545). According to this interpretation, we are dealing with men who were 'writing above their time' and whose genius was neglected. These individuals are victims of 'Stigler's Law of Eponymy' which states that a discovery is always named after someone who was not the first to discover it (S. Stigler 1980). While not taking issue in any way with the fact that this is an important aspect of the phenomena of recurrence, I intend to draw attention to a somewhat different feature of it. This is the fact that there are economic doctrines which had not been ignored when they appeared, but still dropped from sight only to reappear a number of years later. Many examples of this type of recurrence are well known, and I shall review some of them below. This suggests that it would be interesting to try to find an explanation which would explain, not just the neglect of prescient authors, but also the fact that economic doctrines seem to go through cycles of alternating acceptability and abeyance or even oblivion. Yet no general explanation for this phenomenon has been given by historians of economic thought.

This is surprising, since I shall show that descriptions of theory change relating to such phenomena have been made by philosophers of science. Yet, as I shall argue and demonstrate by examples, the recurrence phenomenon is far more pervasive in economics than in the natural sciences. Of course, it is generally accepted today that the history of economic thought is not a cumulative process, but is characterized by discontinuous jumps and the rapid appearance of clusters of innovatory ideas (Dow 1985: 36–9; Hutchison 1978: 312–13; Negishi 1985: 4–5). Even so, this is to be expected, since the so-called 'received view' of the philosophy of science, based on positivist criteria for theory appraisal and a cumulative linear view of the steady progress of science, has been largely replaced among philosophers and historians of science by the new alternative views of science triggered off by Kuhn.[1]

This phenomenon has been termed the 'historical turn' in the philosophy of science. In reaction to Kuhn, a new generation of theorists entered the scene: Lakatos, Laudan, Feyerabend, Holton, Hesse, Cohen, Stegmuller, Shapere and others.[2] The work of older philosophers from outside the Anglo-Saxon empiricist and Viennese positivist traditions, such as Bachelard (1884–1962) and Fleck (1896–1961), also came to appear more relevant.[3] Apart from Lakatos and Laudan, and to a minor extent Feyerabend, this work has had little impact on the history of economic thought and methodology.[4] I shall be referring at times to these newer ideas at several points in this book. In the context of the recurrence phenomenon, the almost exclusive emphasis on Lakatos in the literature relating to economics is unfortunate. This is because it is to him that the epithet 'growth of knowledge theories', sometimes applied to historical philosophy as a whole, is most appropriate. As Ian Hacking, in his lucid commentary on Lakatos, puts it:

> The one fixed point in Lakatos' endeavour is the simple fact that knowledge does grow ... one can see by direct inspection that knowledge has grown. This is not a lesson to be taught by general philosophy or history, but by detailed reading of specific sequences of texts.
>
> (Hacking 1981: 129)

I contend, however, that a detailed reading of specific economic texts does not point unequivocally to the growth of knowledge. This is because theoretical entities of various types can be shown to recur during the history of economics. McCloskey (1983) is amongst the few scholars to have remarked on the similarity between the older and the newer economics. Much modern economics, he points out, is simply the economics of the past in mathematical dress (McCloskey 1983: 501). In fact, he argues that it is not so much the formalization that is important, but what he calls the 'rhetoric', by which he means the new artifices, the new theoretical terms, the new styles of argument and conventions which all determine the way papers are written according to the new fashion.

Thus, the rhetoric may change, but the doctrines remain the same. I should emphasize, however, that it is not recurrence which is the theme of McCloskey's enquiry, but the central role of rhetoric in professional economic discourse. To him, the display of this rhetorical plumage, which does not alter any basic truths of economic life, justifies an anarchistic 'anything goes' view of economic knowledge, similar to that advocated by Feyerabend for natural science. I would argue instead that the recurring nature of economic doctrines suggests the existence not of diversity, but of unity, an inner continuity which suggests that there exists a 'deep structure', to use the terminology of linguistics, which binds economic theories and concepts together.

The first part of this chapter consists of a survey of many of the theoretical entities or doctrines which have recurred in the course of the development of economic thought. It is not my intention to justify the inclusion of these cases by detailed textual exegesis; I will refer usually to cases which have been noted by others. Rather, my purpose is to demonstrate, by the weight of evidence, the pervasiveness of the recurrence phenomenon in the history of economics. My reason for doing this is that it is a basic criticism of individual case studies that, because the history of any field of study is so diverse and contains the bad along with the good, a single case study, or even several, cannot establish any interesting historico-logical or methodological claims.

For just about any claim, no matter how absurd, can be 'confirmed' by some slice of history or other.[5] The large number of examples presented should, however, validate the claim that doctrines recur. The rest of this book does not deal with grand general theories of doctrinal change in economics, but rather is concerned with a detailed case study, in an attempt to make progress in solving the much more general problem. In this chapter I shall show that doctrines do recur; the rest of the book attempts to find out why some of them do so.

The taxonomy of recurring doctrines is also designed to demonstrate that the well-known, noncumulative growth of knowledge theories of Kuhn and Lakatos are simply not applicable to economics because doctrines simply refuse to fade away for ever. This is not to say that historically-orientated philosophy of science is irrelevant to the problem of understanding economic theory change; indeed, the latter part of my discussion in this chapter is concerned with what, if anything, can be learned from the work of philosophers and historians of science, in order to construct hypotheses concerning recurring doctrines which can be tested against a concrete case study.

Before taking up the argument, I think I should say a few words about my use of the phrase 'philosophy of science'. I make no pretence of having undergone formal philosophical training; thus, I have used the key term 'doctrines' for broad, fuzzy, theoretical entities, precisely because it seems to have no technical usage among philosophers.[6] I use 'historical philosophy of science' as a source of inspiration for an economist trying to understand the history of his own subject. It is a potential source of inspiration because both these areas of study are part of the history of ideas, and there are, as Laudan points out, many factors which unify the seemingly disparate areas of research which make up the study of intellectual history. I am also sceptical of the belief, so typical of Lakatos's approach, that we can discover, by deduction from historical examples, an optimal methodology in the form of a maximally general descriptive model of economic research.[7] Therefore I am not concerned with the use of philosophy as an instrument for theory appraisal. I am only concerned with using what Laudan *et al.* (1986) term 'models of scientific change' to generate hypotheses about the recurrence of doctrines, which can be falsified against the historical experience of economics, and thus increase our knowledge of the processes underlying the development of the discipline. Ideally, one would like eventually to construct a theory-like cluster of methodological 'laws' descriptive of the actual practice which determines the transition from one doctrine to another during the course of the history of economics. Something like this has been attempted in a preliminary fashion by Goodwin (1980) and Remenyi (1979). I believe, however, that the cyclical doctrinal dialectic which has taken place in the history of economics presents the potential constructor of any grand historico-methodological system with a serious challenge.

I shall now proceed in the following fashion. First I shall describe numerous examples of the recurrence of economic doctrines, all of these being examples which have been recognized individually in the literature. I will show that these recurrences have taken the form of different theoretical constructs, such as Kuhnian paradigms, or more formal 'theories'. Such recurrences pose problems for the applicability of the ideas of Kuhn and Lakatos, and these problems will be discussed precisely. Then I shall turn to ferreting out some alternative approaches from the philosophy and history of science literature. The ultimate aim is to construct hypotheses which can be tested against a case study. At all points, I illustrate my contentions by brief, compressed references to examples from the history of economics. These are meant to be illustrative examples, demonstrating the relevance or irrelevance of historical philosophical concepts for the historian of economics. They are not meant, in themselves, to be original contributions to historical research.

## Recurring paradigms and guiding assumptions

Literally, paradigm means a pattern, exemplar or model. To Kuhn, in *The Structure of Scientific Revolutions*, the idea of a paradigm derives from some exemplary scientific success. This success serves as a model for the next generation of workers, who try to tackle other problems the same way. Such an exemplar then gives rise to a shared set of methods, standards and basic assumptions which define a particular branch of science. Kuhn is notoriously inexact; one recalls the 22 different ways in which the word 'paradigm' was allegedly used in *Structure* (Masterman 1970). Nevertheless, finding a paradigm is not particularly difficult; one is in the same position when searching for one as the man who says 'I can't describe an elephant but I know one when I see one'.

Aristotelian physics, Newtonian mechanics, Darwinian evolution and relativity theory all usually qualify as paradigms. These are highly general theories dealing with the basic building blocks of the world, and in terms of the economic universe only three similar constellations of beliefs and scientific values qualify as a paradigm: classical economics, Neoclassical economics, and, to a lesser degree, being concerned with macroeconomic problems only, Keynesian economics. However, there have been, over the history of the subject, a number of self-contained sets of established central ideas which have been well insulated against empirical refutation, wide-ranging in application, and highly influential across a variety of the fields comprising economics. These would include ideas as diverse as the labour theory of value and rational expectations (see, for example, Young *et al.* 2004). It is in this domain, somewhat smaller than that of the Kuhnian paradigm in the strict sense, that examples of recurrence can be found.

Indeed, Kuhn himself also uses the term paradigm for smaller schools of thought such as Lavoisier's 'affinity' theory in eighteenth-century chemistry (Kuhn 1970: 130–2). Given these difficulties in defining a paradigm, Laudan *et al.* (1986) use the term guiding assumptions, which takes in not just paradigms, but also other global theoretical entities like Lakatos's 'research programmes' and Laudan's 'research traditions' (of which more below). These are similar to paradigms in that they include both substantive assumptions about the world and guidelines for theory construction and theory modification. What is unique about any set of guiding assumptions is that it has central elements, which are held immune from refutation and which never change until the entire set of guiding assumptions are abandoned. This term is flexible enough to apply to general economic doctrines like classical or Neoclassical economics and to smaller entities like the theory of the firm or trade theory. The concept of guiding assumptions can also be used in the context of the philosophical 'models' of Lakatos and Laudan. However, it is more useful to discuss their schema in conjunction with heuristic ('how to do it') issues, and for the time being my discussion is confined to Kuhn's ideas. This section is concerned, therefore, with the recurrence of what can be termed 'paradigms in the small', or with the recurrence of 'guiding assumptions', a description taking into account the stable factors which are found during the development of a science.

## Examples

It is not hard to find mini-paradigms or guiding assumptions as defined above, which have recurred during the history of economics. One of the most alluring examples is that of the New Classical economics (Lucas, Sargent and their followers; see, for example, Hoover 1988). Various candidates have been proposed as previously embodying this group of modern doctrines, for example, Pigou (Collard 1983), or the Austrians of the 1930s (Kantor 1979; Laidler 1982). There seems to be a strong presumption that this New Classical economics is not so new and, indeed,

Lucas himself has briefly stated that he was reviving older business cycle theories (Lucas 1981: 215–17). Another example is the reappearance of classical theories of value in the 1950s and early 1960s. This recurrence took two forms: first, the Non-Substitution theorem of Samuelson and Koopmans dubbed by Arrow and Hahn (1971: 14) as 'a surprising resuscitation of the classical theory', and second, the revival in the Sraffa version of the theory of value associated with Ricardo (for a survey see Pasinetti 1977). This is not the only way in which sets of guiding assumptions from classical economics have reappeared. Recently, classical models of the competitive process, held to be distinct from perfect competition, have been revived and even formalized (Eatwell 1982; Gareganani 1983; Steedman 1984). It should not be thought that the revival of classical assumptions is a radical preserve, for from Chicago we have had the monetary approach to the balance of payments, according to two of its founders a conscious revival of ideas which date back to Hume and even Cantillon (Frenkel and Johnson 1976: Ch. 1).[8]

Yet the death and revival of guiding assumptions has occurred on an even more fundamental plane. Here I am thinking of the concept of cardinal utility, seemingly 'purged' 50 years ago from economics, as Hicks put it in his *Value and Capital*. As pointed out in a fascinating article by Cooter and Rappaport (1984), it is debatable that the abandonment of cardinal utility was really an advance, and not surprisingly, there has recently been a return to the employment of cardinal utility functions to tackle a wide range of problems. This example suggests that not only the more metaphysical assumptions contained in paradigms recur, but also the heuristic principles they prescribe.

As a final example, consider the theories of household production and human capital. As pointed out by Kiker (1966), there is nothing particularly new about the concept of human capital, which has a long history, but waned after the early 1930s. This is also true of the theory of household production, which dates back at least to an article by Wesley C. Mitchell in 1912, and reached its first apogee in Margaret Reid's *Theory of Household Production* (1934), a good 30 years before Becker reworked this doctrine.

## Kuhnian losses

These examples are rather disturbing for those, like Dow (1985), who believe that Kuhn's account of scientific change is useful for understanding similar processes in economics, because they are completely at variance with Kuhn's insistence that paradigm changes are irreversible, resulting in 'a total victory for one of the opposing camps' (Kuhn 1970: 166). After the battle, the defeated party is then purged with a Stalinist ruthlessness: 'When it repudiates a past paradigm, a scientific community simultaneously renounces, as a fit subject for professional scrutiny, most of the books and articles in which that paradigm had been embodied' (Kuhn 1970: 167).

The unfortunate vanquished also suffer a dismal fate: 'But there are always some men who cling to one or another of the older views, and they are simply read out of the profession, which thereafter ignores their work' (Kuhn 1970: 19).

While this is a suggestive description of the professional relations which existed between Keynesians and Old Classicals, or today between Keynesians and New Classicals, it is in the main contradicted by the examples above. This, in fact, would not have surprised Kuhn. For him total revolution is achieved only at a price: 'There are losses as well as gains in scientific revolutions, and the scientists tend to be particularly blind to the former' (Kuhn 1970: 167). Laudan (1977: 148–9), has provided a number of examples of such losses in the history of science. Hutchison (1978: 314–16) in particular has made much of these 'Kuhnian losses' as being particularly relevant to the history of economics. Indeed, one might expect the losses to be even greater in economics than in the natural sciences. This follows from the fact that, in Kuhn's account, it is empirical anomalies which destroy the edifice of that 'normal science' which is created by paradigm change. Now, as pointed out for example by Kunin and Weaver (1971: 394–5), the amount and destructive potential of anomalies is even greater in economics since it is not only the internal dynamics of the theory which generates them, but external changes in the economy itself.

Although Kuhn admits the existence of losses, he evinces neither regret at their occurrence, nor hints that they are later retrieved:

> The process described as the resolution of revolutions is the selection within the scientific community of the fittest way to practice future science. The net result of a sequence of such revolutionary selections, separated by periods of normal research, is the wonderfully adapted set of instruments we call modern scientific knowledge.
>
> (Kuhn 1970: 172)

The idea that losses take place during periods of paradigm transition (i.e. scientific revolutions) is therefore of only partial relevance to economics, since the reappearance of the lost material is simply lacking in Kuhn's account. It cannot occur because the victors simply rewrite the textbooks in their own image, including accounts of the history of the subject. In fact, Kuhn states that a scientist appears to be, 'like the typical character of Orwell's *1984*', the victim of a history rewritten by the powers that be. Furthermore, that suggestion 'is not altogether inappropriate' (Kuhn 1970: 167).

These statements have, in fact, spawned a vogue for the investigation of 'textbook history' among historians of science influenced by Kuhn, who seek to confirm his account of scientific revolutions (see Schaffer 1986). Kuhn stresses that education in science, even postgraduate education, is rigidly based on textbooks and ignores the creative scientific literature.

Now economics education, even today, involves the reading of current papers and monographs and even, according to a recent survey of graduates, emphasizes the importance of theoretical novelty (Colander and Klamer 1987). This was certainly also true in the past; for example, according to Patinkin's account (Patinkin 1976), drafts of the *General Theory*, including a mathematical formulation of it, were presented at undergraduate lectures in Cambridge in the 1930s, as confirmed by Rymes (1989).[9]

All this suggests a reason why paradigms recur in economics: the indoctrination process is not so complete, and students have always been confronted with the living stuff of current debates.

The above is only a first stab, however, and I shall present several other tentative ideas. Before doing so, I would like to discuss the recurrence of more narrowly focused theories. This phenomenon is even more devastating for the applicability of Lakatos's growth of knowledge theory to economics than recurring paradigms are to the use of Kuhn's account.

## Recurring theories

I shall define a theory in the following way:

> A theory consists of a network of statements which, in conjunction with initial conditions, lead to explanations and predictions of specific phenomena.

Note that this definition, which is taken from Laudan (1981a: 150), describes a theory as being somewhat broader than what economists call a 'model' and philosophers call a 'theory' ('model' in economics describes exactly what is called a 'theory' in the philosophy of science).[10] It can take in not only separate economic models but also broader doctrines, which can be generated by a cluster of related models.

What unites theories is the fact that they are developed methodically from a set of guiding assumptions, utilizing the heuristic principles contained in those assumptions. In this sense, then, a demonstration that theories recur is, in itself, a proof that sets of guiding assumptions recur during the history of economics.

I shall define a recurring theory in the following way:

> A theory recurs if it reappears without its author being aware of its previous existence. This definition, in itself, rules out a huge number of recurrences from examination. I will not discuss examples like Sargent and Wallace's revival of real bills theory, the revival of monopolistic competition theory in the last ten years, the reappearance of Hicksian temporary equilibrium theory in the early 1970s, the attempt by Steedman to revive Ricardian trade theory, R.A. Jones's revival of Menger's theory of exchange, the revived analysis of

Lindahl's concept of equilibrium with public goods, and many more.[11] The fact that so much conscious revival takes place is doubtless in itself a phenomenon which deserves a study in its own right, but the unconscious and unintended revival of theories is, to my mind, more interesting and important. It points to an underlying structure in economic thought which forces theories to resurface, and which obliges researchers to retrace the steps of earlier writers, seemingly without any scientific progress. When a theory is consciously revived, the economist who does so usually wishes to improve that theory in the interest of extending the boundaries of our knowledge. The unconscious reviver, however, may simply replicate an earlier theory; nor is it the case, as some of the examples below will show, that he always presents a version which is mathematically more sophisticated, or where the formalization inherent in the new version of the theory adds anything fundamental to the earlier theory. In the case of the conscious revival, the older theory is probably a limiting case of the new, more general version, something of which there is no guarantee in the unconscious case.

One difficulty should be discussed before enumerating a number of recurring theories. This difficulty relates to the concept of simultaneous discovery and incommensurability.

## Incommensurability of theories

It was claimed initially by Kuhn, and with even greater force by Feyerabend, that scientific theories are incommensurable. This means that they cannot be compared and ranked since there is no natural scale for their ranking, no common measure which all rational men will agree to use and agree how to use. A favourite analogy of Feyerabend is that of different languages. Like them, theories cannot be strictly compared to each other, nor translated exactly into each other. The languages of different theories are the linguistic counterparts of the different worlds we may inhabit. We can pass from one language, embodying a particular worldview, to another worldview only by the 'gestalt-switch' defined by Kuhn in 'structure' (Feyerabend 1975: 72–7, 223–4).

McCloskey, under the influence of Feyerabend, has made much of the alleged incommensurability of economic theories in his *Rhetoric of Economics* (McCloskey 1983: 493, 508). On this view, the idea of recurring theories is simply nonsensical, the theories are incommensurable, especially if there are some shifts in their terminology, and the latter theory thus cannot be seen as an unintended replication of the earlier.

As Shapere (1981) has pointed out, incommensurability drives us to a corner solution: theoretical terms, or sets of them, must either retain precisely the same meaning over time or else must be utterly and completely different with no room for any shades of meaning between them. If this is true, there would be no work whatsoever to do in the history of economics, for we could not compare, classify and draw connections between different epochs in economics; theories are either identical or they are utterly different. That is all that can be said. Rather, I think that incommensurability constitutes a warning. We must realize that the interpretation of theoretical terms depends on context, and that meanings do change over time. Consider the discussion given by Vickrey (1973: 286–90) of the very different use made of the word 'utility' by Bentham, Pareto and eventually Baumol. Nevertheless, with sufficient care, we can pick examples where the differences in meaning are not too great.[12]

## Recurring macro-theories

It is generally accepted that there has been less scientific progress (in the sense of general agreement on the validity of a theory) in macroeconomics than in other branches of economics. Not surprisingly then, macroeconomics provides a number of examples of recurring theories. One of the most interesting is the famous Ricardian Equivalence proposition on debt-based government finance. This has reappeared at least three times since its illustrious author first proposed it. Barro (1974), whose name is most associated with this doctrine today, was incidentally unaware of Ricardo's authorship, and this had to be pointed out by Buchanan (1976).

Pigou (1919 and 1921), however, rediscovered the idea first when discussing the financing of the First World War, again without any reference to his predecessor, Ricardo. Thus Pigou, writing in 1919, declared that:

> On posterity as a whole no direct objective burden is imposed by debt repayment of an internal loan, any more than by payment of interest upon it ... apart from the consequences produced through reaction on the conduct of the persons affected at the time, the choice between the levy and loan method makes no difference to the direct objective burden thrown on future generations.
>
> (Pigou 1919: 251)[13]

Another theory which has had a peripatetic history of this type is that of the political business cycle. Originally, in the hands of Kalecki (1943), this was a left Keynesian deviationist critique of expansionary fiscal policy. When it was independently rediscovered (or re-emphasized) by Nordhaus (1975), it took on a more standard Keynesian appearance before its New Classical manifestations, as surveyed by Alesina and Tabellini (1988). An entirely different theory which has recurred is that of Free Banking, an idea which has a long history, as chronicled by White (1984). Cowen and Kroszner (1987) have shown the large extent to which the 'New View' of the role of money and of banking associated with writers like Fama and

Wallace is an unconscious revival of an earlier theory. Another example, from the microfoundations of money literature, is that of the finance constraint. It is true that this was thought to derive from Keynes via Clower; in fact, as Kohn (1981) has shown, it is in fact a recurrence of Robertson's version of the loanable funds theory.

An interesting earlier case of theory recurrence is that of the Keynesian multiplier. As pointed out by Shackle (1967: 194–7), the multiplier was formulated mathematically in 1896 by a Dane, Julius Wulff, and expounded at length and reformulated as part of the business cycle theory in 1898 by a German, N. Johannsen, who was 'a most complete anticipator' (Shackle 1967: 197), and actually called his theory the 'multiplying principle'. Nor was his theory unknown. His book was known to J.B. Clark, Hobson and Wesley Mitchell (Hutchison 1953: 395). Keynes mentioned Johanssen in the Treatise, critically, briefly and tartly. As Hutchison remarks: 'He should have made some amends by including Johanssen in the very curiously selected gallery of pioneers commemorated in Chapter 23 of the *General Theory*.'

## Some exotic recurrences

One of the most surprising cases of theory recurrence is that of the model of overlapping generations, almost universally attributed to Samuelson. Malinvaud (1987) showed that Maurice Allais (1947), 11 years before Samuelson, provided a fully specified, rigorous mathematical presentation of the model. Since we are talking of a difference of 11 to 13 years, it might be argued that we are on the boundary of a simultaneous discovery. Negishi (1985: 115) pointed out, however, that the basis of the life cycle model was set out by Bohm-Bawerk.

An additional interesting and unexpected case of theory recurrence was discovered and expounded by John Whitaker (1982). Two Danish mathematicians, Bing and Petersen, produced in 1873 a model of economic growth and distribution 'essentially similar' (Whitaker's phrase) to a model produced in 1954 by Bensusan-Butt, and expanded by Champernowne (1961). This example shows just how unexpected theory recurrence can be.

Another example belongs on a different economic planet: the economic system set out by Sraffa (1960) in *Production of Commodities by Means of Commodities*. P. Newman (1962) pointed out that the German economist and mathematician, Robert Remak, studied the problem of exchange in 1929 and offered a mathematical solution formally equivalent to Sraffa's price system for the case in which there is no surplus product (Remak 1929). Judging by the fascinating article by Wittmann (1967), Remak is also responsible for unknowingly originating the more neoclassical mathematical versions of linear economic models developed in the 1950s.[14]

## Recurring microtheories

It might be thought that microeconomics has exhibited some cumulative growth of knowledge, and therefore it is unlikely that we would find any pertinent examples there. In fact, Ault and Ekelund (1987) have recently provided us with a specific study of a particular case of recurrence in the field of peak load pricing. They show that Professor Bye of Harvard had, in the 1920s, anticipated all the results on the optimal structure of pricing for time dependent commodities which were later arrived at by Steiner and Williamson (Steiner 1957; Williamson 1966), who are usually credited with giving the first rigorous results on peak load pricing. In fact, Bye even dealt correctly with relatively complex issues like unequal peak and off-peak time periods and the existence of different types of fixed capital in the relevant technology.

One of the more well-known examples of the recurrence of a theory is in fact the Hicks–Allen (1934) presentation of demand theory, no doubt one of the most fundamental papers ever written on economics. While they arrived at their results independently, they later acknowledged that all of their results were to be found in the work of Slutsky (1915) and Johnson (1913).[15] This is surely one of the more prominent cases of theory recurrence. The history of demand theory, however, also supplies another interesting example: this is the case of the German economist Gossen, who published in 1854 a mathematical theory of utility maximization similar to that developed in the marginal revolution. Now it is true that Gossen influenced Jevons. However, neither Menger or Walras, writing 30 years later, seem to have been aware of his work (Hutchison 1953: 139).

## Recurring trade theories

The number of precedents cited by Viner (1937) for the Hecksher–Ohlin theory suggests that international trade theory may be characterized by recurrences. Viner's examples really are precedents and not full-fledged expositions of the theory which later became prominent. Chipman (1965a, 1965b) provided two rather more concrete examples. The first of these was Mangoldt, who 'foreshadowed much of the modern analysis' (Chipman 1965a: 501) of classical trade theories in the activity analysis mode, such as those of McKenzie. A second example is that of Barone (Chipman 1965b: 699), who, in his *Economic Principles* of 1908 and *Economic Papers* of 1920–1923, discovered most of the analysis of trade using production and indifference curves, well before Lerner (1932) and Haberler (1936; original German version 1933) introduced them.

## The strange case of J.S. Mill

In a well-known paper, Stigler (1965) argued that J.S. Mill produced at least six original theories, which later became important in economics.

Some examples are: Walras's law, noncompeting groups and the first exact statement of the Law of Supply and Demand.

Stigler's explanation for the fact that J.S. Mill received little credit for these innovations was that he had what McCloskey would call a problem with 'rhetoric'. He did not sufficiently emphasize his own originality and paid an equal and exaggerated respect to the achievements of others, thus belittling and drawing attention away from his own work. I am not convinced that this is the only possible explanation. Mill had immediate followers such as Cairnes, who accepted and admired his analysis of issues such as noncompeting groups and protection. Rather, I conjecture that the violent attacks made on Mill by Jevons and Walras, 22 and 40 years later, and the complete victory of their paradigm, led to what was good and original in his work being neglected and forgotten.[16] Here we obviously have a case of Kuhnian losses in economics; the marginalists read Mill out of the profession, as Kuhn would put it, and so successful were they that he survived only to be a favourite butt of Keynes in the *General Theory*.

## Two fallacious arguments (an excursus)

Let me briefly use the Socratic Method and dispose of two arguments which immediately spring to mind as explanations for this very uneven, circular kind of progress in economics. These arguments are the language barrier argument, and what I call the inevitable progress of mathematization argument.

### *The language barrier argument*

Myrdal made a famous remark about 'the attractive Anglo-Saxon kind of unnecessary originality deriving from their foreign language deficiency' (1939 [1933]: 8–9). This surely accounts, for example, for the neglect of the work of an Allais or a Remak. It is nevertheless interesting that such problems have never occurred in the natural sciences. Einstein and Planck were not neglected because their theories were originally published in German. It is true that the mathematical content of scientific work means that less linguistic proficiency is required in order to understand it than is required to understand economics written in a foreign language. In fact, the cases of Remak and Allais suggest that the relatively literary nature of economics is not relevant to the argument. Their works, referred to above, are marked by a high degree of mathematical rigour and content, even by today's standards. Myrdal's proposition is no more than a claim that economists are less well educated than scientists. I know of no sociological study which confirms this. I would think that economists have always had as good a general education as scientists. This language barrier is simply part of a more general problem with the transmission of economic ideas.

### The progressive mathematization argument

It is tempting to suggest that recurrences occur because mathematical economists naturally produce more rigorous versions of theorems previously
advanced in the literature. This is obviously often the case when a theory is
consciously revived by a more technically sophisticated researcher, and this
contention seems to be especially true when one talks about the recurrence
of paradigms. Thus, Hicks has remarked that he could find no way to make
a consistent mathematical formulation of Hayek's schema in *Prices and
Production*. This led him to abandon his interest in Hayek's theories (Hicks
1982: 3–4). One can certainly argue, therefore, that the success of the rational expectations school derives from their ability to solve the type of
problem which defeated Hicks, since they can use new mathematical techniques such as dynamic programming. The problem with this explanation is
that there are too many counter-examples: Gossen–Walras, Remak–Sraffa,
Slutsky–Hicks, Johannsen–Keynes, Ricardo–Pigou, Allais–Samuelson,
Barone–Haberler, to name but a few, are all cases where the recurring
theory exhibits an identical degree of mathematization (or lack of it). It is,
in fact, not hard to find examples of regress in the formal content of economics.

Thus, Walras presented a mathematical monetary growth model in the
*Elements* (see above). He did not totally succeed in formulating a consistent model but his follower, Aupetit (1901) made more progress at a
higher level of mathematical sophistication (see Zylberberg 1987: 3–5).
Nothing similar was attempted until well after the Keynesian revolution. I
would also like to put forward an example of my own. The brilliant Viennese, Karl Schlesinger, is known mainly as a member of Karl Menger's
circle in the 1930s (Weintraub 1985). Although Schumpeter (1954: 1087)
brackets his book on money of 1914 with Aupetit's achievements, the
main body of his work on monetary theory is largely unknown. Examining
his remarkable article of 1931 on the influence of bank credit on the
money supply, we find he derives several alternative money multipliers,
depending on various assumptions about the economic role of banks.
Schlesinger's banks maximize over infinite time, and he therefore solves
the multipliers as infinite sums. Nothing like this, as far as I know, was
attempted in macroeconomics until the late 1980s (e.g. Bernanke and
Gertler 1989). Conventional analysis of money multipliers in the 1950s and
1960s (like Teigen 1965) was mechanical and 'hydraulic'. The classic case
of regression in mathematization is, however, Cournot's treatment of
oligopoly. This was conducted at a higher level of mathematical sophistication than the imperfect competition doctrines of Robinson and Chamberlin.

I conclude, therefore, that the mathematization 'folk-tale' has little in it.
Economists, as a whole, have become more and more technically adept,
but when we talk about individual theories, they themselves are often pre-

sented with the same appropriate conceptual or mathematical tools at different points in time. I am arguing that the problem itself dictates the level of mathematical technique, not the level of technique the problem. For example, the multiplier requires simple algebra and arithmetical examples; this was true for both Johanssen in 1906 and Kahn in 1931, whereas its more complex aspects, that is to say, its dynamic forms, require a more sophisticated level of mathematics (see, for example, Lange 1943; see also Weintraub 2002)

## Theses

Let me now set out what I call, perhaps a little too grandly, some theses on the history of economics which can be distilled from the above examples. These are not 'the truth'; they are simply what these case histories imply.

1   Although theoretical losses are the rule in the development of economics, sets of guiding assumptions themselves are never completely eliminated and may return to a position of dominance.
2   Theory transition, unlike transitions in guiding assumptions, often leads to the total elimination of theories from the collective consciousness of economists. These must be rediscovered, because they totally disappear from the extant body of knowledge subscribed to by practising economists.
3   Scientific progress exists in economics, since some theories are ultimately accepted, such as consumer demand based on utility maximization, but not before a long cyclical process of appearance–disappearance–reappearance has taken place, during which nothing is added to the original theory when it is rediscovered.
4   The rediscovery of forgotten theories shows that what the discipline accepts or rejects at a given moment in time is no measure of the truth of a particular theory. Therefore, economic theories cannot be appraised on the basis of their historical development.

### *Lakatos revisited*

Thesis 1, as shown above, is at variance with Kuhnian tenets on the nature of scientific revolutions. Theses 2–4 play havoc with the relevance to economics of Lakatos's *Methodology of Scientific Research Programmes*. This has been the only philosophical model of scientific change commonly applied to economics (Cross 1982; Hands 1985; Latsis 1976; Weintraub 1979, 1985). Those like Goodwin (1980), who are aware of its limitations, propose to modify rather than abandon it. Let me refresh, briefly, the reader's memory of the subject and state precisely what is wrong.

As I mentioned in my introduction, Lakatos regards the growth of knowledge as the central problem of epistemology. As we have seen, unambiguous cases of knowledge growth are hard to spot in economics, and I shall argue that this is a problem for Lakatosians. Lakatos's description of guiding assumptions is not in itself problematic. These research programmes are characterized by: a 'hard core' of fundamental assumptions, immune from *modum tollens* arguments; a 'protective belt' of collateral and auxiliary assumptions, which are open to revision; and a set of heuristic guidelines which instruct the theorist working in the research programme how to modify theories when they get into difficulty.

Sets of guiding assumptions can easily be fitted into these categories. Yet, when we look at the temporal development of research programmes, it is immediately clear that theses 2 and 4 are totally at variance with Lakatos's account. Thus, in the following passage. Lakatos speaks of the degeneration and death of economic doctrines:

> The great scientific achievements of the past are research programmes which can be evaluated in terms of progressive and degenerating problem shifts; and scientific revolutions consist of one research programme superseding another.
>
> (Lakatos 1981: 115)

This is no different from Kuhn's *'guerre à l'outrance'* between paradigms, and has the same inapplicability. Furthermore, he often states that any phenomenon which has been explained by another is also explained by its successor (Lakatos 1978: 1, 33, 47), which clearly violates 3.

Even more extreme is the view that theories are not regarded as part of the body of science unless they replace earlier theories or themselves are replaced by later ones (Lakatos 1978: 1, 47). On this reading there is simply no science at all in economics, given that Lakatos's strident view contradicts 2–3. Lakatos's historical method of theory appraisal, by which degenerating research programmes cease to be scientific, is also clearly inappropriate in the light of 4. Lakatos's philosophical model is even more inappropriate as advice for the writer of the history of the subject – 'The historian who accepts this methodology as a guide will look in history for rival research programmes, for progressive and degenerating problem shifts' (Lakatos 1981: 19).

I have shown, however, that a degenerating problem shift is extremely hard to identify in the history of economic theories; they are, according to thesis 2, quite illusory. If later generations embrace not just rejected, but totally eliminated theories, how can we possibly claim that research programmes have degenerated? It is easy to show what is wrong with the Lakatosian account as an examplar of theory change in economics. 'Why?' is a harder question to answer. The case study which appears later in the book is designed to provide some tentative answers to this question. It will enable us to identify some of the specific weaknesses of the Lakatosian approach to explaining theory change in economics. Obviously, given

some of my above remarks about the difficulties of demonstrating historical theses by one case study, this one study can only point the way for
others on different examples of recurring doctrines.

## Some alternatives

We have seen that both Kuhn and Lakatos provide accounts of doctrinal
change which are inapplicable to economics. This is because the recurrence of sets of guiding assumptions is incompatible with the Kuhnian
view of total victory for a paradigm, and because the recurrence of theories is incompatible with the Lakatosian account of the tendency to degeneration in research programmes. I have shown that the recurrence
phenomenon is so common that we are not just dealing with a single
counter-example, which can always be found. Should the historian of economics, therefore, cease seeking inspiration in the historically minded
philosophy of science? I contend that the answer is no, at least at this
stage, since there do exist some approaches, less well known to economists, which appear a priori to be applicable to the discipline. As a first
step in explaining the recurrence phenomenon, their relevance should be
discussed by means of appropriate case studies, one of which will be
offered as the meat of this book (Chapter 3). Before starting on this task, I
should like to survey what I have found to be relevant among philosophers' accounts of scientific change. These will provide a group of
hypotheses to be tested against historical experience in the evolution of
economics.

## Bachelard's recurrences

The earliest and, in fact, almost the only explicit discussion of recurring
theories in the philosophy of science literature which I have been able to
find, is that of the French philosopher of science Bachelard. He is often
cited as a forerunner of the 'post-positivist' philosophy of science of the
latter part of the twentieth century.

Concepts such as the theory-laden nature of scientific observations and
the noncumulative nature of the growth of scientific knowledge are prominent in Bachelard's work (see Tiles 1984). In one of his later works,
*L'Activité rationaliste de la Physique contemporaine*, Bachelard traced the
dialectic of two particular theories of light in the hands of Huyghens,
Newton, Euler, Biot and Fresnel (1951: 31–40) among others, with each
one taking up the theory previously rejected by the former over the course
of about 150 years. This might suggest that the phenomenon of a recurring
theory is not foreign to the history of natural science either. However,
Bachelard seems to be alone in claiming this, with the partial exception of
Laudan, as I shall describe later. He also provides only this one example;
nevertheless, he does offer some explanations for this particular cyclical

form of scientific development. He stresses the role of obstacles which are created originally for progressive reasons 'certains barrages que le passe de pensée scientifique aux formes contre l'irrationalisme'. The authority of the Encyclopedia of the eighteenth-century philosophers is a typical example of this. It rewrote the past history of science in much the same manner as did Kuhn's textbooks. What prevents the total destruction of previous concepts is a continuity provided by certain 'concepts si indispensables dans une culture scientifique qu'on ne conçoit pas qu'on puisse être amenera à les abandonner' (1951: 36–7). The dialectic itself is driven along by difficulties of formalizing mathematically the results of a theory and by plain deviations of that theory from common sense observation (1951: 46).

These ideas are suggestive, but no more, of parallel occurrences in the history of economics. The conservative role of the 'Encyclopedie' in the eighteenth century reminds one of Jevons's description of the 'noxious influence of authority' (i.e. Ricardo) in the nineteenth century. The role played by the difficulties of mathematization reminds one of Hicks's problems with *Prices and Production* (see above).

Of particular interest is the idea of key unifying concepts which cannot be totally abandoned, and therefore must be preserved. Shackle has given an example of how such intellectual constants maintain continuity in economics. Thus, Shackle has argued, in a vein similar to Bachelard, that there is in any science which aims to describe the world, a striving for an all-pervasive uniformity, simplicity and unity, and in order to achieve this, perfect foresight, rationality and perfect competition have played the same unifying role in economics as the law of gravity in physics (1967: 4, 293–5). For this reason, economists like Shove and Robertson found it impossible to give up perfect competition, even though they wanted to include the principle of increasing returns (1967: 43–4) in the theory of the firm, and tried to rely on the principle of the representative firm to salvage Marshall's theory of value. Joan Robinson (1933: 337–443) tried another route, and introduced the concept of economies external to the firm. This, therefore, is an example of the tenacity with which a concept like perfect competition can live on, even within the citadel of its detractors (Cambridge).

### Laudan's research traditions

Laudan's account of scientific progress originally appeared in 1977, and has been elaborated on since (Laudan 1981a, 1984, 1986). It is the major system in the philosophy of science which has been constructed since Lakatos and Feyerabend, and it is surprising that its relevance to economics has not been examined [until recently, see, for example Foss 1997; Hands 1996].

Perhaps historians of economics have been influenced by those philosophers who were sharply critical of Laudan's work (e.g. Jarvie 1979 and

Feyerabend 1981). This is partly because Laudan, unlike most philosophers, denies that science is a truth-seeking activity (1977: 5), and also because many of his ideas are sharply at variance with the Popperian tradition from which Lakatos and Feyerabend, in different ways, descend. Perhaps this would make Laudan uncongenial to writers like Weintraub, Blaug and McCloskey who respectively favour Lakatos's, Popper's and Feyerabend's accounts of science. These strictures have not been universal, however (e.g. Butts 1979), and some serious work has been done in testing Laudan's schema on actual historical case studies in the sciences (for references, see the bibliography in Laudan *et al.* 1986).

As I will show, Laudan's ideas appear to be particularly applicable to economics. This is particularly true because of the important role he gives to what he calls conceptual, as opposed to empirical, problems. These, of course, are very much the subject matter of economics, which cannot be defined as a truly experimental science like the natural sciences. Of even more importance is his account of changes in guiding assumptions. These, as we shall see, are held by him to develop over time in a way which can explain the recurrence of scientific doctrines. It is hardly surprising that Laudan's philosophical model turns out to be relevant to economics, since he has always claimed that it can apply to any field of intellectual inquiry, not just science (1977: 189–92; 1981a: 153–4). Three concepts play a major role in Laudan's account; these are the central role of problem solving, the nature and role of empirical and conceptual problems, and the replacement of the ideas of paradigm and research programme as descriptions of guiding assumptions by the new notion of a research tradition. I shall now discuss these in turn, with brief reference to their relevance for economics.

*Problem solving*

Laudan reverses many traditional views of theory appraisal: 'My proposition will be that rationality consists in making the most progressive theory choices, not that progress consists in accepting successively the most rational theories.' Thus, he argues that rationality and scientific progress are linked with the problem-solving effectiveness of theories, not their verisimilitude, corroboration, falsifiability and the like. Theories are not appraised by any absolute criteria; rather, scientists choose pragmatically between all currently available options rather than searching for the theoretically possible best option (Laudan 1984: 27–8). Theories, themselves, are appraised in terms of their overall problem-solving effectiveness, and this is determined by estimating the number of problems which the theory solves and by subtracting the number and importance of the anomalies and conceptual problems which the theory generates. With regard to scientific change, this is held to be of a progressive nature when theories which are even better problem solvers are accepted (Laudan *et al.* 1986: 208). As he puts it: 'The aim of science is to secure theories with a high problem solving effectiveness' (Laudan 1981a: 145). This down-to-earth 'cost–benefit' (Laudan's usage) approach to appraisal is consistent with much that has been written about neoclassical theories, albeit perjoratively; they are, after all, only Joan Robinson's 'box of tools' (Robinson 1962: 70), or Clapham's 'empty economic boxes', which are 'handled with beautiful ingenuity, but never actually opened' (Clapham 1922: 201).

Diverse critics such as Hollis and Nell (1975) and Boland (1982) make much of this conventionalism, to use a philosopher's word. Lakatos described conventionalism as a system of pigeon holes which 'organizes facts into a coherent whole', but is not 'provenly true' but only 'true by convention' (Lakatos 1970, 1981: 111). One is immediately struck by the similarity between these pigeon holes and Clapham's 'boxes on the shelves of his [the economist's] mind labelled with theoretical terms like monopoly or constant returns'. We therefore have two lines of criticism deriving from Clapham's classic piece, from, on the one hand, Joan Robinson and younger radicals like Hollis and Nell who dislike the neoclassical emphasis on technique to solve formal problems and, on the other hand, from followers of Popper and Lakatos, like Boland, who dislike conventionalism. From the perspective of Laudan's problem-solving approach, all these anticonventionalist, pigeon hole and box-burning criticisms misfire badly. Neoclassical economics is naturally only an apparatus for solving problems, as is any line of scientific or intellectual inquiry. To understand this point more fully, I must proceed to elucidate the nature of the problems being solved.

Laudan defines problems which must be solved by scientific theories in two ways. First, empirical problems 'about the world', which are divided into three categories: solved problems, unsolved – that is potentially solved problems – and anomalous problems – those empirical problems which a particular theory has not solved, but which one or more of its competitors have solved. He places more emphasis, however, on conceptual problems which are the 'characteristics of theories', which 'have no existence independent of theories which exhibit them, not even the limited autonomy which empirical problems sometimes possess' (Laudan 1977: 48). Conceptual problems are divided into those which arise within a particular system, such as inconsistency, vagueness and unclarity (these he calls internal problems), and external problems which arise from a conflict between two rationally well-founded doctrines or theories (Laudan 1977: 49). This is all highly attractive as a description of economics, since much more time is spent on conceptual debates than on empirical research (judging by data on citations; see Liebowitz and Palmer 1984). The following paragraph describing the nature of internal conceptual problems can serve as a description of much that has gone on in economics:

> The increase of the conceptual clarity of a theory through careful clar-
> ifications and specifications of meaning is, as William Whewell

observed more than a century ago, one of the most important ways in which science progresses. He called this process 'the explication of conceptions' and showed how a number of theories, in the course of their temporal careers, had become increasingly precise largely as a result of the critics of such theories emphasizing their conceptual unclarities. Many important scientific revolutions have depended largely on the recognition, and subsequent reduction, of the terminological ambiguity of theories within a particular domain.

(Laudan 1977: 50)

Laudan's reference to William Whewell, the polymathic Master of Trinity, is entirely appropriate to the context of the history of economics, for it was Whewell who, in 1829, attempted to translate the doctrines of Ricardo and Smith into mathematics (Hutchison 1953: 64–6). This was the pioneer attempt at a mathematical economics. It is, therefore, hardly surprising that a model of scientific development inspired by Whewell's overall philosophy is appropriate to economics, since it was Whewell who first attempted to introduce formal conceptual order and precision into the subject.

Conceptual debates of the Whewell–Laudan type are perhaps too common in economics to justify their enumeration here. One need only note the perennial question of 'what microfoundations for macroeconomics' to generate a score of examples. One should not deny that empirical anomalies are important in economics; the Philips Curve and the debate in the late 1940s and early 1950s on the consumption function are two such examples. I only claim that conceptual debates are more prevalent, and this is a great advantage for Laudan's approach, since Kuhn, Lakatos and Popper are persistently concerned with the details of scientific experiments. Their models of scientific change were never meant to deal with the evolution of abstract sets of mathematical theories which are not subjected to vigorous testing in the laboratory.

## Recurring research traditions

Underlying and generating the theories which sort out conceptual and empirical problems are a broad set of guiding assumptions, a complex of presuppositions and beliefs which Laudan calls research traditions. These identify the objects in a domain of inquiry and the methods suitable for studying them. In addition, they provide guidelines for modifying and improving theories to improve their problem-solving effectiveness (1977: 79, 92).

A research tradition consists of a general, not easily testable, set of doctrines and assumptions, including a number of contemporaneous and predecessor theories, and a set of metaphysical and methodological commitments which individuate it. Like a 'research programme', a research tradition is not, strictly speaking, explanatory, predictive, or even easily testable, but its constituent theories are. Unlike theories, a research tradition goes through a number of different (and often mutually contradictory) formulations. It evolves both by the successive replacement of its constituent theories and by changes in some of its most basic core elements. These metaphysical and methodological commitments mark out a research tradition at any point in time, but can change gradually over time (1977: 94, 96, 99).

To understand why Laudan's account is so different from that of Kuhn, we must go back to the issue of conceptual problems. According to Kuhn, these are debated only during a crisis which precedes a scientific revolution; while normal science holds sway, a paradigm is, as we have seen, enforced by a dictatorship with an iron will. According to Laudan, conceptual debates go on all the time and therefore 'the co-existence of research traditions is the rule rather than the exception'. From this co-presence of research traditions, the route to explaining their recurrence is clear. One such tradition needs only fade into the background for a time:

> At any given time, one or other of these may have the competitive edge, but there is a continuous and persistent struggle taking place, with partisans of one view or another pointing to the empirical and conceptual weaknesses of rival points of view and to the problem-solving progressiveness of their own approach. Dialectical confrontations are essential to the growth and improvement of scientific knowledge; like nature, science is red in tooth and claw.
>
> (Laudan 1981a: 15)

Here we have an account of the recurrence of guiding assumptions. This can also explain the recurrence of theories; these are solutions to the conceptual problems which are the temporally revolving objects of debate. It seems to me, however, that in order to explain the unconscious revival of forgotten theories, one must add to this account Kuhn's description, referred to above, of the way protagonists of one research tradition read protagonists of the other out of the profession and suppress knowledge of their theories by means of textbooks.

Laudan's prize example of a recurring Research Tradition, amply documented in his *Science and Hypothesis* (1981b) is, not surprisingly, that of a perennial conceptual, or even methodological, dispute. He shows how the hypothetico–deductive method, the very stuff of logical empiricist accounts of science, was favoured by Descartes, seventeenth-century scientists and the Port-Royallogicians, only to be replaced by inductive methods under Newton's influence. In the later eighteenth century, hypothetic–deductive methodology came back into favour. What is particularly interesting about this tale for economists is that Jevons emerges among Laudan's dramatis personae as the author of a last attempt to salvage induction in his *Principles of Science* (1874). Significantly, Mays (1962) has shown the strong, albeit implicit connection between Jevons's philosophy of science and his economic methodology.

Furthermore, Laudan regards Keynes's work as a theorist of probability as being in the tradition of Jevons (Laudan 1981b: 200). J.S. Mill was also an important protagonist in these debates (Laudan 1981b: 140–8).[18] The exact implications of this dialectic in science for the history of economics has not been worked out, yet it is easy to see how the type of account given by Laudan immediately transfers itself to economics. Whether we are concerned with the Jevonian revolution, the Keynesian or with James Mill and Ricardo's 'methodological revolution' (Hutchison 1978: Ch. 2), we are inevitably directed to the changes in the conceptual foundations underlying the struggle between research traditions.[19]

### The perspective of the sociology of knowledge

One group of scholars, of whom Barry Barnes and David Bloor are the most well-known members, have elevated not scientific revolution but Kuhn's account of the authoritarian nature of normal science into the centrepiece of their description of the development, or as they would say 'the production' of scientific knowledge.[20] What is particularly striking about their views is an extreme relativism, which leads them to assert that assessment of a body of knowledge cannot be undertaken except in so far as it reflects the interests of a social group. Coats (1984) has ably summarized this 'Strong Programme' in the sociology of knowledge for the benefit of historians of economics, so I shall not go over the same ground here. Suffice it to say that from this perspective our investigations should be purely sociological; the adoption of theories is determined by the socialization and training undergone by scientists, together with the interests of the social group to which they belong. A typical sociological study of the type undertaken by adherents of the Strong Programme will analyse the adoption of a particular knowledge claim first by considering the technical and esoteric professional considerations of a group of researchers, and then go on to examine the wider social context.[21] Such analyses of theories are based on an inversion of the typical definition of a theory, which is not 'a system of statements perhaps, or a formal mathematical structure ... a theory is defined by its applications: it is simply the cluster of what are called its "applications"' (Barnes 1982: 63).

Needless to say, the emphasis on the class interests of a profession should not deceive the reader into thinking that the Strong Programme is simply a form of vulgar Marxism. In fact, its epistemological nihilism is much more radical than that of the Marxists.[22]

What implications does this view of the production of knowledge have for the issue at hand? Clearly, its implication is rather trite: we should explain the recurrence of theories with reference to the replication of the sociological characteristics of the economic profession. This, however, neglects the all-important point of the interaction between economists and society at large, and it is a truism to say that this interaction, in most areas of the subject except the most abstract reaches of theory, conditions the tasks which a policy-orientated science like economics must perform. Some of the most suggestive ideas with respect to this issue are to be found in Kuhn's great forerunner, Ludwig Fleck (1935 [1976]). Fleck's view of knowledge appears to me to be identical to that of the Strong Programme.

Claims to empirical knowledge, 'facts', as Fleck calls them, are simply whatever the scientific community chooses to regard as relevant to its preservation. Thus, 'the signal of resistance opposing free arbitrary thinking is called a fact' (Fleck 1935 [1976]: 101). These facts are produced by what Fleck calls the 'Thought Collective', which 'can exist whenever two or more individuals are actually exchanging thoughts' (102), but may develop into more stable social structures – 'communities maintaining intellectual interaction' (1935 [1976]: 39).

A Thought Collective is divided into two parts: an esoteric side consisting of experts, and an exoteric circle of laymen influenced by the theories produced by the experts. The role of the Thought Collective is to be the articulator of what Fleck calls the 'Thought Style' and which 'provides the special "carrier" for the historical development of any field of thought, as well as for the given stock of knowledge and level of culture', but also influences facts since it is 'directed perception, with corresponding mental and objective assimilation of what has been so perceived' (1935 [1976]: 101). In effect, it conditions cognition within the Thought Collective. A Thought Style radiates from the esoteric circle, and becomes more and more reified the further away a member of the Thought Collective is from its centre. We therefore have a model not just of the generation of scientific facts, but also of the influence of a science on society.

Philosophically minded historians of science have difficulty with a concept as sociological, concrete and relativist as the Thought Collective. Kuhn tries to get round this by endorsing Fleck's view as a 'hypostasized fiction'.[23] I think this idea is much less of a 'fiction' in the history of economics, where 'external history', to use a Lakatosian term, looms large indeed. Let us take an example.

Classical Economics clearly fits appropriately into the concept of a Thought Style. One has to go through a lot of convoluted arguments to claim that it did not have a strong ideological component.[24] Ricardo and those who closely followed his doctrine, like James Mill, Senior and McCulloch, constitute the esoteric circle. Those who attended the Political Economy Club constitute the overlap between the esoteric and exoteric circles, while politicians in parliament who endorsed some of their ideas, from Huskisson (a Tory) through Francis Place (a Radical), belong to the exoteric circle.[25] Further out from the esoteric circle we find the populariz-

ers such as Harriet Martineau and Jane Marcet, and right on the circum-
ference of the exoteric circle are to be found the propagandistic versions
of Political Economy taught in schools for the working class.[26] In addition,
this Thought Style overlaps with another, that of the philosophic radicals,
and a figure like Bentham, who is notoriously difficult to place, can be
regarded as embodying both.[27] Probably a similar sketch could be made
for Keynesianism in the 1950s or monetarism in the 1980s. From this
perspective, the idea of a Thought Style is much more relevant than that of
a paradigm, and exists concretely as a technical examplar of successful
scientific practice.[28] Sets of Guiding Assumptions in economics, however,
have all too often been part and parcel of wider social and political ideologies. One has only to think of Bohm-Bawerk as a Minister of Finance or
J.S. Mill as the parliamentary spokesman for the working man, to be
aware of this. The concept of a Thought Style, through the connection
with the Thought Collective, embodies this sociological and cultural aspect
of the history of economics which displays 'the close association that exists
within the attitude of the public ... with the kind of problems that at any
given time interest analysts and form the general attitude or spirit in which
they approach their problems' (Schumpeter 1954: 39).

To further grasp the relevance of these ideas for economics, one should
look at the surprising degree of congruence between Fleck's concepts and
those of Schumpeter in Chapter 4 of his *History of Economic Analysis*,
entitled 'The Sociology of Economics'. While Fleck is not mentioned, one
should perhaps not be surprised at this similarity, since Schumpeter was
explicitly writing from within that particular European tradition which
derives from Karl Mannheim. Fleck is clearly related to this tradition,
although he, unlike Schumpeter, does not actually cite Mannheim.

The idea of a Thought Style corresponds remarkably to Schumpeter's
'vision', which is 'ideological almost by definition' and 'enters in on the
ground floor of the pre-analytic cognitive act', and like a Thought Style
'embodies the picture of things as we see them' (Schumpeter 1954: 39–42).
This recalls Fleck's description of Thought Style as a form of perception.
Schumpeter also has a concept similar to that of the Thought Collective. This
is 'Economic Thought', 'the sum total of all the opinions and desires concerning economic subjects' (Schumpeter 1954: 38). This, in turn, is divided up into
an esoteric part – 'Economic Analysis' – and an exoteric – 'Economic
Opinion' – the 'less completely systematized set of opinions on economic
subjects that "float in the public mind"'. There is certainly an interest, from
the point of view of the historiography of economic analysis, in these connections between Schumpeter's framework and that of Fleck's, but what is
particularly interesting for our problem is Schumpeter's suggestion that a
Vision or Thought Style may recur during the development of economics:

It is interesting to note that vision of this kind not only must precede
historically the emergence of analytic effort in any field but also may

re-enter the history of every established science each time somebody teaches us to see things in the light of which the source is not to be found in the facts, methods and results of the pre-existing state of the science.

(Schumpeter 1954: 41)

Schumpeter, himself, made less use of this idea than he might have. He did, however, find one striking example, the stagnationism of the classicals which he held to be part of their Vision, and the stagnationism later recurring as the Vision of some of the Keynesians (1954: 570, 1172).

Now we can answer the question: what can be learnt from the literature on the boundary between the sociology of knowledge and the historical philosophy of science? I think there are two things.

First, by using Fleck's much more well-articulated and structured version of the concepts used by Schumpeter, we arrive at the hypothesis of a recurring Thought Style. Second, from the Sociology of Science proper and its Strong Programme, we have a pragmatic emphasis on the role of research techniques, materials and instruments for the dissemination of the knowledge which determines the nature of scientific 'facts'.[29]

## Interim conclusion and working hypotheses

To conclude this chapter, let me systematize certain potentially fruitful hypotheses about the recurrence of theories and guiding assumptions, which I have distilled from the historical philosophy of science. These will be tested later against an actual case study. They are the following:

1   Theories recur because of the continuity of certain basic scientific concepts, often linked to a reaction against some particularly monolithic body of ideas which has outlived its usefulness (Bachelard).
2   Theories recur ostensibly in conjunction with continuous debate over conceptual problems. In fact, this reflects a dialectic of Research Traditions (Laudan).
3   Theories recur because a Thought Style reappears (Fleck, Schumpeter). This is related both to technical factors special to the subject and to its external history (Strong Programme).

None of this should be taken to imply any agreement on my part with these hypotheses. Rather these, and the subtle concepts which underlie them, such as Research Traditions and Thought Collectives, direct one to write a structured and analytical type of history of economic thought.

As Kant put it: 'Mere polyhistory is a cyclopean erudition that lacks one eye, the eye of philosophy' (quoted by Hacking 1983). Hopefully, this eye will help us to examine this problem of recurring doctrines.

# 3 A survey and reconstruction of the modern intertemporal approach to international macroeconomics

Progress in economics consists almost entirely in improvements in the choice of models.

J.M. Keynes (1973: 296)

Applications of intertemporal general equilibrium analysis have become increasingly popular in international macroeconomics. The analysis of raw material or input shocks is something to which the traditional tools in the area, like the Mundell–Fleming framework and the Monetary Approach, being designed to deal with other problems, are not very well suited. If one wants to incorporate resource allocation effects such as those mentioned above, an application of general equilibrium analysis seems important, if not indispensable. The intertemporal aspects of the problem, on the other hand, notably the responses of private saving and investment and government borrowing, are important for analysing the process of balance of payments adjustment. An advantage of general equilibrium is that it presents macroeconomic adjustment in a framework which is explicitly consistent with private optimizing behaviour; if a welfare analysis is required, this approach makes it much easier to arrive at precise results.

A related literature, in the 1980s, has discussed the monetary aspects of international payments problems within the context of intertemporal general equilibrium analysis. In particular, it has been concerned with exchange rate theory. This literature, exemplified by Helpman (1981), Lucas (1981) and Helpman and Razin (1979), has clarified the welfare properties and general features of equilibria under alternative exchange rate systems. Further studies, such as Stockman (1980) and Helpman and Razin (1982), have tried to isolate the determinants of exchange rate movements in terms of an intertemporal approach.

The theme of this chapter and the following one is that this approach is not really new; there exists a research tradition in the history of international monetary economics which utilizes the concepts of intertemporal trade. This body of doctrine constitutes a rival research tradition to what, for want of a better description, I shall call the 'traditional' or 'received' research tradition. The received research tradition consists of those works which always regarded current account and balance of payments equilibrium as synonymous. The term research tradition itself should be understood in Laudan's sense: 'A set of guidelines for the development of specific theories' (1977: 79).

To recap the account of Chapter 2, remember that these guidelines are divided into two parts: an ontology which constitutes a set of assumptions about the entities and processes in a domain of study, and a heuristic, which specifies the legitimate methods of inquiry open to a researcher within that tradition.

The purpose of this inquiry is to see if the concept of a research tradition provides an adequate explanation of the recurrence of doctrines in economics, but before carrying out this historical inquiry I must provide an adequate metatheoretical description of the cluster of models which are to be found within this research tradition.

This description will rationally reconstruct the interrelated theories of intertemporal trade which are of 1980s vintage. My reconstruction will serve to illuminate, compare and contrast the earlier theories which are described in the next chapter. My particular method of reconstruction derives from the 'Structuralist' approach to theory analysis applied to economics by the authors in Stegmueller *et al.* (1982), especially the less formal applications of the approach presented by Kotter and Hamminga in that volume. This type of metatheoretical approach is structuralist in the sense that a theory is defined as a whole interrelated model or group of models, and this construct is taken as the unit of analysis. Such a procedure marks this approach off from that of Popper and Lakatos, who are concerned with the statements and predictions made by a particular theory where the term theory is synonymous with what economists call a model. They are not concerned with the formal interconnections between models. (The term 'structuralism' is here used in a different sense from that associated with Levi Strauss and his followers.) Hopefully, the structuralist approach will yield useful insights into the functioning of these models which will make it possible to pick out theories from the past of economics which belong to the intertemporal trade research tradition.

My exposition proceeds as follows: I shall set out some rather crude but basic distinctions between the intertemporal and received approaches to international macroeconomics. This type of classification is often made in expositions of the subject, and it will be seen that it does not really get to the heart of the differences between the two approaches.

Next, harking back to the previous chapter, I shall give a brief description of the thought style underlying the theory to be articulated later. A formal reconstruction of the theory is not in itself sufficient, I believe, to explain the recurrence of intertemporal trade theory which I shall be discussing later in the book. Following from this, I undertake an analysis of the theory where the full panoply of the structuralist approach is employed, particularly with regard to its monetary aspects.

## Received versus intertemporal international monetary theory

The received approach to international monetary economics follows a time-honoured methodology in economics, and this consists of selecting those aspects of economic behaviour which appear to the researcher to be essential for explaining a particular problem and then welding them together into a coherent whole. This is very much the approach of the General Theory for example, where a 'universal psychological law' (underlying the consumption function) is used extensively. Keynes did not invent such a procedure, however; Ricardo's theory of growth and distribution or Fisher's version of the quantity theory, to quote two examples at random, are both based on subjective judgements about the behaviour of economic agents. Most international monetary economics since Ricardo can be characterized as being of this type. It has been surveyed with great scholarship by Viner (1937), provocatively by Frenkel and Johnson (1976: Ch. 1), and by Flanders (1989). The intertemporal approach uses a quite distinct methodology; it uses the methods and tools of intertemporal general equilibrium theory, and like all general equilibrium theory has a microeconomic foundation based on axioms of rational behaviour by consumers and firms.

This is enough to distinguish the intertemporal theory from the received one from the point of view of any economist, yet the fact that such a thought style (to use the terminology of Chapter 2) is used in itself tells us very little about the distinctive functioning of this theory. To demonstrate the truth of this contention, consider the following characterizations of models of the international economy given by Krueger (1983: 21–8). These characterizations are:

1    The questions these models ask, such as what are the properties of fixed as opposed to flexible exchange rate systems in handling external shocks? or what are the alternative means of adjustment to external or internal disturbances?
2    The assumed nature of the international environment. Are we dealing with a small or a large country, therefore are world prices and interest rates given?
3    The assumed macroeconomic structure of the economy; in particular, are we dealing with a flexprice or fixprice economy, and therefore, are we dealing with an economy which can exhibit unemployment?
4    How is the capital account treated, in particular can domestic consumers hold domestic money but not foreign money, can they hold foreign bonds but not foreign money?

5   What are the links between the current account and the domestic economy? In particular, are traded goods produced domestically, perfect or imperfect substitutes for goods obtainable from the rest of the world, and is there a set of nontraded goods in the economy?

6   Are changing asset positions and therefore international indebtedness, analysed as they develop over time?

7   Expectations formation: is it rational or static, and more particularly in this context, are developments such as devaluations or external shocks anticipated or unanticipated?

It is safe to say that the models created by the intertemporal approach are in no way different with regard to 1, 2, 4 and 5. 3 is also a relevant characterization, since there exists a disequilibrium strand in this literature (Cuddington *et al.* 1984: Ch. 2; Cuddington and Vinals 1986). Point 6, which one might think is the province of the intertemporal approach, can also be covered by models which allow scope for capital or asset accumulation but do not assume optimizing behaviour by individual agents. For the case of flexible exchange rates these models are surveyed in detail by Obstfeld and Stockman (1985), and for fixed exchange rates by Frenkel and Mussa (1985: Sec. 3).

The way the intertemporal approach treats 7 expectations, is, surprisingly, less distinct than one might expect. While perfect foresight or rational expectations are usually assumed, Persson and Svensson (1983) have shown how this approach can be applied to a situation where expectations are systematically wrong. Where, then, other than the question of how models should be built, lies the difference between the intertemporal and received approach? The answer, I believe, lies in the conception or vision of balance of payments equilibrium underlying the two bodies of literature.

In the traditional literature, current account balance is a necessary condition for equilibrium of the balance of payments. This is true under the price–specie flow mechanism, traditional Keynesian multiplier models, the monetary approach to the balance of payments, or a sophisticated model of capital and asset accumulation like Dornbusch (1980: Ch. 7). In the most simple cases, such as those treated by classical economists like Ricardo or Thornton or by the basic 'proto-model' (to borrow Flanders' 1989 terminology) of the monetary approach, the requirements are more rigid and the trade account must be balanced in equilibrium.

In the intertemporal approach, these requirements are relaxed; all that is necessary for equilibrium is that the current account be balanced over time, in the sense that the present value of a country's obligations cannot exceed the present value of its assets. It has been argued that this definition of equilibrium is the appropriate one to use when analysing the problem of the impact of fiscal policies and supply shocks in an international context (Dornbusch 1980). This change in the conception of the equilibrium of an open economy is what truly marks off the intertemporal approach from the received approach.

There now follows a formal reconstruction of modern work on intertemporal trade. This reconstruction will be carried out by tracing out the research strategies economists commonly pursue when constructing a theory. We shall see that this results in the development of a series of models of increasing realism and complexity. Ultimately, it will be seen that the intertemporal approach can be summed up by three alternative models and a number of theorems.

## The structuralist approach

The next part of this discussion then enters upon the reconstruction proper of our contemporary theory. Initially, I should like to set out the type of structuralist approach I am going to use in this undertaking. As stressed above, the approach is called structuralist in that the unit of analysis is the structure of the theory as a whole, not just the hypotheses it generates. In order to do this therefore, one needs to devise a terminology which unambiguously describes the architecture of the models. In metatheories of this type, one starts initially with what is left unsaid by the participants in a field of research. I thus start with the informal concepts which characterize the thought style of a group of researchers. For the purposes of this inquiry I shall treat a thought style as consisting of two parts. The first part is the vision, which represents the intuitive idea underlying a particular theory. In the work of Schumpeter, this term and thought style are more or less interchangeable, but I shall add a second component to the concept of a thought style, and this consists of a set of presuppositions. This idea was first introduced, as an amendment to Lakatos's research programme, by Zahar (1976), and applied to economics by Fulton (1984). These presuppositions consist of the methodological commitments of the authors. Related to these presuppositions, which are basically those of intertemporal general equilibrium analysis, are the set of standard conditions on technology, preferences and factor endowments (Hamminga 1982: 3; Kotter 1982: 108–9). In intertemporal trade theory, for example, these form a domain from which a functional system determines a set of range of variables, which are the equilibrium prices of factors of production and commodities in different time periods, and likewise the equilibrium quantities of factor inputs used by firms and their equilibrium outputs of commodities. These will be an equilibrium set of prices and quantities, in so far as they support a set of consumption plans for consumers and production plans for producers such that: (a) each producer's plan has maximum present value given his production possibility set; (b) each consumer's plan maximizes his utility within the consumption possibility set, subject to his intertemporal budget constraint; (c) for each commodity at each date, total world demand equals the total world supply. Note that (c) does not hold for any individual economy, as it must do within a closed economic system.

So far I have done no more than to describe the underlying thought style. It is possible to construct a very general model, of the Arrow–Debreu type, on the basis of the standard conditions (a), (b) and (c). Such a procedure is often not the appropriate one for a researcher to take, since it is well known both among philosophers (Hausman 1981: 203–5, 117–20) and economists (Hahn 1973: 323–4), that these models are far too broad and their assumptions too removed from reality to provide scientific explanations of economic events. (The term 'scientific explanation' has a precise philosophical meaning in this context. It refers to the covering law model of scientific explanation (Hausman 1981: 198–200).) Their generality is also such that they lack any clear predictive power (Hausman 1981: 152–3). To overcome these problems, economists then specify an additional set of explanatory ideal conditions (Hamminga 1982: 4) which cope with the specific situation they are seeking to describe. An example of these are the assumptions in trade theory that factors are immobile between countries, and the more specific assumption in the Hecksher–Ohlin variant that production functions are identical across countries. Another example is the assumed demographic structure of overlapping generations models. What is important about these conditions is that they remain constant throughout the variants of a particular model. They are therefore the means by which a class of models with a specific and restricted structure is extracted from the most general type of Arrow–Debreu framework, and the means by which unity is maintained within a class of models.

An important adjunct in economics to these explanatory ideal conditions is a specialized condition termed 'the field' (Hamminga 1982: 4). The field is determined by the number of countries, commodities, factors and time periods assumed in the initial conditions of a model. A classic case is the $2 \times 2 \times 2$ field of basic trade theory. Such a field, together with a set of ideal conditions, enables the economist to devise a set of applications for a theory. The purpose of these applications, however, is to devise meaningful theorems which follow from these conditions. These theorems can be either internally interesting or externally interesting. By internally interesting, I mean that the theorem clarifies certain conceptual problems created by the theory. An example of these are existence theorems, which were originally devised to clear up severe inconsistencies in Walrasian accounts of general equilibrium (Weintraub 1985: Ch. 6). On the other hand, theorems can pack a political punch, like the Stolper–Samuelson theorem of real trade theory, or rational expectations results on the irrelevance of monetary policy. Such theorems are called externally interesting.

In order to derive theorems it is usually necessary not just to specify the field, but also to introduce an additional set of special conditions. These involve restrictions on the form of production and utility functions, and what distinguishes them from the explanatory ideal conditions is that they can be altered from model to model.

We now have a description of the structure of an economic theory; but this structure is a useful conceptual device only if it can be used to describe a set of research strategies adopted by economists to develop a theory. I shall discuss these in more detail below; yet it is immediately evident what such strategies might be. First, we have the possibility of field extension, an obsession of real trade theory for example. Second, the special conditions may be weakened in order to increase the generality of a theorem. A third possibility is to construct alternative conditions and prove the same theorem under these assumptions. Fourth, one may try to alter the special conditions, not in order to make the theorems more rigorous and general, but to make them less abstract and more meaningful in relation to economic life. All of these strategies are in effect plausibility strategies, aimed at increasing the probability that theorems may be true in the real world. Finally, we have what I term implementation strategies, aimed at altering the conditions so that empirical tests of the theorems can be performed. Such strategies may contradict the more theoretical plausibility strategies; for example, in econometric work it is usually necessary to use strong special conditions and assume specific functional forms.

## Intertemporal international macroeconomics

I now begin my sketch and structuralist examination of intertemporal trade theory. First, I sketch out what I conjecture is the basic 'vision' – that is to say, as I have stated, the intuitive idea in the minds of economists using this theory. Next, I try to isolate the presuppositions which underlie this vision. These presuppositions are often unstated and taken as understood; however, they constitute the body of fundamental ideas around which a new school has crystallized. Next, this idea is extended to set out the concepts I have attributed to these economists by means of simple two-period diagrams. This is done because two-period analysis is a useful expository device, widely used in the literature I am discussing. In addition, this model was greatly used by Irving Fisher, and by Milton Friedman in his analysis of the consumption function. These facts say something about the intellectual provenance of the new approach. Then this approach is generalized in a manner which demonstrates its relationship to real trade theory. Next, monetary intertemporal literature is discussed. The purpose of the analysis is to emphasize those features which demonstrate the unity of these studies with those that deal with monetary issues. Finally, I compare the approach of the 1980s, during which the modern intertemporal literature developed, with material which appeared about two decades earlier, and is similar in some respects.

The next step is to derive a group of criteria which, taken together, are sufficient to define whether the work of a particular economist fits into the intertemporal approach to international macroeconomics. These criteria are derived from the above investigation of the methodology and results to be found in the research of the 1980s. As such, they constitute a measuring rod against which the work of the earlier group of economists can later be judged.

## The basic vision

I have described the first component of any thought style as being a basic vision, an intuitive picture of how the economy functions. The basic idea of the intertemporal approach is that individuals derive an optimal savings programme over time in an open economy context. Just as this theory provided capital-theoretic underpinnings to the idea of the consumption function, so it is hoped that it will do the same for the analysis of the balance of payments.

Consider a country consisting of a single representative consumer who maximizes a multiperiod utility function discounted over time, subject to an intertemporal budget constraint. There is only one nonstorable good available, although a country or representative individual receives new endowments in each time period. This country has access to a perfect world capital market at each point in time and is assumed to be small. The condition for the allocation of consumption along the optimal path will be that the ratio of marginal utility of future consumption to that of present consumption will be equal to the marginal cost of borrowing, which under the above assumptions equals one plus the world rate of interest. This condition fixes the optimal quantity of debt at each point in time. At any point in time, the borrowing abroad means in effect that the consumer good is being imported into the country in exchange for claims by foreigners on its future output. The repayment at later dates of foreign debts with interest likewise requires the export of commodities. The two sets of transactions can be regarded as one act of intertemporal commodity trade. It follows from this discussion that international lending and borrowing are subject to the same basic principles as static trade, with the difference that it is not different commodities at the same date which are traded but a single commodity at different dates. This implies that trade is not required to be balanced at any moment in time. I have already identified this above as the central difference between intertemporal and textbook international monetary theory. The existence of the intertemporal budget constraint does imply that trade must be balanced, but this is only in the sense of being balanced in present value terms over the country's entire horizon. At any moment in time, there can be a trade deficit (surplus) financed by a capital inflow (outflow). This result translates a variant of microeconomic trade theory into a theory of trade imbalance, and hence into an analysis of the problems of balance of payments financing and adjustment dealt with by international macroeconomics.

If explicit assumptions are made about the form of the utility function, it is possible to relate a model of this type more directly to the current account. A solution can be found for the consumption demand function in terms of the parameters of the utility function and initial wealth (as for example in Frenkel and Razin (1985)). With output given exogenously, the balance of payments can be derived and comparative dynamic exercises can be carried out. Such exercises can be further facilitated if the conditions can be found for a stationary equilibrium of the system. In this way, appropriate technical assumptions make it possible to use the optimal international borrowing and lending model for an analysis of various international issues. Examples of these are Dornbusch's study of real exchange rate effects (Dornbusch 1983), and Frenkel and Razin's study of the international consequences of government budget deficits (Frenkel and Razin 1985).

## The presuppositions

Fulton (1984) has pointed out that there are usually a set of common concepts underlying any economic theory. These constitute the structure of ideas from which that theory is derived. These concepts are often more general than formal assumptions; they may be only vague generalizations shared by the whole of economics, or they may actually be metaphysical propositions with no scientific content. This is a wider classification than Lakatos's idea of the 'hard core' and, as mentioned previously, it originates in the work of Zahar (1976), who calls such a set of ideas 'presuppositions'. It can be shown that a common set of presuppositions underlies the recent intertemporal general equilibrium studies. Many of these may seem both obvious and commonplace. Despite this, they have an importance which derives from the fact that they have previously received no emphasis in international macroeconomics. There follows a list of relevant presuppositions, in order of decreasing generality, although not necessarily in order of importance:

1   Good economic theory is based on individual entities such as the consumer, the firm or worker; therefore, International Monetary Economics should explicitly analyse the behaviour of these economic actors.
2   The behaviour of economic actors in the international economy is rational. Rational conduct is defined as that conduct which the individual can demonstrate, at least to himself, to be the most advantageous for him.
3   Households and firms are maximizing agents and exhibit optimizing behaviour not only with regard to the present, but also with respect to the future.
4   When forming expectations about the future, individuals have full knowledge of the relevant circumstances of their economic situation,

including those circumstances which will occur in the future. This statement includes the possibility that individuals act in terms of a known probability distribution.

5    Permanent and temporary changes in economic variables must be taken into account. A permanent change is defined as a disturbance which occurs over the entire time horizon specified in an individual's decision problem.

6    Money is held because of particular functions it fulfils for individuals at the microeconomic level. Money demands should therefore be derived from individual utility maximizing behaviour.

7    Welfare evaluations should be performed with demand functions derived from utility maximization. This makes it possible to use the criteria of Pareto optimality.

Most of these requirements were previously considered unimportant in International Monetary Theory. Sometimes some of them have been met; for example, Frenkel and Rodriguez (1975) incorporated an investment decision grounded in rational choice, but did not extend this to all economic agents when they used a saving–consumption decision based on a mechanistic wealth adjustment process. Likewise, the many models basing themselves solely on the rational expectations hypothesis but using an ad hoc microeconomic framework fulfil the criteria of rational decision-making and expectation formation, but neglect the element of basing the analysis on a bedrock of individual utility or profit maximization. Intertemporal general equilibrium theory will, on the other hand, satisfy the above presuppositions, although this often requires a careful specification of the model, especially when money or uncertainty are included. The studies discussed below all use such a methodology and in addition, as in the case of Helpman and Razin (1979) or Persson (1982), openly declare that they hold many of the presuppositions listed above.

## The two-period models

I believe that the vision described above, in which a forward-looking, rational consumer who carries out optimal saving and consumption decisions over time while enjoying access to an international capital market, constitutes, together with the presuppositions, the essential thought style of economic activity in an open economy which is the basis of the modern approach. Unfortunately, explicit infinite-horizon maximizing models become difficult to handle, however, when additional factors such as investment and intermediate inputs are introduced. Analysis can also involve a retreat from the most general model to special cases. The most fruitful of these has been to use a two-period finite horizon approach. This makes the approach identical to the standard Fisherian model of capital and interest.

### The Fisherian approach

The extension of the Fisherian closed economy analysis of interest rate determination to the theory of current account adjustment is relatively simple, and essentially involves no more than treating countries as if they were individuals in Fisher diagrams. It is surprising then that this approach was neglected until the advent of the new approach. No analysis using this device appeared until Webb's (1970) analysis of the determination of the current account, and it did not become common until Sachs (1981) made extensive use of it. This fact suggests that technical advances in model building did not play a role in creating the new school. Rather, the adoption of the set of presuppositions discussed above was the essential prerequisite for the adoption of an intertemporal capital-theoretic approach to balance of payments problems. Until this was done, economists did not see the relevance of the Fisher diagram to international macroeconomics issues.

The simplest framework to illustrate an intertemporal general equilibrium approach is therefore not the multiperiod paradigm sketched in the first section but a two-period, one-good model. Figure 3.1 depicts the autarchy equilibrium of this model. The one good, call it 'corn', is perfectly malleable and is capable of being consumed or invested in order to grow

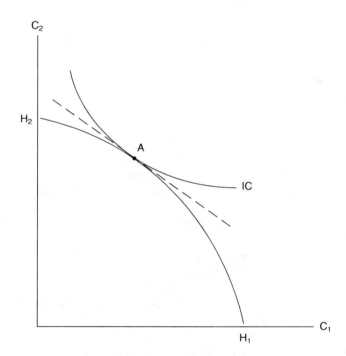

*Figure 3.1* Two-period one-good model equilibrium.

corn next year. $H_1$ represents this year's harvest. The concave curve $H_1H_2$ depicts the frontier of transformation between current corn consumption and next year's harvest of seedcorn. It is concave because the technology exhibits diminishing returns, given, for example, a constant labour force. Curve IC displays a community indifference curve between current consumption and future consumption of corn. (If we assume a constant distribution of income and homothetic preferences, we can construct a community indifference curve and do not need to assume a representative consumer.) Point A represents the Pareto efficient competitive equilibrium. The slope of the curve at A reflects the intertemporal preferences for present as opposed to future consumption. If preferences had been more directed to first-period consumption, equilibrium would have occurred to the southeast of A, where the future is discounted more with respect to the present.

Figure 3.2 describes the position of the economy once it has been opened to a perfect international capital market. The line IT, whose slope is equal to one over one plus the world rate of interest, now represents the new intertemporal consumption possibilities frontier. With homothetic tastes, consumers will move along the straight-line wealth expansion path (WE) from A to B. Clearly, a higher level of utility can be attained. We immediately see that this approach readily permits welfare analysis of the effects of foreign borrowing. This diagram, when carefully interpreted, yields several further insights. First, the tangent between IT and $H_1H_2$ shows that the marginal product of corn–capital should be equated with the marginal cost of capital represented by the world discount rate. This is in fact the standard cost–benefit condition for investment projects in a small open economy. Regardless of the consumption stream, we see that the country should invest so as to equate the marginal product of capital, evaluated at world market prices, with the cost of capital, also at world market prices. A second point is that we note that a country moving from A to B will run a current account surplus of $C_1 - X_1$ in the first period and a deficit of $C_2 - X_2$ in the second period. This demonstrates what Frenkel and Razin (1987: 149–50) call the 'consumption augmenting' effect of international borrowing. The possibility of lending to the rest of the world through a current account surplus and reducing home investment augments the level of consumption in both periods. (Investment at home falls from the horizontal distance between A and $H_1$ to $X_1 - H_1$. Note that savings and investment are always equal in this one-good world with perfect foresight.) Alternatively, a country initially at C has a strong preference for present consumption; under homothetic tastes and the expansion path given by WE', this country will run a current account deficit $C_1' - X_1$ in the first period and a corresponding current account surplus in the second period. The important conclusion is that countries which exhibit high (low) rates of time preference will tend to run initial deficits (surpluses) and future surpluses (deficits). This discussion illustrates what

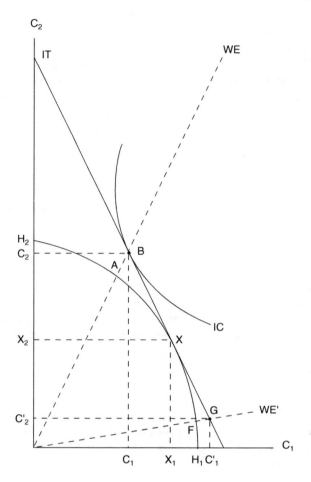

*Figure 3.2* Intertemporal trade equilibrium.

Sachs (1981) has called the 'time preference motive' underlying the determination of current account surpluses. When home rates of time preference are below interest rates on the world capital market, households have an incentive to accumulate wealth, that is to save and to enjoy the benefits later by running a current account deficit and enjoying net imports of the consumption good. This wealth is accumulated by lending abroad, acquiring foreign securities which will be cashed in during the second period. On the other hand, people in a country with relatively high rates of time preference will want to borrow now to finance a current account deficit and pay for this current consumption by running a surplus in the second period. There is also a trade-theoretic interpretation of this result in terms of 'comparative advantage' with regard to intertemporal preferences. Countries with high rates of time preference will initially tend to be capital importers, while countries with low rates of time preference relative to the rest of the world will export capital.

The intertemporal budget constraint for the country enables us to easily illuminate some of these points, in particular the relationship between first-period deficits (surpluses) and second-period surpluses (deficits). The representative consumer in this economy maximizes his utility from consumption in the two periods, subject to the present value budget constraint:

$$C_1 + \delta C_2 = W$$

where $\delta = 1/1 + r$ is the discount factor and $W$ is the country's wealth. Wealth is defined as the present value of net outputs (gross outputs minus investments):

$$W = f(\bar{K}) - I + \delta f(\bar{K} + I)$$

Here $I$ is investment and the second-period output depends on the initial stock of seedcorn and that added by first-period investments.

Substituting this expression for wealth into the consumer's budget constraint yields the relationship that the discounted sum of trade balance surpluses ($TA_1$ and $TA_2$), must equal zero:

$$TA_1 + \delta TA_2 = 0$$

Under the assumption that the country has no initial debt, the first-period trade account equals the first-period current account, so we find that the discounted sum of current account surpluses must equal the debt service account, $DA_2$ in the second period:

$$CA_1 + CA_2 = DA_2$$

The two equations I have just set out exemplify the definition of balance of payments equilibrium required in the intertemporal approach. Trade must be balanced over time in present value terms: there is no reason for the current account itself ever to be in balance.

### *Temporary and permanent disturbances with homothetic and nonhomothetic tastes*

A great advantage of the intertemporal approach is that it enables the effects of real disturbances such as changes in productivity or the availability of raw materials to be easily analysed. The crucial distinction here is that between temporary and permanent disturbances, a distinction that could not be analysed without taking an explicitly intertemporal approach.

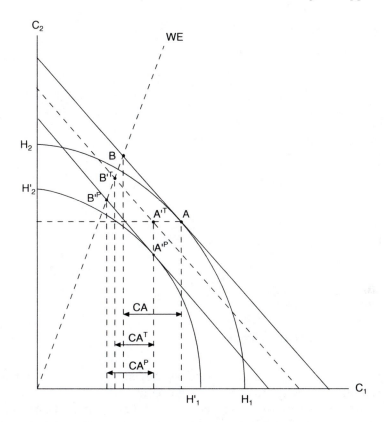

*Figure 3.3* Shocks and intertemporal trade equilibrium.

In Figure 3.3 the permanent shock is represented by a parallel inward shift of the intertemporal transformation frontier from $H_1 H_2$ to $H_{1'} H_{2'}$. Production moves from $A$ to $A^{'P}$. In the case of a temporary real shock in the first period only $A$ shifts to $A^{'T}$. The temporary decline in output leads to a much larger fall in the current account surplus than does the permanent decline. This is because in this case the current account is acting as a shock absorber, smoothing the path of consumption over time in the event of disturbances. The temporary discrepancy between consumption and income is made up for by a current account deficit, financed by a capital inflow.

In order to make this point even more explicit, consider the extreme case of Figure 3.4, where initially there is no balance of payments deficit. In this case, a permanent shock, which reduces $H_1$ and $H_{2'}$ by equal amounts, will leave the current account unchanged and trade will remain balanced as before. On the other hand, a temporary productivity decline from $A$ to $A^{'T}$ again leads to a current account deficit. This brings home

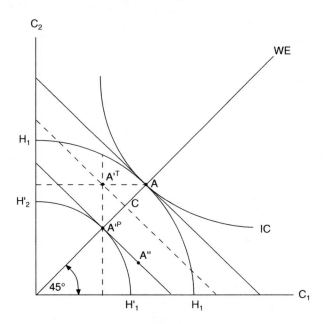

*Figure 3.4* Shocks and productivity decline.

the important point that it is temporary deviations from permanent income that have a strong effect on current account imbalances.

In the first case, where there is an equal shock in both periods, permanent income is changed, while in the case of the temporary disturbance households dissave by means of the current account deficit, spreading some of the loss in consumption to the second period.

### The effect of nonhomothetic preferences

To conclude then, the intertemporal approach emphasizes three causes of current account imbalance. The first is the consumption-augmenting motive, which depends on different returns to investment at home and abroad; the second is the time preference motive which depends on international differences in discount rates; and the third is the consumption-smoothing motive, which depends on the response of consumers to real disturbances which do not affect permanent income.

The breakdown between these motives is harder to sustain if we drop the assumption that preferences are homothetic. For example, if the rate of time preference is high at low levels of wealth and falls as wealth rises, then the consumption expansion locus intersects point $A$ from below, and a permanent negative supply shock will induce a current account deficit shown by a move to a point like $A$ in the diagram (Frenkel and Razin 1987: 152–3). In this case, the time preference motive also operates with respect to real shocks. A similar indeterminacy can also occur in the case of the consumption-augmenting motive. If, following Obstfeld (1981), one assumes that the rate of time preference is a monotonically increasing function of the level of utility, then the new consumption point in Figure 3.2 will be to the right of *B* and the current account surplus is reduced. The time preference motive emphasizes the substitution effect between present and future consumption, and the consumption-smoothing motive emphasizes an income effect caused by an external shock whose influence varies over time. If time preferences are taken to depend on the level of wealth or utility, these distinctions break down, because a direct link between the two effects now exists.

### Some 'externally interesting' theorems

The existence of investment in real capital means that the current account is not just dependent on the consumption-smoothing behaviour discussed above, but also depends on the investment motive. In two sector models in particular, such as that of Bruno (1982), the effect of real disturbances is likely to be ambiguous. For the Fisherian models it is possible to construct cases, as in Razin and Svensson (1983), where saving remains unchanged in response to a shock, while investment is reduced. Thus, the optimal response to, for example, a permanent reduction in productivity is actually to run a current account surplus.

Another important result is that the 'Ricardian' equivalence proposition holds in this context (see Bruce and Purvis 1985; Frenkel and Razin 1985). If government spending increases in the first period and taxes are collected in the second, households, foreseeing the higher second-period taxes, will save more. This saving exactly cancels out the current account deficit induced by government expenditure, so the neutrality of government extends to an open economy intertemporal equilibrium world.

## Field extension: the trade theoretic approach

The natural way to extend the field of the Fisherian model is to add one country and thus abandon the small country assumption. This immediately raises the problem of determining world equilibrium, and it is not surprising that the natural tools to use for this are those of real trade theory. This can be done in several ways: Norman Miller (1968) used Leontief's version of the Fisher diagram to generate trade indifference curves, offer curves and finally world trade equilibrium in the manner of Meade's classic *Geometry of International Trade*; Frenkel and Razin (1987), 19 years later, used the Edgeworth box. The Meade technique, however, has the drawback of being rather cumbersome (it requires four quadrants), while the Edgeworth box requires separate diagrams to analyse differences in discount rates and growth rates between countries.

The most convenient trade theoretic tool to use is the free trade version of the Baldwin (1948) envelope. This permits the derivation of a maximum number of results in a simple framework, while underlining the relationship between intertemporal international macroeconomics and basic trade theory. Figure 3.5 is analogous to a diagram used by Baldwin (1948: 754) and shows the transformation curves for two countries superimposed on one diagram. $X_1X_2$ is the foreign country's (Country II), intertemporal transformation curve and $H_1H_2$ is that of the home country. As in static real trade theory, we can derive an offer curve, $OP$, for the foreign country; this indicates what exchanges that country is prepared to make of current goods for future goods at the intertemporal terms of trade. The diagram has current goods, $C_1$, on the horizontal axis, future consumption, $C_2$, and quantities borrowed on the vertical axis, since the foreign country is prepared to sell securities of value $QR = QP/1 + r$ in order to procure $QR$ of current goods. Choosing different terms of trade in succession, we can then trace out the Baldwin availability locus $B_1B_2$ for country I, which is the home country. In each case, we will derive a new triangle like $EKG$ in Figure 3.5, which is derived by finding the point of tangency $G$, between the price line and country I's transformation curve. Then we measure a triangle whose horizontal and vertical distances are identical to $QR$ and $PQ$. Doing this for all prices, we obtain the line $B_1B_2$ which represents II's offer at various prices. At $F$, the foreign country prefers financial autarky. To the left of $F$, the foreign country borrows and runs a current account surplus in the second period; to the right of $F$, it will be a creditor in the first period and run a current account deficit in the second period. In order to derive the full world intertemporal equilibrium, it is necessary to derive the locus $CHSI$, which represents the different demands by the home country for period 1 goods and securities at different intertemporal prices of consumption. For example, $H$ represents the demand vector corresponding to the world discount rate which induces financial autarky in the home country. Similarly, when the intertemporal terms of trade are given by the slope of $EG$, the home economy's consumption vector is represented by point $E$. To the left of $H$, the home country wishes to export period 1 goods, i.e. be a creditor, to the right she is a debtor. For any terms of trade, the economy will seek the highest indifference curve, such as $I_{CI}$ in the diagram.

Now in order to determine the international equilibrium, two conditions must be fulfilled:

1   Demands and supplies of the commodity must be equal in both periods.
2   The balance of payments must be in equilibrium in one country. (This automatically ensures equilibrium in the other.)

Condition 1 can clearly only be met where the $CHSI$ locus of demands will equal available resources given by the envelope $B_1B_2$. Either points $S$ or $E$

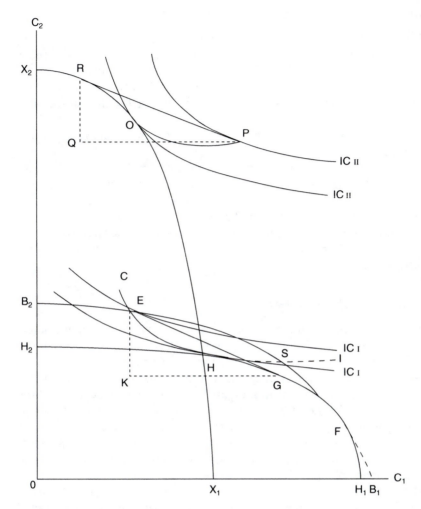

*Figure 3.5* Superimposition of two-country transformation curves.

are possible equilibria. In fact, condition 2 rules out $S$, since at this point, as explained above, both countries wish to run a current account deficit (i.e. they are both offering goods, not securities). This is because to the right of $H$, the home country runs a current account deficit, while to the left of $R$, the foreign country runs a current account deficit. With only one good, this rules out balance of payments equilibrium in a two-country world. Therefore, as in the diagrams drawn, $E$ is the equilibrium intertemporal terms of trade; the foreign country initially runs a current account deficit (as is dictated by the equilibrium at $E$), while the home country initially runs a surplus.

A number of simple theorems follow from this analysis. These are discussed below.

## Externally interesting theorems

1    A country is more likely to be a creditor the lower is the marginal product of its investment. (Where both countries' indifference maps are identical, Country II, with great efficiency in the production of the future goods, will be a debtor in the first period. As in the one-country analysis, a country where it is optimal to invest for the future must finance this by current borrowing.)

2    World interest rates (i.e. intertemporal prices) are equalized by trade in debt.

3    Equality of world interest rates does not imply current account balance. This is contrary to what prevails in conventional macroeconomic models of the open economy, such as the Mundell–Fleming model. Dornbusch (1980: Ch. 10, Sec. 3) shows that under perfect capital mobility, world equilibrium requires current account balance in the traditional framework as long as all traded assets are perfect substitutes.

## Internally interesting theorems

1    Pre-trade relative prices and marginal efficiency of investment determine the pattern of current account surpluses and deficits; autarky prices play the same role as in the theory of comparative advantage. (The more productive is investment in the foreign country, the more likely is the autarky point *R* in Figure 3.5 to be over to the left, and the higher is the likelihood that equilibrium occurs to the left of *H*, so that the home country runs an initial current account surplus.)

2    The determinants of intertemporal trade are essentially the same as those of commodity trade: the form of production functions; initial endowments of capital; and intertemporal preferences.

3    The formal similarity to real trade theory means that 'transfer problem criteria', analogous to those in the static case, can be derived in this model (Frenkel and Razin 1987: 163–5).

## Further field extension

The two-country model outlined above is special in the same way that the two-country, two-factor, two-good model of real trade theory is special. Intertemporal trade, by adding an extra time dimension to the field, complicates matters considerably. The only way to make the two-country model easily tractable is to assume a model like the basic space trade model, with only two goods, period one and period two goods. When the goods field is extended, we immediately run into the familiar trade-theoretic problems of having more goods than factors. Just as in real trade theory, unambiguous results cannot be obtained when many goods are assumed to be traded (Razin and Svensson 1983). Backus and Kehoe (1987) purport to show that they have demonstrated the existence of consumption smoothing and time preference motives in a many-country, one-good and many-time period world without production. In fact, they are able to prove only the existence of an international equilibrium, and have to rely on very special assumptions about functional forms to demonstrate the existence of consumption-smoothing behaviour and the time preference motive. Special conditions must always be added to the model if any analysis is to be carried out in the many-commodity case. The weakest assumption, as shown by Razin and Svensson (1983), is that when there are two goods, one must assume that they are weakly separable over time. This means that the temporal and intertemporal allocation of spending can be separated. Unless such an assumption is made, we must deal with four commodities in each time period when we carry out intertemporal analysis.

Under the above special condition, we can treat intertemporal problems in the same way as in the $2 \times 2 \times 2$ model. It is worth pointing out, however, that extending the field without adding special conditions proved a viable research strategy in real trade theory. I venture to suggest that the inherent bias in the examination of macroeconomic problems towards producing externally interesting theorems and examining the conditions under which they are true or false mitigates against a strategy based on examining the formal conceptual problems involved in field extension. The research strategy followed, as seen in some of the examples above (Ricardian equivalence, supply shocks), has been rather to develop externally interesting theorems which are economically meaningful, even at the expense of adding special conditions.

## Monetary models

The framework discussed above is open to the criticism that it provides a theory of the current account but not of the overall balance of payments. This can be remedied by adding assets such as money and bonds. Previously, the capital account reacted only passively to current account changes; now, with the explicit introduction of asset determination, its composition can be treated as a portfolio choice problem which influences the balance of payments in conjunction with the behaviour of the current account. An even more important consideration is that money must be included if the theory is to be extended to cover the analysis of exchange rate movements. This follows from the fact that an exchange rate is the relative price between two national monies. The previous framework has been extended to monetary environments in a number of ways. It is not my intention to survey what is already a fairly large literature, but merely to comment on the connections which exist between the real and monetary studies, as seen in the literature of the 1980s.

In the most general sense, the studies surveyed by Obstfeld and Stockman (1985), and the similar but more welfare-orientated work of Helpman and Razin (1979), Helpman (1981) and Persson (1982), have much in common with the nonmonetary analyses discussed until now. They share the general set of presuppositions set out above, which is borne out by the fact that they all rest on a framework where intertemporally optimizing agents with perfect foresight interact in a Walrasian general equilibrium setting. In addition, since many of these presuppositions are similar to those which underlay the theory of the firm and the theory of consumer behaviour, this approach uses specific microeconomic theories of money. This microeconomic bias means that all demand functions, including those for money, will be derived from individual utility maximization. It is therefore possible to make precise welfare analyses of the effects of monetary disturbances in the same way as the real framework permits direct welfare analyses of the effects of capital movements and real shocks.

At a more specific level, it emerges that exchange rate movements can be determined by the same forces as those discussed in the previous section. This will be true of any approach that, first, shares our common set of presuppositions, and, second, emphasizes the role of the current account in exchange rate determination. In this way, Obstfeld and Stockman (1985: 982) show how exchange rate movements depend on movements in the current account. These current account movements depend first on deviations between home discount rates and world interest rates, and second on external borrowing and lending in the face of deviations of disposable output from its 'permanent' level. These two factors are of course the time preference and consumption-smoothing motives, which underlay the determination of the current account in a nonmonetary model.

The monetary and nonmonetary frameworks seem therefore to be fairly closely connected, when one takes the approach to modelling money adopted in the discussion by Obstfeld and Stockman (which is based on Obstfeld 1981). This consists of treating money as a utility-bearing asset, in the Patinkin–Sidrauski tradition. The connection is not so clear when the 'cash-in-advance' or finance constraint approach to monetary theory is taken. Even so, Helpman and Razin (1987) do show that exchange rate movements are influenced by the intertemporal pattern of savings and investment, although this must be taken in conjunction with other factors such as the type of payments system operating in the world. Furthermore, differences in interest rates as between home and foreign countries are also shown to play a role in determining exchange rates, as they do in determining the current account.

To understand fully how results of this kind are derived, I would like now to use the structuralist method to seek an understanding of the workings of these monetary models.

Having carried our this brief summary of the way money was incorporated into intertemporal trade theories in the 1980s, I would like to reconstruct one particular variant, the cash in advance approach, using the structuralist framework outlined earlier. The formal development of the theory is drawn from Persson (1982), Obstfeld and Stockman (1985), Frenkel and Razin (1987) and Backus and Kehoe (1987). The material is, however, rearranged in a manner which gives insight into the development and architecture of the theory. By constructing a picture of the theory, it will be possible to see to what extent it is distinct from the trade-theoretic approach.

I start with a review of the presuppositions. These are the same as before, with one exception: some friction or constraint on the functioning of the market for future goods must be introduced into this Arrow–Debreu type of model, in order for money to be held in intertemporal equilibrium. The trick, of course, is to make this friction as mild as possible, so that the basic canons of rational behaviour are not violated. In other respects, the type of underlying standard conditions are no different from what they were before. Thus, consumers have increasing concave and differentiable utility functions which satisfy the Inada conditions. If one wants to include uncertainty, a factor certainly relevant in many contexts where one wants to prove the existence of a monetary equilibrium, it is assumed that the probability of any uncertain event pertaining to a future commodity is known. The consumption possibility set includes a complete set of contingent commodities. Under these conditions, it is of course easy to show that it does not matter whether all trading in future commodities takes place at the initial date, or whether trading takes place in a market which reopens at each future date (Lucas *et al.* 1989: 29–36). The role of firms, however, requires special treatment in the cash in advance framework.

Next, we have the explanatory ideal conditions, whose significance was explained above. The crucial point about these conditions is that they do not vary across a large class of models. Here one must diverge to some extent from the assumptions of the trade-theoretic approach, and introduce conditions necessary for the application of the general framework to international monetary economics. These explanatory ideal conditions concern government, households, firms, markets and the international environment.

1   I start with government, since in a monetary economy some authority must create fiat moneys. The government therefore creates a home country money; it makes purchases or transfers which it finances by issuing new money or lump sum taxes. The government also plays a role in exchange rate policy, but as this depends on the assumed exchange rate regime, and this assumption can vary from application to application, this function is not part of the explanatory ideal conditions. The government must satisfy a budget constraint for all of its operations.

2    Consumers. Households can trade in bonds, which are issued by the private sector and traded on an international capital market. A crucial assumption is made – that interest rates on these claims are positive. Households then carry out a sequence of trades, beginning in the assets market where bonds, home and foreign currency are traded. It is assumed that each household consists of a shopper and an owner. The shopper visits different countries and purchases goods from their workers. The owner sells his endowment in exchange for local products while receiving profit from his firm. Note that cash must be used for every transaction in goods; there are no IOUs. This cash in advance requirement is the distinctive feature of the theory. The shopper then returns, bringing goods and unspent cash. The household then uses its remaining cash holdings and any new money it may acquire from government transfers to restart the sequence of trades. Notice that at this stage, one cannot specify the exact form of the cash in advance constraint as an explanatory ideal condition. This is because its form depends upon the exact timing of the trading sequence and will vary across models.

3    Firms. Firms are rather passive in this formulation: there are no investments or stocks. We can even think of all production as exogenous and costless. The only role of the consumer firm owner is to accumulate money from sales and hold this money at the end of a sequence of trades.

4    Markets. The domestic money market is assumed to be always in equilibrium, so that foreign and domestic demand for home money must always equal its supply. It follows from the presuppositions that goods and bond markets must always clear in each period. For an intertemporal monetary equilibrium to exist, goods allocations, money and asset positions and government policies must be such as to satisfy these market clearing conditions and be consistent with consumer utility maximization over time.

5    The international environment. World markets for goods and financial assets are fully integrated and open to all individuals. Therefore, the law of one price holds:

$$P_t = e_t P_t^*$$                                                         (1)

where $P$ is the home price level, $P^*$ the foreign price level, $t$ is the time period and $e$ the exchange rate. Covered interest rate parity also holds:

$$1 + r = \frac{e_{t+1}}{e_t}(1 + r^*)$$                                     (2)

Here $r$ is the home interest rate and $r^*$ the foreign interest rate.

Most of these conditions are quite general. There are only three specific explanatory ideal conditions: PPP, the law of one price and money market equilibrium. The other conditions are all constructed so that the cash in advance requirement will be the 'monkey wrench thrown into the machine' of intertemporal general equilibrium theory (*pace* Milton Friedman), in order to create conditions under which rational individuals endowed with perfect foresight will hold money.

The field consists of one consumption good and two countries, each with its own money and bond denominated in its country, with one representative household in each country. There are two time periods, an assumption which makes it impossible to discuss a sequence equilibrium in which trading in short-term assets occurs in markets which reopen in each period; with two periods, one cannot distinguish between short- and long-term bonds. The fundamental equivalence under perfect foresight of a standard intertemporal equilibrium (date zero equilibrium, where all future trades are made at the beginning of the first period) and a sequence equilibrium suggests that this is not a limitation of the analysis. The assumption of a finite horizon has one important but often neglected implication; this is that at the end of the last period no money will be held, for it has no function to perform and its value is zero. By backward induction, we would find that money has no value at any previous time. It must therefore be assumed that the government is prepared to hold all the money left over at the end of the second period, in other words the 'chips are cashed in' at the end of an individual's life. This problem obviously cannot occur with an infinite horizon.

By specifying appropriate special conditions, it will be possible to set out the equilibrium of the economy and to derive the externally and internally interesting theorems which are the central results of this approach. At each stage we will indicate how, as part of a research strategy, these conditions may be modified in ways that alter the central theorems. There are three important special conditions which determine the final theorems: these are (a) the status of the currencies, (b) the timing of the sequence of transactions, and (c) the exchange rate regime. I shall deal with these in turn.

a) It is assumed that purchases of goods must be carried out in the seller's currency. A plausible research strategy would be to modify this requirement later so that the buyer's currency must be used, e.g. Helpman and Razin 1984). The timing of the sequence of transactions is that in any period, households first trade money for bonds, after having received a cash transfer from the government. Households then trade cash for goods, so the cash in advance constraints have the form:

$$P_1 C_1 = M_{1H} \tag{3}$$

$$P_1^* C_1^* = M_{1H}^* \tag{4}$$

for period 1, where the star denotes the foreign country, and likewise for the second period. These equations state that planned holdings of domestic currency must equal planned purchases of domestic goods, and planned holdings of foreign currency must equal planned purchases of foreign goods. Equivalent constraints hold in the second period:

$$P_2 C_2 = M_{2H} \tag{5}$$

$$P_2^* C_2^* = M_{2H}^* \tag{6}$$

and for foreign consumers. These constraints hold with equality because of the explanatory ideal condition that interest rates are positive. The money market ideal equilibrium condition implies that:

$$P_t Y_t = M_t \tag{7}$$

This follows from consolidating the home and foreign cash in advance constraints and the fact that in this model, everything produced is consumed at home or abroad. Thus, the strict quantity theory with velocity of one holds in this model.

(c) Initially I assume a flexible exchange rate regime, so the government has no role to play other than to produce domestic currency. So the money supply is given by:

$$M_t = M_{t-1} + D_t \tag{8}$$

where $D_t$ is the new issue of home currency. We can now set out the maximization problem of the home consumer as follows:

Max $U = U(C_1, C_2)$

s.t. $P_1 C_1 - B = M_0 + D_1$

$P_2 C_2 = P_1 Y_1 + D_2 - (1 + r)B$

By (1) and (2), all goods and asset price yields are equivalent from the home country's point of view, so $C$ and $B$ have not been disaggregated into their separate components. $M_0$ is the holdings of domestic money initially held by consumers. It is simplest to consolidate the budget constraint and use the households' dual expenditure functions. (This is a well-behaved maximization problem and all the duality theorems hold. Again, this is a result of the condition of positive interest rates, which insures that budget constraints hold with equality.)

$$E(1, d, u) = M_0 + D_1 + \frac{1}{1+r}(P_1 y_1 + D_2) \tag{9}$$

where $d$ is the discount factor $\left(\dfrac{1}{1+r}\right)\dfrac{P_2}{P_1}$.

Note that $P_1 y_1$ is the household's income in period one available in period two. There is an analogous condition for the foreign country. Market clearing conditions must also be satisfied:

$$E_1 + E_1^* - y_1 + y_1^* = 0 \tag{10}$$

By Walras's law, I shall omit the market for period-two goods, but we also have a market clearing condition in the bond market:

$$B_1 + e_1 B^* = 0. \tag{11}$$

and the interest rate parity and law of one price conditions:

$$P_1 = e_1 P_1^*$$

$$1 + r = (1 + r^*)\frac{e_2}{e_1}.$$

and finally the quantity equation in both countries:

$$M_1 = P_1 y_1, \ M_1^* = P_1 y_1^* \tag{12}$$

Note that all conditions except the quantity theory are in fact explanatory ideal conditions; in this sense, the quantity theory is not part of the theoretical core of the model.

We can now state some externally interesting theorems:

*Theorem 1: neutrality of money*

The trick here is to show that the wealth of consumers in their budget constraint does not depend on the quantity of money.

This wealth is:

$$W = \frac{M_0 + D_1}{P_1} + \frac{1}{1+r}\frac{P_1 y_1 + D_2}{P_1} \tag{13}$$

The first part of this equation represents $y_1$ by the quantity equation. The second expression is $d(M_1 + D_2)/P_2$ but $M_1 + D_2 = P_2 Y_2$, so the budget constraint in fact is $y_1 + dY_2 = W$, dependent on real variables only. The beauty of this proof is that it underscores the relationship between the strict quantity theory and the neutrality of money.

*Theorem 2: monetary theory of exchange rate determination.*

By purchasing power parity 1) and the quantity theory 2) we find:

$$e_1 = \frac{M_1 y_1}{M_1^* y_1^*} \tag{14}$$

and likewise for $e_2$. If output is held fixed, we have a theory of exchange rate determination which goes back at least to Ricardo's *High Price of Bullion* (1810) ('I know of no cause why gold is dear other than a redundant currency').

This model has stipulated the precise conditions under which such a theory will hold. In fact, as shown by Stockman (1980) for example, if one follows the research strategy of altering the timing of transactions so that the goods market opens at the beginning of the period, and the asset market after it, one can derive a variable velocity of money. This research strategy of altering the timing of transactions, and by implication, the cash in advance constraints, was followed by Svensson (1985) and Svensson and Stockman (1987).

Another research strategy is to alter the special conditions concerning the status of the currencies. The most illuminating move is to assume that each currency can be used to purchase either good, making them, in effect, perfect substitutes. This leads to the following key theorem:

*Theorem 3: indeterminacy of exchange rates*

Under such an assumption, the form of the cash in advance constraints for the countries are altered so that they can use either currency:

$$M_{H1} + e M_{H1}^* = P_1 C_{1H} + P_1^* C_{1H}^* \tag{15}$$

$$e M_{F1}^* + M_{F1} = P_1 C_{1F} + P_1^* C_{1F}^* \tag{16}$$

(15) represents the home country's first-period constraint and (16) is the foreign country's first-period constraint. These constraints can be consolidated into a world quantity equation in the spirit of global monetarism:

$$M_1 + e M_1^* = P_1 y_1 + w P_1^* y_1 \tag{17}$$

Since we have one good and the two moneys are now perfect substitutes, we can in fact add the expressions on each side to construct the world demand for money. Reasoning of this type once played a role in the analyses of Hayek, as I shall show in the next chapter. To continue the analysis note that given the form of the cash in advance constraints, equilibrium requires that neither currency dominates the other in rate of return. Otherwise no agent would hold the dominated currency. A sufficient condition for this is that the returns on the currency are equal, which implies:

$$e_1 = \frac{P_1}{P_1^*} = \frac{P_2}{P_2^*} = e_2 \tag{19}$$

so exchange rates are constant over time.

To show that exchange rates are indeterminate, one consolidates the home and foreign country budget constraints:

$$W + W^* = \left[ \overline{M}_0 + \frac{D_1}{P_1} + \left( \frac{1}{1+r} \right) \frac{P_1 y_1 + D_2}{P_1} \right]$$

$$+ \left[ \frac{e_1 M_0^* + e_1 D_1^*}{P_1^*} + \frac{e_2^*}{e_1^*} \left( \frac{1}{1+r} \right) \frac{P_1^* y_1^* + D_2^*}{P_1^*} \right] \tag{20}$$

The first plus the third terms are simply the world real money supply in the first period which is equal to:

$$\frac{M_1}{P_1} + \frac{M_1^*}{P_1^*} = y_1 + y_1^* \tag{21}$$

which is arrived at by dividing (17) through by $P_1$ and using (19).

Turning to the second and last terms, the foreign nominal interest rate equals the home nominal interest rate, since $e_2/e_1 = 1$ by the constancy of exchange rates. Then, by the same argument as that in the neutrality of money theorem:

$$W + W^* = y_1 + dy_2 + y_1^* + dy_2^*$$

Since we only have one good in this analysis, this consolidates into one equation for the whole world:

$$W = Y_1 + dY_2$$

$$Y = y + y^* \tag{22}$$

Likewise, with constant exchange rates over time, we have from (17) a global quantity equation in both periods

$$M_1 = P_1 Y_1 \qquad M_2 = P_2 Y_2 \tag{23}$$

The model has been reduced to a one-country, one-consumer model, an observation borne out by the fact that interest rate parity now plays no role with constant exchange rates over time. Since our two-country model is equivalent to a one-country model, there is nothing to pin down exchange rates, which can take on any value. This simply follows from the fact that with no restrictions on the transactions which can be carried out with two moneys, they will be perfect substitutes with nothing to determine their relative price. There is room for only one fiat money, which is used to observe the global cash in advance constraint; the exchange rate is just an arbitrary conversion of units between two equivalent fiat moneys, of no more significance than the exchange rates between pounds and pence.

The aggregation procedure which underlies this result would not, however, have been possible if any restriction had been put on the transactions which could be performed with either money. This suggests another plausible research strategy, that of altering the restrictions which are placed on the uses of different denominations. Thus, what if, as in Helpman and Razin (1984), the buyers' currency must be used for all transactions?

They find that saving and investment behaviour (which I have ignored) have radically different implications for exchange rate behaviour under the two systems.

The last result is one of the most important in this literature, and is due to Helpman (1981). It is a theorem of particular external interest:

### Theorem 4: equivalence of fixed and floating exchange rate regimes

To demonstrate this theorem, we must alter the special conditions to take account of the revised role of government. If exchange rates are fixed, the government needs a policy to finance pegging of the exchange rate. I assume that the government issues bonds which are denominated in foreign currency and held by the foreign country's monetary authority. In order to finance a balance of payments deficit, the government sells these bonds for foreign currency. We also have an additional special assumption that the government's financing operations must be balanced over time, and therefore it must pay back any borrowing with interest in the next period. Interest rates on the bonds are now equal worldwide; the revised ideal condition under a fixed exchange rate is:

$$1 + r_H = 1 + r_F \tag{2'}$$

I call $b$ the value of the government's sale of bonds, and we have a revised definition of the money supply:

$$M_1 = M_0 + D_1 = b = P_1 y_1 \tag{24}$$

$$M_2 = M_1 + D_2 - (1 + r)b = P_2 y_2 \tag{25}$$

Here we again use the ubiquitous money market equilibrium condition which is derived from the cash in advance constraint.

If one substitutes for $\bar{M} + D_1$ and $P_1 y_1 + D_2$ in the original budget constraint using (24) and (25), where the original constraint was:

$$W = \frac{M_0 D_1}{P_1} + \frac{1}{1+r}\left(\frac{P_1 y_1 + D_2}{P_1}\right)$$

one finds that:

$$W = y_{1+} dy_2 \tag{26}$$

Therefore, money is neutral under both fixed and flexible exchange rates. As a corollary to this, the real welfare effects of the two regimes are obviously identical.

This result is in fact rather special, being tied to the nature of the government's financing scheme for a balance of payments deficit. This suggests the plausibility strategy of altering the special conditions on the role of government. This research strategy was followed by Persson (1984), but one can demonstrate the idea with an even simpler example than those given in his paper. Suppose that the government has a large amount of foreign exchange reserves, which it can use to finance the deficit, and assume the quantity is so big that a nonnegativity constraint on these reserves always holds. Also suppose that the government does not care how many reserves it holds at the end of time (the second period). Call $\Delta R$ the change in reserves. Then (24) and (25) become:

$$M_1 = M_0 + D_1 + \Delta R_1 = P_1 y_1 \tag{27}$$

$$M_2 = M_1 + D_2 + \Delta R_2 = P_2 y_2 \tag{28}$$

In this case, substituting in the budget constraint yields:

$$\omega = y_1 + dy_2 - \left(\Delta R_1 - \frac{1}{1+r}\Delta R_2\right)\frac{1}{P_1} \tag{29}$$

The last term can be positive or negative, depending on the pattern of surpluses and deficits as well as the interest costs of holding reserves. Therefore, there are potential welfare costs associated with this balance of payments financing scheme and furthermore, the exchange rate equivalence theorem does not hold nor is money neutral. This shows again how subtle variations in the special conditions can create results which have more plausibility in the real world.

It is worth saying a few words about the implications of this theory and its models for the trade-theoretic approach. Note that under the strong neutrality properties of the model, with complete dichotomy of the monetary and real sides of the model, all the previous theorems about the time preference and consumption-smoothing motives for balance of payments behaviour will still hold, although under a flexible exchange regime, the impact of different rates of time preference will be on the exchange rate, as in Helpman and Razin (1982). Such conclusions must be modified, of course, if special conditions are introduced on transactions timing or the exchange rate regime which obviate the neutrality of money. It is also worth mentioning in passing that extending the field to an infinite horizon makes no impact on the results (see, for example, Helpman 1981). Extending the number of goods would modify the results by introducing Marshall–Lerner type elasticity criteria into the analysis. These, for example, will affect the formula for exchange rate determination (Obstfeld and Stockman 1985). Such effects, however, will again be of crucial theoretical importance only in situations where the neutrality of money does not hold.

An alternative to the cash in advance exemplar is to take a more revolutionary step and alter the explanatory ideal conditions by introducing a different friction into the intertemporal equilibrium model, in order to rationalize the existence of money. This is what those researchers who use the Allais–Samuelson overlapping generations model have done. In fact, this approach adds no new insights; exchange rate indeterminacy holds in such a context (Sargent and Wallace 1981), as does the exchange rate equivalence theorem (Helpman and Razin 1979). If one introduces more complex monetary regimes, as in Greenwood and Williamson (1989), one obviously can negate the strong neutrality and equivalence results in this model as well. Cash in advance models have, however, an overriding advantage over the overlapping generation exemplar; unlike the latter, they justify the coexistence of money and interest-bearing assets under perfect foresight, thereby resolving a central problem in monetary theory.

### A summing up

I have given a comprehensive description of the structure of the cash in advance variant of the monetary theory of intertemporal trade. It has been shown how the explanatory ideal conditions, which are characteristic of monetary theory (e.g. restrictions on the timing of goods versus asset trade) or of international monetary theory (e.g. interest rate parity), interact with carefully specified special conditions on international transactions in goods, exchange rate regimes and the nature of the cash in advance constraint to produce interesting theorems. I have shown how altering these conditions constitutes a plausible research strategy which leads to results which are more externally realistic. The neutrality of money is the central theorem of this theory: from this other implications for exchange rates and their regimes follow, and it supplies the reference point from which modifications to the structure should be made. Significantly, neutrality is also the core theorem in the sense that it requires only one very weak special condition in order to follow from the ideal conditions.

Of the other theorems, exchange rate equivalence has the greatest properties of external interest. This result cuts through the Gordian knot tied by years of debate on the properties of exchange rate systems, a debate which was sparked off by the propositions of the Mundell–Fleming model. Exchange rate indeterminacy is the theorem which is of internal interest; it is connected with the deeper questions of the role of money in the economy, and in effect it specifies those conditions which are necessary for internationally traded monies to serve only as units of account, despite the fact that money has a transaction role and the international economy is more than a mere clearing house.

I have shown that exchange rate indeterminacy is a theory which follows in an entirely characteristic way from the structure of the theory, since slightly altering the special conditions on the role that fiat monies play in purchasing commodities is sufficient for it to ensue.

Finally, I have shown at several points how research strategies which create more complex and realistic theorems can be constructed by altering the conditions which are the building blocks of these theorems.

## Comparison with previous approaches

Finally, it seems appropriate to contrast theory of international monetary relations, developed in the 1980s, for the most part, with some earlier work, developed two decades before, to which it bears certain similarities. By doing this, we will first place it in context, and second emphasize exactly what is unique about this approach.

First, we consider the work of Baldwin (1966), Miller (1968) and Webb (1970). These writers had the idea of using a variant of the Fisher diagram due to Leontief (1958) in order to analyse international capital flows. Webb at least showed some awareness that balance of payments relationships can be derived from this type of diagram, but on the whole the impulse of these authors seems to have been to integrate their analysis with static trade theory. Thus, Miller uses Leontief–Fisher diagrams to generate trade indifference curves in the manner of Meade. Baldwin used that diagram to develop a theory of physical capital movements. Baldwin did not show that intertemporal general equilibrium theory allows capital movements to take place via trade solely in claims to future output. The essential difference between their approach and the recent one therefore lies in the fact that they regarded Fisherian capital theory as a means of extending traditional trade theory, not international macroeconomic theory. Formally, however, there is no difference between their work and what I have called the trade-theoretic approach.

The work of Bardhan (1966) and Hamada (1966) is at first sight very close indeed to the multiperiod, infinite horizon versions of the studies discussed above. In fact, these models are formally identical to the one briefly sketched above. Even so, they had a different conception of the use to which these models should be put. They did not conclude that the optimal borrowing behaviour of an individual can be treated with the same tools one uses to derive an optimal borrowing programme for a government.

The conclusion from this discussion then is that the writers in the 1980s changed the emphasis in an already existing literature, since there existed a small literature in the 1960s which used intertemporal concepts. The important point, however, is that the macroeconomic analysis of the balance of payments in an intertemporal general equilibrium is new. Once the step of analysing balance of payments issues in this way has been taken, a whole host of new results emerge, which were unknown previously.

## Interim conclusion and summary

### The characteristics of an intertemporal approach to international macroeconomics

Having surveyed the literature of the 1980s, I am now in a position to summarize the exact characteristics which mark it off from the type of international macroeconomic models which were current before the 1980s. The most important new characteristic, to my mind, is that represented by the new methodology of intertemporal general equilibrium and intertemporal welfare maximization. This is the case because such a methodology clearly distinguishes this approach from the crude Keynesian models of the 1940s and 1950s, or the monetary models of the 1970s.

The other foundation of the new approach is, as we have seen, the totally different definition of balance of payments equilibrium whereby the current account only needs to be balanced over time in a present value sense, as opposed to the unequivocal current account equilibrium required in the traditional approach.

As I have shown, on these foundations there arises an interrelated network of assumptions and conditions which, despite its complexity, combines to prove some sharp-edged propositions about the role of the current account and the determinants of exchange rates. The structuralist account of this framework, which I have delineated, provides a complete compartmentalized description of the theory of intertemporal trade. Such a set of compartments furnish a group of criteria, in effect a checklist, by which one can identify how similar were theories constructed by earlier economists. The writings of these economists produced from *c.*1900 through 1940 are the subject matter of the next chapter. In order to establish whether a research tradition exists in this field, I shall compare this structure with the structures, albeit more primitive, which they built. I shall now recap in turn each component and pigeonhole of this structure, noting where each piece of contemporary theory fits in the overall picture. It is worth pointing out, however, that this framework can easily be extended without tampering with the original structure. As an example, one can introduce uncertainty and incomplete markets, as in Svensson (1988), into not just the real but also the monetary version of the theory. Such extensions may prove relevant later; for the moment, however, it is necessary to finish this chapter with a complete mental picture of the relevant theory structure in one's mind.

To reiterate then, economic theories with strong foundations in the bedrock of the neoclassical paradigm have five components:

1 a thought style consisting of a heuristic and metaphysical character which are linked to:
2 a group of standard basic conditions derived from economic theory as a whole;
3 a set of explanatory ideal conditions derived in this case from other monetary and international monetary theories;
4 a field of commodities, factors of production and time periods and finally
5 the alterable special conditions, which in combination with 1–4 generate a set of externally or internally interesting theorems.

This structure does not alone define intertemporal trade theory. Cutting across it are three models which serve as exemplars for successful research. Each model is derived from a different specification of the explanatory ideal conditions. These models are the basic Fisherian model; the trade-theoretic model with an extended field and; the monetary model, a hybrid of the real model with the theory of money.

I shall now briefly summarize my findings on each model. I shall also say something about their real world policy and empirical implications.

## The basic vision

This is derived from intertemporal general equilibrium theory, and is a constant to be found in each of our three exemplars. One can of course abandon this vision of the economy by adopting a fix-price method, while continuing to use an intertemporal model as in van Wijnbergen (1987), or Cuddington *et al.* (1984) for example. When such an approach is taken, one not surprisingly reverses the conclusions along with the vision of intertemporal equilibrium. Thus, Cuddington *et al.* (1984: Ch. 5) vindicate Mundell and Fleming in a fix-price setting with cash in advance constraints, in utter contradiction to our neutrality theorems. In the next chapter we shall have to gauge, in the case of Mosak, the extent to which deviations like this cast an economist out of the intertemporal brotherhood.

## The basic presuppositions

In the above discussion, therefore, presuppositions have been isolated which underlie the modern theory. They can be briefly summarized as follows:

1    we must begin our analysis with individual entities such as consumers and firms;
2    their behaviour must be treated as rational;
3    they must exhibit maximizing behaviour with respect to the present and future;
4    these individuals possess complete information about their current situation;
5    they possess perfect foresight with regard to the future or, alternatively, knowledge of the probability distributions of all relevant variables.

As was noted above, these presuppositions have been explicitly stated in a number of papers, of which Helpman and Razin (1979) and Sachs (1981) are outstanding examples. Taken together, they can be condensed down to a requirement that the tools of intertemporal general equilibrium theory should be employed in international monetary theory. In my view, this is the essence of the approach of the 1980s, and everything else, the complex models and surprising results included, follows from these simple injunctions.

### The Fisherian model

By drastic reduction of the field, one arrives at a very tractable model which nevertheless generates two results of great external interest on consumption smoothing as an influence on the current account and the time-preference motive for running surpluses or deficits. This has a strong real world implication: current account deficits are not a policy problem in a first-best world. Consumption smoothing is a feature of the permanent income theory of consumption. One can, therefore, carry out econometric tests of the validity of this type of result by using tests taken from empirical work on the consumption function.

### The trade-theoretic model

If one follows the research strategy of real trade theory, and adds just one country, one arrives not surprisingly at a framework which is a complete analogue of the basic real trade model. Naturally, one can then build up a set of 'analogue theorems' in an intertemporal context. Some relevant analogies are comparative advantage, factor-price equalization, the Marshall–Lerner conditions, and so on. These theorems have played an unobtrusive but significant role in the development of the theory. Examples are the use of 'transfer problem criteria' in Frenkel and Razin's (1987) analysis of the international transmission of fiscal deficits, or the use of Stolper–Samuelson magnification effects to derive results on supply shocks in a world with nontraded goods, as in Bruno (1982).

### The monetary model

Adding money to the real trade model involves altering the basic conditions to allow for the existence of money in a perfect foresight general equilibrium, this with the proviso that the basic neoclassical 'vision' be left undisturbed. Therefore, market clearing in each time period is retained in the model. The explanatory ideal conditions must be extended to cover:

1   The sequencing of markets.
2   The role of government as producer of fiat money.
3   Consumer behaviour in Clower's world, where 'money buys goods but goods do not buy money' and therefore a transactions constraint operates.
4   The international environment, both from the institutional point of view and from the point of view of the implications of global arbitrage (law of one price, etc.).

These conditions then interact with special conditions on government, the form of the cash in advance constraint and the rules for making purchases with country-specific moneys to generate four key theorems which are central for identifying followers of this approach. If a writer adheres to the basic vision and some of these conditions and theorems, he adheres to the intertemporal trade approach to international monetary theory. These theorems are:

1   The neutrality of money in an open economy.
2   A monetary theory of exchange rate determination.
3   Exchange rate indeterminacy.
4   The equivalence of fixed and floating exchange rate regimes.

The great merit of a structuralist exposition, however, is that it shows how small changes in the special conditions, integrated with the ideal conditions of the explanatory exemplar, are themselves sufficient to produce broad variations of these four theorems.

### Identifying research traditions

To sum up then, we must, when studying any writer whom we wish to place in any particular research tradition, look at four facets of his research practice. These are his overall thought style and the basic conditions derived from it, the model which serves as his exemplar and its explanatory ideal conditions. Ultimately, we arrive at a research strategy characterized by a process of formulating new theorems, modifying them on the grounds of plausibility and even testing them empirically.

The recent work which uses intertemporal methods has been thoroughly categorized in this way. It remains to do the same for the literature of the 1920s, 1930s and 1940s which bears a similarity to it. The description of the modern theory given in this chapter will serve as a yardstick with which to measure the extent to which the earlier work is similar to it.

# 4 The research tradition in intertemporal international trade theories

Conspicuously absent from the literature were attempts to develop a normative intertemporal theory of international capital transfer.

Maurice Obstfeld on 'International Finance: The Interwar Period', in *The New Palgrave* (1987)

Foreign lending merely indicates that present utilities are exchanged for future imported utilities produced at home.

Carl Iversen (1935)

## Introduction

Maurice Obstfeld, the contributor to *The New Palgrave Dictionary of Economics* on the subject of 'International Finance', expressed a representative view of the nature of international monetary theory in the interwar years. He stated that the intertemporal approach to the analysis of the balance of payments was a recent invention:

> International capital movements were discussed increasingly in the theoretical literature, but they were viewed for the most part as an adjunct to the classical balance of payments mechanism. The theoretical discussions merely formalised a mechanism that had long been exploited by the Bank of England to regulate gold flows ... Such short term or interest-sensitive capital movements were generally discussed separately from 'long term' international capital movements which directly financed investment or government expenditures.
>
> Theoretical discussions of long term capital movements focused mainly on the transfer mechanism, the balance of payments and terms of trade adjustments that would accompany an intercountry transfer of capital.
>
> Conspicuously absent from the literature were attempts to develop a normative intertemporal theory of international capital transfer. Such a theory naturally would have extended the prevailing external balance concept to comprise changes in a nation's overall

indebtedness rather than just changes in the central bank's foreign assets. This gap in the literature is surprising in view of the developments in international capital markets over the previous century. In the world assumed by Hume, specie flows had been the only means of settling current account imbalances, and a concept of external balance based on balance of payments equilibrium had been defensible. Such a concept of external balance was outmoded, however, in a world where other types of asset trade could finance the current account. The necessary change of perspective did not occur for several decades.

(Obstfeld 1987: 900)

This chapter will demonstrate that this view of the history of international monetary theory is an exaggeration. Significant research, using a methodology identical to that of the 1980s, was done in the 1920s, 1930s and 1940s. I shall draw attention to the work of writers who produced, in the two decades from 1925–1945, work well grounded in the 'normative intertemporal theory of international capital transfer'. Furthermore, I shall show that even nineteenth-century economists were quite cognisant of the implications of long-term lending and had begun to adjust their ideas accordingly. I am of course in total agreement with the way in which Obstfeld contrasts the intertemporal approach with what I have called, in Chapter 3, the 'traditional approach'. I shall attempt to show, however, that this account of the history of international monetary economics is inaccurate. What we have here, I shall argue, is a classic and illuminating example of the recurrence phenomenon, in which the methods and models of a group of earlier writers have been rediscovered, although their names are forgotten.

This chapter then consists of a demonstration of the striking similarity which exists between the intertemporal thought style and its theories, described in the previous chapter, and much of the international economics that predates it. To make this comparison accurate, I shall use the framework developed there, emphasizing that the doctrines of Iversen's book of 1935, for example, which was quoted initially, have a similar structure to those of a modern work like Frenkel and Razin (1987). Naturally, we shall also find some modern theorems in archaic dress. It is well to remember, nevertheless, that the structuralist approach in the case of the modern theory, defines a full-fledged mathematical theory with a complete logical architecture. This will never be quite true of the older writers; my history will reflect Schumpeter's dictum that 'there has been scientific progress in economics from J.S. Mill to Samuelson in the same way as there has been scientific progress in pulling teeth' (1954: 11). Thus, I shall demonstrate a steady progression of theoretical and mathematical sophistication, from the theoretically jejune efforts of Cairnes (1874), through to Mosak's *Intertemporal General Equilibrium Theory and International Trade* (1944). My discussion therefore proceeds roughly in chronological order, emphasizing points of structure in the case of each writer. I shall show how, writer by writer, the whole structure is gradually filled in until we eventually arrive at a close approximation to the modern theory. Nevertheless, I shall show that many of the key insights of intertemporal trade theory had appeared long before its fruition.

### Theoretical background: the origins of intertemporal theory

Before commencing my exposition of the work of these earlier theorists, it is worth saying a few words about the wider intellectual background to their thoughts, in particular in connection with the interwar years which are, in the field of macroeconomics, primarily thought of as being characterized by the rise of Keynesian doctrines. Such a viewpoint, however, only results from viewing the past through the lens of what Joan Robinson (1971: 95) called the 'bastard' Keynesian paradigm, which was dominant in the 1950s and 1960s. In fact, the macroeconomics of the 1920s was complex and diverse, much as the subject is in the late 1980s. In particular, the period saw a rebellion against the classical notion of economic equilibrium so graphically described by Adam Smith:

> The natural price ... is as it were, the central price, to which the prices of all commodities are continually gravitating. Different accidents may sometimes keep them suspended a good deal above it, and sometimes force them down somewhat below it. But whatever may be the obstacles which hinder them from settling in this centre of repose and continuance, they are constantly tending towards it.
>
> (Smith 1776 [1961]: 65)

This notion of equilibrium was continued by Marshall, Walras and indeed Wicksell (Milgate 1979: 2–3). As Milgate (1979) has shown, first Hayek and then Lindahl rebelled against this tradition, particularly in the context of trade cycle and capital theory, and substituted for it the notion of intertemporal equilibrium. This involves, as we saw in the last chapter, the determination of $nt$ market clearing prices over time ($n$ commodities and $t$ time periods) in order to establish an equilibrium. The discovery of intertemporal equilibrium was truly an upheaval in the development of economic thought, leading of course to the Arrow–Debreu model and Malinvaud's theory of capital accumulation (Milgate 1979: 3–7). Yet intertemporal equilibrium theory was not the only development in dynamic economic theory in the years prior to the Second World War which is relevant to our theory. Hayek's work led directly on through Hicks's (1933) response to Hayek to the temporary equilibrium theory of *Value and Capital*. This 'half way house', as Bliss (1975: 23) calls it, is nevertheless connected to intertemporal general equilibrium theory because it uses 'incomplete Arrow–Debreu structures' (Weintraub 1979:

104). Another theory of older provenance which nevertheless was prominent in the 1930s was Austrian capital theory, whose development culminated in Hayek's *Pure Theory of Capital* (1941). Like Hicks's temporary
general equilibrium theory, Austrian capital theory can plausibly be interpreted as an intertemporal general equilibrium theory to which some
restrictions have been added (Hausman 1981: 98–101). I shall show that
what Obstfeld calls 'an intertemporal normative theory of international
capital transfer' indeed arose in the context of the more general intertemporal theories referred to above. This should hardly be a matter for sur-
prise, since the traditional view of international equilibrium as being
defined by the equilibrium of the trade or current account is the natural
application, to the open economy, of static equilibrium concepts referred
to above, such as Adam Smith's 'natural price' and Marshall's long-run
equilibrium. It is hardly surprising then, that the notion of an intertemporal trade equilibrium emerged at the time when intertemporal general
equilibrium theory itself emerged.

   This discussion in itself indicates how I shall define the group of writers
I am going to discuss. There existed no school of cooperating researchers
in the sociological sense. What did exist were economists who belonged to
the same research tradition in that they shared, often unknowingly, the
same methodological commitments. They thus came, as Laudan's account
(see Chapter 2) would predict, face to face with the same conceptual and
empirical problems. Occasionally, however, we shall brush up against a
school in the narrowly defined sense of the sociology of science. Sociology
views a school as being a group of researchers who interact socially, and
Hayek and his followers fit this definition. The personal coherence of this
group. imparted by their adherence to the Master, means that they can be
treated as a 'school' from the sociological point of view.

## The forerunners

First, I would like to discuss some important figures in the history of economics who, largely under the impact of the large-scale capital movements
of the nineteenth century, adopted the foundations and some of the vision
of the intertemporal approach. In particular, they broke with the classical
notions of balance of payments equilibrium. This identified such an equilibrium as being identical with trade account equilibrium, as J.S. Mill realized. However, the major break was made by Mill's pupil and follower
Cairnes; it was then taken up and given precision by the great Austrian,
von Wieser.

### *Cairnes*

The prehistory of intertemporal international macroeconomics begins with
Cairnes's *Principles of Political Economy* (1874), which is usually regarded

as the swansong of the Classical School. Cairnes got some credit for his doctrine of noncompeting groups (Schumpeter 1954: 605), but his contribution to dynamic trade theory has been forgotten today, although, in his *Theory of International Prices* (1926: 94–5), Angell acknowledges the originality of his contribution.

Cairnes broke with classical definitions of balance of payments equilibrium as being identical with the equilibrium of the trade account; indeed, he argued that this is never the case:

> It very rarely happens that the whole exports of a country, even if we take an average of many years, exactly pay for the whole of its imports; nor can it only be said that there is any tendency in the dealings of nations towards this result.

> (Cairnes 1874: 354)

Cairnes was also the first economist to describe systematically the dynamic process of international lending. The assumptions of his analysis make it clear that he was inspired by the massive long-term British lending to South America and the colonies, which was going on at the time. Cairnes was the originator of the 'stages of the balance of payments analysis', an idea which is not complex enough to constitute a theory in the sense of Chapter 3, but nevertheless is a conceptual foundation of the thought style of international trade theory.

This hypothesis states that a country goes through a number of distinct balance of payment stages, starting as an immature debtor and ending as a mature creditor. It was prevalent in the development literature of the 1950s and 1960s, and has been analysed in a rigorous intertemporal framework by Bazdarich (1978). From the point of view of the history of economic thought, this approach is interesting because it constituted the first ever attempt to analyse international trade in assets being carried out as a process over time. As pointed out in Angell's (1926) comprehensive survey of doctrine, the theory originates in Cairnes's *Leading Principles of Political Economy* (1874), along with the discussion of the balance of trade just surveyed. Cairnes's treatment, however, was descriptive and lacked any analytical content. Its importance derives from the link that exists between his contribution and that of Wieser.

### Wieser

Schumpeter says of Wieser that 'the great thing about him was a spacious vision that went deep below the surface' (Schumpeter 1954: 848). It is in Schumpeter's hands that Cairnes's ideas begin to evolve into the thought style characteristic of intertemporal trade theory. Indeed, to borrow Laudan's terminology to describe research traditions, some clear ontological definitions and heuristic statements begin to appear in Wieser's writing. Even so, his contribution appears to have gone largely unnoticed. Schumpeter believed that *Social Economics* (*Theorie der gesellschaftlichen Wirtschaft* 1914, English translation 1927) added nothing 'essentially new' to economic analysis (Schumpeter 1954: 649). Other accounts such as those of Hutchison (1953) do not mention the open economy aspect of his thought. Despite this, I have come across the claim by Mahr (1951), an economist who published mainly in German in the 1930s, to the effect that Wieser originated the specifically Germanic tradition in balance of payments analysis. Be that as it may, given that *Social Economics* was widely read as a textbook, one may suppose that it provides a link in the chain of theoretical development. Wieser in fact gives two twists to Cairnes's doctrines, which he repeats almost verbatim although without acknowledgement (1927: 454). The first is that he uses it to make a sharp attack on the classical school. The second lies in the fact that he insists that behind the process of lending and borrowing lie the decisions of rational individuals.

Wieser opens his analysis with a sharp attack on the classical economists. He calls the classical exposition of balance of payments equilibrium a half-truth of genius and he suggests, in a similar manner to Cairnes, 'that it appears to be merely accidental that equilibrium is maintained once capital movements are taken into account' (Wieser 1927: 449). Wieser then argues that the correct way of analysing the problems posed by the capital account is, in a manner similar to that of the vision of the modern school, to begin with the behaviour of individual economic actors who are rational agents: 'The problem of the balancing of (international) accounts offers no fundamental difficulties for a theory that has reduced the national economic community of payment to the participating individuals' (Wieser 1914 [1927]: 451).

Since individuals must satisfy their own budget constraints in equilibrium, von Wieser argues that a country must be in a similar position:

> The international balance of payments is nothing more than the sum of the personal balances of payment for all the people; the commercial balance is only a similar sum of the personal balances of wares. As soon as we have recognised the motives that lead to an equilibrium in the individual economy, there can no longer be a riddle in world economic relations, if we assume ideal national economics, consisting of none other than well regulated individuals (economies), the equilibrium of all personal balances-of-payments and consequently the equilibrium of their net foreign payments, i.e. the international balance-of-payments, must prevail undisturbed.
>
> (Wieser 1927: 452)

It is unfortunately not clear from Wieser's account whether these individual decisions are forward looking or not, and his account is therefore reduced to a plea for giving the balance of payments a choice theoretic foundation. To actually analyse the process of international lending and borrowing he falls back on a historico-logical account very similar to that of Cairnes. Wieser therefore added one piece of the vision – individual utility maximization – to the equilibrium concept advanced by Cairnes.

### Fetter

With F.A. Fetter we come to a case of an economist who devoted much of his theoretical research to elucidating the determination of interest rates, and moreover grasped the implications of his own research for the behaviour of the balance of payments.

In the first two decades of the twentieth century, Fetter was regarded in the United States as the leading representative of the Austrian School. His writings also have an institutionalist tinge, and the influence of Veblen's evolutionary economics can also be seen. Nevertheless, his prestige was so great in his time that his 1927 paper 'Interest Theory and Price Movements' was presented as the main item in the A.E.A. proceedings of that year and was discussed by the leading American theoretical economist, Irving Fisher, and the leading American empirical economist, Wesley C. Mitchell. Despite the slightly exotic features of Fetter's economics, mentioned above, Fisher concluded in his comments that there was no fundamental difference between his approach and that of Fetter, and that in effect Fetter had demonstrated the similarity of Fisherian and Austrian interest theory.

Fetter's general theory of time valuation was, unlike Fisher's, an explicitly general equilibrium theory, and his whole style of thought was essentially not different from the modern one. One can see this because he insists that interest theory should be integrated with general equilibrium theory:

> There is but little evidence in the large volume of recent discussions of price movements and the business cycle that the implicit question of interest has been explicitly considered as an integral part of the price system. Interest theory receives attention only incidental to or aside from the price system.
>
> (Fetter 1927: 131)

In the manner of Malinvaud (1953) and Debreu (1959: Ch. 2), Fetter argues that the price system should be used to determine the value of future goods in exactly the same way as it determines the value of present goods. Strikingly, Fetter realizes that in order to do this he must adopt the concept of own rates of interest, used in the postwar literature on intertemporal general equilibrium:

> Some rate becomes automatically involved in every price of durable goods (or series of incomes and of products) where time location in

any degree affects the valuation of the constituent elements making up the whole price of the thing.

(Fetter 1927: 8)

One special aspect of Fetter's thought is that the rate of time preference is treated as endogenous. As the economy advances and more present goods are produced, the preference for present goods is lowered, and the 'time discount' falls (Fetter 1927: 75; Rothbard 1977: 16). In other words, the discount rate is negatively related to the current level of wealth. Similar assumptions appear in some modern works. Obstfeld (1981) assumed that the rate of time preference rises with the level of utility, the opposite of what Fetter assumed. Lucas and Stokey (1984) formulated a rigorous intertemporal general equilibrium model with endogenous preferences and show that an equilibrium exists in such a model. Fetter believed that the economy would attain an intertemporal equilibrium with endogenous time preference, although he does not use this term as such:

> Capitalizations, the relative prices of present goods and durable agents, and normal rates of profit in active business investments, as well as rates of interest must, through the operation of competition and substitution, be brought into some measure of consistency, in regard to the time discounts in various goods and employment.
>
> (Fetter 1927: 74)

This system of intertemporal prices is stable, although it may be disturbed by exogenous shocks:

> Whatever the relative prices of particular classes of goods these prices would all be interpenetrated more or less consistently by the time discount rate peculiar to each market or group. Any such system of prices having become fairly stable at any time and in any country, may be disturbed and altered by changes originating (1) in the medium of exchange mechanism or (2) under conditions of time valuations, actual time prices and capitalizations; or (3) under special conditions of demand and supply determining relative prices.
>
> (Fetter 1927: 75)

Notice in (2) that there exists a potential for changes in the rate of discount which perturb the equilibrium, in line with the endogenous nature of time preferences. It is the study of the comparative statics of such disturbances, especially (1) and (2), which takes up about half of Fetter's paper. What I am concerned with are those disturbances which take place in the context of an open economy.

The origins of intertemporal general equilibrium theory are not the subject of this chapter, but I think enough has also been said to show that the title of originator should not go to Hayek, as Milgate has claimed, but to Fetter, who describes such a 'coherent' and 'stable' system of prices.

Enough has certainly been said to show that Fetter's vision was also that set out in Chapter 3 for modern intertemporal trade theory. Rothbard (1977) and O'Driscoll (1980) have both ignored this connection between Fetter and the dynamic structures found in modern economics.

Fetter goes on to argue, in a manner analogous to that of contemporary macroeconomics, that the basic conditions which form the first building block in the structure (see Chapter 3), of a macroeconomic (or any) theory, should be derived from intertemporal general equilibrium theory:

> A unified time-valuation theory makes it clear that time discounts and premiums enter into the formation of all prices both of direct and of indirect goods, and are an inseparable part of even the earliest price systems. This view gives a clear, consistent criterion by which to test various notions with respect to price changes and policies with respect to the fixing of discount rates by government and banks.
>
> (Fetter 1927: 132)

Fetter, having set out his 'time-valuation theory' at great length, then makes five applications of it to macroeconomic problems, all of which of are covered by disturbances (1) and (2) quoted above. They are: price fixing by government under a paper money regime; an examination and critique of Wicksell's cumulative process; the Bank of England's discount rate policy under the gold standard; international borrowing in time of war and; foreign borrowing to finance postwar reconstruction. It is the last three with which I shall be concerned. Starting with the last application, Fetter shows himself to be aware that differences in marginal rates of intertemporal substitution will give rise to beneficial trading opportunities which take the form of international borrowing and lending. He argues that a country which has suffered war damage will have the marginal product of investment so adjusted that profit-maximizing individuals will find it profitable to import capital, and thus the country is rebuilt by means of a current account deficit:

> in this situation no doubt large loan funds could be 'profitably' borrowed from more prosperous nations. The price system is such in the devastated country that all sorts of goods with future uses are so priced that investors can 'profit' (individually) by contracting to pay abroad high interest rates to buy, build and increase the number of long-time durable bearers of future uses.
>
> (Fetter 1927: 104)

Here we are face to face in 1927 with the 'normative intertemporal theory of international capital transfer', whose alleged absence at that time was so regretted by Obstfeld.

In this particular application, however, Fetter does not seem to be describing the time preference motive for current account behaviour but rather what Frenkel and Razin (1987) have called the 'consumption augmenting motive' for international borrowing.

According to this motive, which was demonstrated in Figure 3.2 in Chapter 3, a country with a higher marginal return on investment than the rest of the world can increase its level of consumption by borrowing, without introducing variability into its time profile. There is a difference, however, between Fetter's treatment of the consumption-augmenting effect and the exposition in Chapter 3, since he appears to be assuming that a supply shock – a war – leads to a change in the productivity of investment. This would be represented, not just by an inward movement of the intertemporal transformation frontier, but also by a change in its curvature. An effect like this cannot be derived by a one-good model like the one I employed in the last chapter; however, while Fetter's scenario can be derived in a two-sector model, that is beyond the scope of this chapter.

The problem in identifying the precise nature of Fetter's result lies in the fact that he jumps straight from his basic conditions to the derivation of theorems. He explains the institutional and monetary set-up in each case, but details such as the field and the exact situation of the economy before trade is opened are left unexplained in his informal account.

Despite this theoretical weakness, he is able, without the full apparatus of a well-structured theory, to give a precise description of the time preference motive, this time in the context of war borrowing. The obvious way to treat the immediate need for huge increases in present consumption on the outbreak of war is as a temporary increase in government expenditure, a case naturally studied extensively by Frenkel and Razin (1987: Chs 7–9). Instead, Fetter treats this occurrence as a comparative static increase in the country's rate of time preference (as in Frenkel and Razin 1987: 152–3). This naturally occurs in his theory because the need for war expenditure will reduce the level of current wealth, thus increasing the rate of time preference. In a closed economy, this would require an increase in the official bank discount rate to maintain intertemporal equilibrium within the country. Such a policy can, however, be avoided by running a surplus on the capital account: 'countries with large saleable or pledgable assets may for a while retard a rise by selling claims, securities, credits, against other assets or against themselves, to wealthy neutral nations' (Fetter 1927: 100–1).

These possibilities for intertemporal trade disappear once the conflict becomes general, because then an equalization of rates of time preference occurs: 'it may happen that most of the capitalistic world becomes involved and the fundamental time-variations are everywhere raised' (1927: 101).

In this situation, the intertemporal international trading possibilities caused by the war cease. With no more possibility of financing current consumption by capital imports, he insists that governments must not adopt a policy of keeping interest rates artificially low, as this can be done only by an inflationary monetary policy. It is better to allow the interest rate to rise to the level dictated by the new world rate of time preference. Fetter is arguing, in effect, that mutually beneficial intertemporal trade is impossible in a situation where all countries have suffered the same shock to their wealth (i.e. they are all now at war), and as a result, their new higher rates of time preference are identical.

As is very well known, during the gold standard era central banks, and in particular the Bank of England, ironed out temporary fluctuations in the balance of payments by raising their discount rates and attracting short-term capital from abroad. According to the classic statement of this policy, the British Cunliffe Committee Report of 1918, this policy would have the added effect in the longer term of removing the underlying causes of a deficit by bringing about a monetary deflation. These practices were much discussed by the leading economists of the day such as Hawtrey and Keynes, and its role and significance also figure in the most recent retrospectives on the gold standard.[1]

Fetter's comments are interesting, because they contrast so sharply with received static discussions of bank rate policy, and because he views this mechanism in ways similar to what one would expect from a modern 'equilibrium business cycle theorist'. His first point is one of criticism; the discount rate mechanism will distort international intertemporal relative prices, although his example is given in the context of a low rate causing inflationary conditions when

> [t]here would have been the constant tendency not only for the discount rate but for the whole price system in this [banking and commercial] world to get out of accord with the underlying forces of time-valuation, and with the previous 'normal' scheme of capital – values and prices.
>
> (Fetter 1927: 101)

Despite this criticism, he accepts that 'this plan really works'. The reason for this is that raising the discount rate when a country is running a current account deficit, simply involves the Bank of England as behaving in the same way as individuals endowed with perfect foresight:

> In our view, in accord with the general theory of time valuation, this process is nothing more than an anticipation of the bank-fund deflation that would otherwise be forced by the continued exports of gold. Raising the rediscount rate merely puts springs under the commercial prices to prevent their dropping later with a jolt.
>
> (Fetter 1927: 101)

As in the rational expectations exemplar, individuals are aware of the balance of payments adjustment mechanism. Notice, however, that for Fetter this is a consequence of 'the general theory of time valuation' – intertemporal general equilibrium. He was nothing if not consistent in pursuing the logic of intertemporal equilibrium analysis through to the end of every application.

It is clear from all of the above that Fetter embraced the entire vision and the associated general or basic conditions associated with the intertemporal approach. He applied this to the open economy, and in so doing anticipated elements of the Fisherian and trade-theoretic models. Two things are conspicuously lacking from this discussion. The first is a role for consumption smoothing; the argument is all conducted in terms of the endogenous changes in time preference induced by external shocks. The second is the lack of the explanatory ideal conditions which should articulate a well-structured model. This lack of a tightly specified framework meant that he missed the full range of results presented in the previous chapter.

The historian of economics is faced with the intriguing possibility of where these remarkably prescient results originated. There is every possibility that Fetter, known for his immersion in the classic Austrian texts of Menger, Bohm-Bawerk and Wieser (see Rothbard 1977, which is an introduction to a collection of Fetter's papers), was influenced by Wieser. Unfortunately Wieser's discussion, suggestive as it is, did no more than sketch out certain aspects of a vision of the balance of payments based on microeconomic foundations, as I have emphasized above. One therefore needs to look further afield, and I have been struck by an interesting debate which occurred between Fetter and Harry Gunnison Brown in 1914. This debate was not about intertemporal trade: it was an argument, after the fashion of Bohm-Bawerk, about the validity of the various grounds for a positive rate of interest. (See Negishi 1985: Ch. 9 for a modern discussion and summary of the debate about Bohm-Bawerk's theory of interest.) These debates about capital theory are absolutely characteristic of the time, and in the course of his article Gunnison Brown introduced the elements of intertemporal trade theory into the discussion, without any apparent intention of actually contributing to international economics. Gunnison Brown wanted to defend, in the anachronistic language of the time, the 'productivity theory of interest' against Fetter, who at that time (1914) believed that interest depended on time preference. To justify his position, Gunnison Brown introduced a second individual, a Spaniard, into a Robinson Crusoe economy where the only input is labour and the only good is fruit which takes time to grow on trees. He shows that the Spaniard will trade fruit (present goods) with Crusoe for trees, future goods, depending on the time preference motive:

> His position is analogous to that of a lender. If he buys trees, he will
> be giving up present fruit for future fruit. What is the most he will

give? He will be guided in his decision by two considerations. One of these is his impatience or time preference. The other is the cost-of-production of the trees.

(Gunnison Brown 1914: 343)

Here we seem to have an exact description of the behaviour which takes place in the Fisherian model. Gunnison Brown, however, missed his opportunity to develop a theory of intertemporal trade. His purpose was quite different. Because he has a labour-only economy, he is able to reduce all future goods to present labour. Gunnison Brown seemed to think that this means that cost of production is the ultimate cause of interest.

Fetter, of course, in his reply pointed out that this argument could never hold in an economy with more than one primary factor (Fetter 1914: 856). Fetter does not here evince an awareness of the possibilities opened up by Gunnison Brown, but the following statement by Gunnison Brown may have lodged in his mind:

Trade was supposed to take place in kind. The producer of present goods desired future goods; and the producer of future goods desired present goods. There was specialisation and trade. In spite of the assumed absence of complicating factors, it is believed that the essential elements of the problem have been included.

(Gunnison Brown 1914: 347–8)

All that Gunnison Brown needed to do was to describe Crusoe and the Spaniard as the representative individuals in two countries, in order to arrive at the time preference motive for international asset trade. It was left for his critic, Fetter, to take this vital step. Gunnison Brown never became aware of the potential of these ideas. His *Economics and the Public Welfare* (1928) repeats the above discussion of capital theoretic problems. The chapters on trade and international payments simply repeat standard classical doctrines on these subjects. Gunnison Brown, unlike Fetter, made no connection between international economics and capital theory.

### Iversen

Iversen's *International Capital Movements* (1935) is a tortuously difficult book to read. It is neither a survey of the then state of the art, nor is it an original monograph. I shall be concerned with Part 1 – the first 200 pages of a 500-page work. This part purports to be a survey of most that had been written on international capital mobility, with the emphasis mainly on nonmonetary analyses. (Part 2 is a survey of the transfer problem literature.) Part 1 includes a melange of just about everything written on the subject, from the point of view of the Hecksher–Ohlin theory of trade through to the Austrian theory of capital. This encyclopaedic survey is interspersed with Iversen's critiques of individual writers and his own thoughts and apercus on the subject.

In order to derive original insights from the text, the reader is forced to pan for gold. Ultimately, Iversen's own intertemporal, trade-theoretic view of the subject can be sieved out from the other deposits.

Iversen opens his account with a strong criticism of the classical theory of international trade: he believes that the classical economists never got beyond analysing the transfer of goods, and did not think at all about the special problems associated with capital movements:

> it was not intimated that their existence might necessitate a reformulation of the traditional trade theory. Not even Taussig has taken up these problems. Just like J. S. Mill, he refers his discussion of the transfer mechanism to tributes rather than to ordinary capital movements.
>
> (1935: 7–9)

(Taussig being a leading and subtle expositor of the classical approach in the 1920s; see Flanders 1989.)

The ontological preoccupations of Iversen's vision are also contradictory; although openly intertemporal, he also introduces issues of expectations formation:

> Among the data by which the price structures are determined, *anticipations of the future* play an important role. If all future changes could be fully anticipated they would, in due time, be taken into account in all economic dispositions. Now, a good many changes in the price system are in fact almost completely foreseen – many seasonal fluctuations, for instance ... if on the other hand, completely unexpected changes occur the previous anticipations of the future are modified. This means that gains and losses are entailed upon the owners of the capital values that have changed as a result of these unexpected events.
>
> (Iversen 1935: 14)

Iversen then makes explicit reference to Myrdal's *ex ante/ex post* method, which is found in the latter's *Monetary Equilibrium* (1939), although Iversen's reference is to the original Swedish version of 1931. (There was also a German version published in 1933.) Marion and Svensson (1984) made a full application of these ideas to the open economy. They show how, in a three-period model, unforeseen shocks in the second period influence outcomes in the third. Iversen therefore suggested an application of Myrdal's method which has been found fruitful in modern theorizing.

Iversen, similarly to Marion and Svensson, believed that expectations of the future and their possible disappointment would influence outcomes in the open economy. The reason for this is that unexpected capital movements 'will occasion capital gains and capital losses which in their turn may release secondary transfers of capital' (Iversen 1935: 15).

Later on, however, in discussing the nature of the concept of capital, he adopts the intertemporal equilibrium version of this problematic notion:

> The stock of capital goods in existence at any moment is the result of past saving and investment. But in order to maintain this stock of capital goods intact the 'saving' must be continued. The sacrifice of present satisfactions for future satisfactions which people undergo in order to reap the advantages of capitalistic production is not something done once and for all, it is a continuous sacrifice.
>
> (Iversen 1935: 23)

This passage shows that Iversen recognized, as opposed to Keynesian 'animal spirits', for example, that saving and investment decisions are bound up with intertemporal utility maximization – 'the sacrifice of present satisfaction for future satisfactions'. He therefore believes that 'waiting or capital disposal has two dimensions: amount and time'. The former is embodied in capital goods, the latter in what he calls 'free capital disposal' and 'the productive factor which moves in the case of international capital flows is free capital disposal' (Iversen 1935: 24).

It is apparent, therefore, that Iversen's vision, that is to say, his intuitive ideas, are those of intertemporal equilibrium. This position leads him to establish the time preference motive for foreign lending. He begins by criticizing the view that welfare losses are caused by foreign loans. This obviously cannot be the case if they are part of optimal forward-looking decisions:

> Pigou and Taussig ... seem to imply that foreign investments, by creating an export surplus reduce the supply of goods available for domestic consumption, thus raising their prices and inflicting a special loss or sacrifice on labourers and consumers in general. It is not a peculiarity of foreign investments, however, that they reduce the quantity of goods ready for immediate consumption. Had the same amount of capital been invested at home rather than abroad, the same proportion of the productive agents would have been diverted to the creation of future, instead of present, utilities.
>
> (Iversen 1935: 166)

In his characteristically eclectic manner, he then brings in the concept of 'roundaboutness', or time intensity of production, used in Austrian capital theory, which effectively means that production functions are themselves increasing functions of time (see Negishi 1985: 103–5, for a

fuller explanation). Nevertheless, he recognizes the role which time preference plays in decisions to lend:

> The decisive question is to what extent the productive resources shall be
> used in roundabout ways; that will depend on the terms on which present
> and future goods are to be exchanged for one another, i.e. on the rate of
> time preference. The higher return expected from investments abroad
> may obviously affect this choice between the present and the future, but,
> apart from the immediate export surplus which emerges, the case of
> foreign lending merely indicates that present utilities are exchanged for
> future imported utilities, instead of future utilities produced at home.
>
> (Iversen 1935: 166)

This is a statement, albeit a not very clear one, of the distinction
between the time-preference motive, described in the first sentence, and
the consumption-augmenting motive, described in the second sentence.
Iversen ends by using the analogy of static trade theory surveyed in the
last chapter, by which borrowing constitutes the import of future goods.
The argument would be clearer if Iversen set out whether we are dealing
with a small country or a two-country world, and whether the rate of time
preference equals the rate of interest under autarky, as it does in the Fisherian and trade-theoretic models. It is the lack of structure, the absence of
any explanatory ideal conditions, which makes Iversen's work hard to
interpret, and means that despite his powerful intertemporal methodology,
there are no clear-cut results of the type Fetter produced.

At one point, Iversen is forced to be more explicit. This occurs at the point
where he criticizes Keynes, who argued that foreign investment might reduce
'the national gain' because it could turn the terms of trade against the home
country. Iversen suggests here that Keynes should have specified some of the
explanatory ideal conditions which are part of the trade-theoretic model of
the previous chapter, in particular with regard to the time period field: 'To
make the equation valid, two different periods of time must be taken into
account: (1) the period in which the loan is made and (2) the subsequent
period when interest payments are received' (Iversen 1935: 168).

Iversen argues that we must introduce an expression for the second-
period trade balance, evaluated using the second-period prices of imports
and exports. He also argues (as the modern view demonstrates) that we
must take intertemporal terms of trade effects into account:

> The more favourable shifts in trade terms due to interest and amorti-
> sation payments lie in the future, whereas the less favourable terms
> apply to the present. It might be argued that the process of discount-
> ing renders the present value of the future benefits less than the value
> of the immediate loss.
>
> (Iversen 1935: 169)

It can be concluded that Iversen certainly adopted the same methodological position as Fetter, and arrived at an awareness of the time preference motive.

In particular, these passages state clearly that in accordance with intertemporal theory, it is the normal state of affairs under utility maximization over time that one country should have a surplus and another a deficit. Lastly, I note that Iversen, in response to Keynes, sketched out briefly some aspects of the two-period trade-theoretic model.

## Hayek

If one looks at Hayek's work from the perspective of the modern Austrian School (Rothbard, Kirzner, Dolan, Lachmann, O'Driscoll and others), it would appear that he has little in common with the intertemporal tradition in general equilibrium theory. For the neo-Austrians, that research tradition errs because it assumes the very thing to be explained – the availability of information. Yet until his famous article of 1937, *Economics and Knowledge*, Hayek was a committed general equilibrium theorist who stated that 'it is my conviction that if one wants to explain economic phenomena at all, we have no means available but to build all the foundations given by the concept of a tendency towards equilibrium' (Hayek 1937: 31). By this he explicitly meant the Walrasian concept of equilibrium (Hayek 1933: 42–3), whose horizons, as I have remarked at the beginning of this chapter, he expanded into the dimension of time. His authorship of the great article of 1928, *Intertemporal Price Equilibrium and Movements in the Value of Money* (English translation 1984), is in itself enough to demonstrate that he adopted the thought style with which this research is concerned; indeed he originated it. Yet already in this work he is worrying over the implications of the open economy for his grand theory, and he initiates a train of thought which he carried over into *Prices and Production* (1931, second edition 1935), and which culminated in *Monetary Nationalism and International Stability* (1937). It must be said at the outset that Hayek, who laid all the conceptual foundations of the complete monetary theory of intertemporal trade, never took the opportunity to derive firmly based theorems from them, choosing instead to write a loosely structured work like *Monetary Nationalism*. The material which is not in *Monetary Nationalism* is essentially an adjunct or subtext to the themes of 'Das Intertemporale' and *Prices and Production*. The reader should be warned then, that applying the structuralist approach to Hayek's work gives it the appearance of a theoretical coherence that it actually lacks.

As Milgate (1979) noted, Hayek set out the complete vision of an intertemporal equilibrium for the first time. In his article of 1928, Hayek made the decisive innovation of defining an intertemporal equilibrium as a market-clearing equilibrium in a temporal sequence of markets. The salient features of Hayek's conceptual framework are those of modern economic theory. First, commodities are specified by their location in time as well as by their qualitative characteristics; second, an equilibrium is defined by the set of market-clearing prices determined simultaneously over the interval from time $t$ to time $T$.

Hayek contrasted his methodological approach to the theory of capital with what he saw as the older static theory of the early neoclassical economists: 'The examination of the necessity for the existence of an intertemporal price system is not only incompatible with the wide-spread assumption of the temporal constancy of prices but strongly contradicts such an assumption' (Hayek 1928 [1984]: 74).

The idea of distinguishing the prices of the same commodity at different points in time is introduced (1928 [1984]: 73), and it is envisaged that the multiplicity of commodity own rates of interest or intertemporal terms of trade should be adopted as the basis of the theory.

Of course, all this requires the assumption of perfect foresight, for 'to enable the use of equilibrium analysis it is necessary to assume, as we have done, that no deviation from the expected course of events take place' (1928 [1984]: 72). He later elaborated this idea into a definition which is identical to a rational expectations equilibrium, 'in which everybody foresees the future correctly and that this foresight includes not only the changes in the objective data, but also the behavior of all other people with whom he expects to perform economic transactions' (1939: 140; also see Young *et al.* 2004, for a fuller discussion of Hayek's contribution).

Unfortunately Hayek never resolved the problem of how or why money might be held in such an intertemporal economic system, and it was this point which was seized on by Hicks in his criticism of Hayek's system (Hicks 1933). Later, this issue led Hicks to adopt the method of temporary equilibrium.[2] Hayek in effect sidestepped the problem by accepting that a monetary economy would never be Pareto optimal – 'the prices established with the existence of money do not correspond to the equilibrium prices of the hypothetical system which does not possess a medium of exchange and therefore must yield the same outcome as any other price system inconsistent with equilibrium' (1928 [1984]: 99). The ideal economic system would have no money at all, and the object of monetary policy, once government had forced money into the system, was to allow the economy to approximate its real intertemporal equilibrium as closely as possible. Hayek articulated this idea by means of the concept of neutral money. This had two interpretations – as a theoretical tool and as a policy proposal. The theoretical tool permitted real analysis to be conducted in monetary terms, and served as a benchmark against which to make normative judgements about monetary regimes. As he put it, 'the tendencies towards equilibrium depicted in general economic theory are to remain operative in a monetary economy, all the conditions which it is the task of neutral money to indicate must be realized' (Hayek 1928 [1984]: 160). For Hayek, this is only possible if the quantity of money is kept constant. The method of Hayekian analysis is this: analyse the intertemporal general equilibrium of the economy as if money is neutral and list the various characteristics of the economy under these conditions, then look at the real world and ask if these conditions are reproduced there. If they are not, condemn real world monetary arrangements as being suboptimal.[3] As one of Hayek's best interpreters, the Frenchman Jean Pierre Reynaud, put it: 'Neutral money is precisely that which permits the real relations of production to manifest themselves, which will permit the economy to maintain its natural structure in a fashion which will attain the position of optimal equilibrium' (Reynaud 1937a: 1197). When reading what Hayek has to say about international monetary systems, one must keep this concept in mind; he is trying to recommend an optimal rate for the money supply only in the sense that it should cause a monetary economy to rule the intertemporal barter equilibrium. It is true, however, that many contemporaries continued to interpret neutral money as a kind of monetary policy (Reynaud 1937a: 1191 lists some of this literature), while in effect it was a conceptual device for devising policy. This interpretation is reflected by some of Hayek's statements to the effect that keeping the money supply constant is the appropriate policy rule under certain carefully specified circumstances:

> The relationship between the theoretical concept of neutrality of the money supply and the ideal of monetary policy is that the degree to which the latter approximates to the former provides one, probably the most important but not the sole, criterion for assessing the maxims of monetary policy. It is perfectly conceivable that monetary influences would always give rise to a 'falsification' of relative prices and a misdirection of production unless certain conditions were fulfilled, e.g. (1) the flow of money remained constant, (2) all prices were perfectly flexible and (3) in the conclusion of long-term contracts in terms of money, the future movement of prices was approximately correctly predicted.
>
> (Hayek 1933: 151)

Neutral money and the constancy of the money supply as a method of achieving it are also defined in the same way as they are above in the policy-orientated section of *Prices and Production* (1935: 131). Neutral money and intertemporal equilibrium are therefore the basis of Hayek's thought. As the earliest (and in my opinion the best) commentator on Hayek, H.S. Ellis, put it: 'From a doctrinal angle Hayek's entire work pivots on one distinctive thesis, that a constant effective volume of money is the unique prerequisite of intertemporal equilibrium' (Ellis 1934: 350).[4]

This concept carries with it the corollary that if the quantity of money is held constant, added savings, whether from increased frugality or productive efficiency, automatically go into actual investment of an economically correct nature; but that if the money supply is increased, although savings still go completely into investments, ultimately all of the saving forced by the process of inflation is economically wasted, with the likelihood of additional real losses to the economy. The weakness of these ideas lies in the fact that, on the basis of Hayek's assumptions of rationality, any announced and persistent policy with regard to the price level of consumer goods would be appropriately discounted into the present and cause no resource misallocation. This was pointed out early on by Ellis (1934: 352). Individuals therefore exhibit money illusion in the face of any monetary disturbance, which causes a deviation from intertemporal equilibrium.

Hayek's discussion of the open economy in *Monetary Nationalism* is based on these foundations, but we need a little detective work to prove this. On p. 30 of *Prices and Production* (1935 edition) he cites the article on 'Intertemporal Equilibrium' as the basis of his monetary theory.[5] Later on in *Monetary Nationalism* he explains that it is his adherence to the model of *Prices and Production*, whereby misdirections of investment due to credit inflation are the cause of the trade cycle, which distinguishes him from his theoretical opponents (1937: 47). It is evident then that the concept of intertemporal equilibrium, at one remove, underlies *Monetary Nationalism*. The short section in *Prices and Production* itself which deals with the open economy cites the 1928 article on 'Intertemporal Equilibrium' as the original source of his ideas on this subject (1935: 110).

'The fundamental thesis that a constant effective volume of money alone secures intertemporal equilibrium' (Ellis 1934: 358) is not all that underlies Hayek's treatment of the open economy. Of crucial importance is a distinction between the effects of exogenous real and monetary shocks: real changes (for example in productivity) lead to changes in money expenditures, which in turn bring about equilibrium reallocations, while monetary changes are 'self-reversing' and the equilibria created by such changes are 'not stable' (1941: 34 and 1937: 50). (See O'Driscoll 1977: 79–80 for an elaboration of this interpretation.) From the point of view of the international economy, this implies that monetary flows will and should take place because of country specific real disturbances:

> The increase of the product of any one country is regularly accompanied by an increase of the quantity of money circulating there ... What appears to be an absolute increase of the amount of money in circulation consequent upon an increase of production, if viewed from the standpoint of a single country, proves to be nothing but a change in the relative local distribution of the money of all nations, which is a necessary condition of the change in the distribution of the product of the world as a whole.
>
> (Hayek 1935: 111)

On the other hand, Hayek holds that exogenous changes in the world money supply also have real effects, albeit undesirable ones: 'such changes in the quantity of money must give rise to disturbances in quite definite ways' (Hayek 1928 [1984]: 109).

Before continuing with this theme of the differing consequences of real and monetary shocks, I would like to describe the model-theoretic context in which Hayek's discussion takes place. Since Hayek's treatment of the open economy developed from his article of 1928, some of his concepts can be seen as forming a system which is a partially formed version of the monetary intertemporal model. The first piece of evidence for this claim is simply that the action takes place in the context of an intertemporal equilibrium model. The second piece of evidence is that he assumes a perfectly integrated world economy. This is clear because he assumes that initially the 'ideal distribution of specie' of classical theory holds (1928 [1984]: 106), something which can only be the case under conditions of purchasing power and interest rate parity. Lastly, while the transactions structure is not explicit, the role of money is a cash in advance one: 'so far as the individual in the monetary economy is concerned, the increase in his money income is only a necessary link in the chain of processes which enables him to obtain an increased share in output in return for an increase in his participation in production' (1928 [1984]: 107).

It is evident, however, that Hayek did not accept that money is neutral in the world economy, a result which obtains in the model of the last chapter. There are a number of reasons for such non-neutralities which are, as we shall see, dealt with more explicitly in *Monetary Nationalism* than in the 1928 article.

We now come to Hayek's main point, which is that while the quantity of money may change in any one country in response to real changes in accordance with 'the theory that ... can be traced back to North and Hume' (1928 [1984]: 109), there is no validity in the idea that the quantity of money in the world as a whole 'must grow in proportion to the volume of transactions effected by it' (1928 [1984]: 106). Hayek therefore distinguishes sharply between the need for changes in the country-specific money supply and the need for stability of the world money supply:

> In the first case, the changes in the relative quantities of money in the individual countries are a necessary precondition for the restoration of equilibrium, namely for the change in the relative price levels in the two countries which has become necessary. But there is no change in the absolute quantity of money in the two countries now linked together into one economic system. A change in the total quantity of money would not imply at all that the equilibrium that has been upset within the economy is now restored, but merely that a temporary disturbance of equilibrium in the production of goods has been created for the purpose of bringing about a new equilibrium with the output of gold.
>
> (Hayek 1928 [1984]: 106–7)

Hayek elaborates his view of the necessary role of 'local redistributions of money' with an example of a country which enjoys a productivity improvement:

> A little reflection will show that ultimately our country's share in the value of total world output has increased to the same extent as the relative level of the money income of the inhabitants of our country has risen by comparison with that of other countries because of the gold inflow. The change in this share will be due partly to the fact that the people of our country retain for their own use an absolutely and relatively greater part of their increased agricultural output and an absolutely and relatively greater share of their unchanged output of other exportable goods, and simultaneously can import more of other goods.
>
> (Hayek 1928 [1984]: 108)

He goes on to give a view of the adjustment process, which appears to be that of the 'monetary approach to the balance of payments', with a dominant role for money income, not price movements:

> After the conclusion of the transition period within which the gold movements have taken place and exerted their influence upon prices, the share of our country in the value of world output will therefore have risen by precisely as much as the value of the total output of the commodity whose output was initially increased, and the precondition for this increase in the share of world output was precisely a corresponding rise in the sum of money incomes in the country. The flow of gold from one country to another, and the rise in the 'money supply' thereby brought about in the latter, therefore merely constitute a necessary and intermediate step which in the monetary economy must precede a change in the market positions of the two countries.
>
> (Hayek 1928 [1984]: 109)

Nevertheless, Hayek explicitly rejects the view of the monetary approach to the balance of payments that changes in the demand for money can explain current account imbalances (e.g. Frenkel and Mussa 1985: 691):

> The fact that the money income of a group linked together in a particular place rises proportionately, and indeed not merely in terms of that part of it composed of sales to foreigners but also that originating in the original exchange within this group, must result in a relatively greater quantity of money permanently remaining within this group. This phenomenon can certainly be described as an increase in the demand for money, but to do so offers no explanation of it. Nevertheless, it is precisely this description which renders it easy to conclude

that these so-called changes in the demand for money are independent causes of the gold movements, and further that an adjustment of the quantity of money to the changed demand for it under all circumstances is a prerequisite for the maintenance of equilibrium.

(Hayek 1928 [1984]: 109)

Hayek contrasts this case with one where one sector of the world economy experiences a productivity improvement, and the fall in price resulting from the increase in output gives rise to an expansion of gold output and associated with that an expansion in the quantity of money (1928 [1984]: 110). This expansion of the money supply has real effects:

The temporary rise in the profitability of the production sectors first affected by the gold inflow slackens because of the rise in prices which takes place as a result of it. Hence the branches of production concerned will ultimately have to be contracted back to their level at the beginning of the gold inflow.

(Hayek 1928 [1984]: 110)

It appears that Hayek is arguing that changes in the world money supply (under a commodity money system) cause confusion between a relative and nominal price change which leads to undesirable changes in output. On this basis, Hayek argues that while the money supply of an individual country may vary in response to a real change through the medium of a current account imbalance, no such change should take place for the world as a whole:

In contrast in the case of a movement of gold within the economy, therefore, changes in the total quantity of money in the economy do not provide a basis for the individual economic subjects to alter the extent to which they satisfy their needs. Rather in this context the change in the quantity of money is the definitive and conclusive outcome; and so, when the money supply is expanded, the individual is forced to accept as final payment something which he had no desire to take as such.

(Hayek 1928 [1984]: 110)

('The economy' means the world economy in this context.)

It must be said that Hayek's argument for keeping the world quantity of money constant is open to Ellis's criticism of Hayek's proposal for keeping the money supply constant in a closed economy. It is simply not compatible with rational expectations (see footnote 4, pp. 141–2).

There is no detailed or clearly articulated argument as to why monetary shocks can have real effects in a world where people have perfect foresight. It may be that Hayek is referring to unanticipated random shocks, but in the above example of a global productivity improvement we would expect people to know that increases in the output of gold represent no underlying real change (unanticipated shocks cannot occur under perfect foresight). Unanticipated stochastic shocks can be treated in a framework with uncertainty and rational expectations, but Hayek does not clearly distinguish this case from that of perfect foresight. Hayek's analysis suffers from the fact that he did not know of the way in which the concept of rational expectations translates the concept of perfect foresight into an uncertain environment. Whatever Hayek had in mind, his treatment here was too brief to clarify the mechanism by which a monetary change causes a welfare loss, and the reader is thrown back on assuming that the real effects result from the money illusion which characterizes this article.

*Monetary Nationalism and International Stability* (1937) considerably elaborates the themes begun in the 1928 article – the difference between real and monetary shocks and the need to hold the world money supply constant. Here the focus is on how government intervention, particularly attempts to control the money supply or manipulate exchange rates, prevent the necessary international transmission of real shocks and create unnecessary monetary shocks. The exposition is much more elaborate than in the 'Intertemporal Equilibrium' article in the more familiar world of Hayekian business cycle theory. As pointed out earlier, Hayek's explicit statement of intertemporal equilibrium is situated two removes away from this work. What are much more in evidence are some scenarios which are familiar from much of Hayek's work and from much Hayekian exegesis. Business cycles are caused by the familiar Wicksellian mechanism, by which the existence of a market rate of interest below the natural rate causes a general distortion of resources toward future production from that which is economically optimal (1937: 28), as in *Monetary Theory and the Trade Cycle* (Hayek 1933: 102–6; Ellis 1934: 342–3). Entrepreneurs confuse temporary changes in the supply of capital for permanent changes, and revise their production plans mistakenly (1937: 31, 47), as in the important article *Price Expectations, Monetary Disturbances and Malinvestments* (Hayek 1939: 143) (for an exegesis see Kyun 1988: 43, 83–4). Changes in the money supply cause the economy to be in an unstable temporary equilibrium (Hayek 1937: 50) as in *The Pure Theory of Capital* (Hayek 1941: 34; O'Driscoll 1977: 80).

Nevertheless, Hayek's exposition continues to centre on his distinction between real and monetary shocks and his policy programme for instituting a regime of 'neutral money' through holding the world money supply constant. I shall consider the treatment of each of these themes in *Monetary Nationalism* in turn. Looking first at Hayek's view of the relation between developments in the real economy and international movements of money, one finds a statement of the views already expressed in 1928. Inter-country flows of money are responses to real shocks and should not be prevented by controls. They should be distinguished from exogenous monetary shocks caused by government action:

There is no reason why one should not expect the self-reversing effects of monetary changes to be connected with the changes of the quantity of money in a particular area which is not part of a wider monetary system. If a decrease or increase of demand in one area is offset by a corresponding change in demand in another area, there is no reason why the changes in the quantity of money in the two areas should in any sense misguide productive activity. They are simply manifestations of an underlying real change which works itself out through the medium of money.

(Hayek 1937: 49)

The great error of 'nationalist' policies, which manipulate exchange rates in order to stabilize the price level by controlling the quantity of money in a particular country, is that they prevent such 'redistributions of money', which 'are the only ways of effecting the change in real income with the minimum of disturbance' (1937: 52).

Turning now to Hayek's view of monetary shocks, one finds that this part of Hayek's argument, as already stated, is concerned with what he called the 'self-reversing character of the effects of monetary changes. It emphasizes the misdirection of production caused by the wrong expectation created by changes in relative prices which are necessarily only temporary' (1937: 52). The mechanism by which these effects come about is more clearly specified than in the 1928 article and is consistent with fully rational behaviour.

The basis of these unwelcome responses to monetary inflows is the potential effect the creation of bank loans that, 'to any significant effect, are only made for investment purposes, have in increasing investment activity' (1937: 28). The gold exchange standard, for example, to the extent that it allowed changes in credit conditions under fractional reserve banking, therefore also prevented the smooth functioning of changes in the international distribution of specie and caused these international gold movements to have real effects on the capital stock:

the equipment which has been created will cease to be useful ... revised plans which will be made are bound to be disappointed in the reverse direction and the readjustment of production which has been enforced will prove to be a misdirection.

(1937: 31)

Underlying all this is Hayek's programme for the creation of a regime in which money would be neutral, one with a 'homogenous international currency' lacking 'that most promiscuous feature of our present system: namely that a movement towards more liquid types of money causes an actual decrease in the total supply of money and vice versa' (1937: 82). Hayek thus continued, in *Monetary Nationalism*, to maintain that the quantity of money in the world, as opposed to that in individual countries, should always remain constant:

> The aim, as we have just seen, must be to increase the certainty that one form of money will always be readily exchangeable against other forms of money at a known rate, and that such changes should not lead to changes in the total quantity of money.
>
> (1937: 84)

It is not made explicit whether all this is meant to be compatible with rational behaviour. Nevertheless, Hayek constantly emphasizes the 'temporary' and 'self-reversing' nature of the monetary disturbances which occur under both the gold exchange standard with fractional reserve banking and under a managed exchange rate regime (1937: 24–5, 28–9, 31–2, 47–8, 50–1). Real changes, in response to a change in the money supply, therefore occur only along the adjustment path back to the original equilibrium. This also occurs in modern models of investment in a monetary economy, but neither in those well-worked out theories, nor in Hayek's description are entrepreneurs making permanent real changes in output.[6] In both Hayek's theory and modern equilibrium business cycle theories, these temporary non-neutralities occur because of the 'wrong expectation created by changes in relative prices which are necessarily only temporary' (1937: 52). In this sense, individuals in Hayek's treatment do not suffer from money illusion and Hayek's analysis is consistent with rational behaviour and the existence of intertemporal equilibrium. In modern parlance, money is assumed to be neutral (a monetary shock returns the real sector of the economy to its original dynamic equilibrium), but not 'superneutral' (that is to say, monetary shocks cause real adjustments along the economy's adjustment path).[7]

*Monetary Nationalism* also contains a discussion of real fluctuations in the open economy which is closer to recent work and focuses on the consumption-smoothing motive; indeed, the following is an exact statement of it:

> The possibility of credit transactions, the exchange of present goods against future goods, greatly widens the range of advantageous exchanges. In international trade it means in particular that countries may import more than they export in some seasons because they will export more than they import during other seasons. Whether this is made possible by the exporter directly crediting the importer with the price, or whether it takes place by some credit institution in either country providing the money, it will always mean that the indebtedness of the importing country to the exporting increases temporarily, i.e. that net short-term lending takes place.
>
> (Hayek 1937: 58)

Stockman (1988: 543) presents an identical exposition of consumption smoothing, using a simple example of two otherwise identical countries that have different deterministic seasonal variations in production opportunities: the home country produces more in the winter and the foreign country in the summer. He concludes that: 'With complete financial markets consumption would be perfectly smoothed over time' (Stockman 1988: 543).

Hayek then attacks the idea, characteristic of the received view on capital movements, that they respond to interest rate differentials:

> We can also see how misleading it may be to think of capital movements as exclusively directed by previous changes in the relative rates of interest in the different money markets. What directs the use of available credit and therefore decides in what direction the balance of indebtedness will shift at a particular time is in the first instance the relation between prices in different places.
>
> (Hayek 1937: 59)

These price differences are caused by what are apparently largely seasonal shocks, and 'short-term international indebtedness' therefore proceeds largely with the 'normal fluctuations of international trade' (1937: 56). Hayek still intends the argument to apply to international capital movements in general, since he states that in effect, 'with the exception of non-funded long-term loans almost any form of investment may have to be regarded as short-term investment' (1937: 56). Formally, Hayek's argument is a correct statement of consumption smoothing, even if he views it as an explanation and justification of short-run capital movements. From the point of view of the main argument of *Monetary Nationalism*, however, the point is that managed floating interferes with this optimal behaviour, which is derived from Hayek's vision of intertemporal equilibrium. In fact, in the chapter of *Monetary Nationalism* on 'International Capital Movements', one sees exactly how Hayek's method of analysis works. First, he describes the intertemporal barter equilibrium characterized by consumption-smoothing behaviour in a trading world where individual countries are subject to seasonal fluctuations. The effects of various managed monetary regimes on that equilibrium are then worked out.

Again, the emphasis is on the need for the adoption of a Hayekian monetary policy. This is because:

> It is difficult to see how, under a homogenous international standard, capital movements, and particularly short-term capital movements, should be a source of instability or lead to changes in productive activity which are not justified by corresponding changes in the real conditions.
>
> This conclusion has, however, to be somewhat modified if, instead of a homogenous international currency, we consider a world consisting of

separate rational monetary and banking systems, even if we still leave the possibility of variations in exchange rates out of account.

(Hayek 1937: 60)

('A homogenous international currency' is defined by Hayek to mean a world monetary system with a 'pure metallic currency', no banking system and no government creation of money (Hayek 1937: 20). The world money supply is clearly constant under such a system as long as the supply of precious metal remains unchanged.)

Hayek's contribution is difficult to assess when it is considered in relation to the modern work surveyed above. The intertemporal perfect foresight equilibrium of his pathbreaking article of 1928 should imply the existence of the neutrality and exchange rate regime irrelevance theorems presented in Chapter 3. Nevertheless, Hayek vaulted over the basic monetary model and enmeshed his exposition in the complications which arise when money is not neutral in an optimizing framework. The non-neutrality of money can be derived in a much simpler way than those suggested by Hayek. As pointed out in the last chapter, all that is required is to change the sequence of transactions from that which prevails in the basic cash in advance model (Obstfeld and Stockman 1985: 967–8). In the most general of such treatments, only some of Hayek's intuitions can be shown to hold, for example, country-specific monetary shocks, leading to increases in the money supply, may be correlated with current account surpluses or deficits depending on the size of various parameters (Stockman and Svensson 1987: 187–8).[8] [In the basic monetary model presented in Chapter 3, which is due to Helpman (1981), no correlation whatsoever exists between the behaviour of the money supply and real shocks; see Stockman 1988: 539 and Backus and Kehoe 1987: 34. This follows from the complete dichotomy between the monetary and real parts of the economy which is characteristic of this model. This means that stochastic processes for the money supply can be chosen to yield any desired correlation between exchange rates, the current account and real shocks to the economy.] In a complex model, there also exists a correlation between real shocks and international redistributions of money as Hayek expected (Stockman and Svensson 1987: 190). Despite these results, it is usually the case that in a fully specified general equilibrium model, in which investment and consumption decisions are both created and asset-holding decisions are fully specified in the context of uncertainty, the connections between various economic variables and the current account are ambiguous and depend on the relative size of parameters like the degree of intertemporal substitution in consumption, the sign and magnitude of net foreign assets, the marginal product of capital and the degree of risk aversion in a particular country. Like Hayek, modern theory takes an intertemporal general equilibrium approach, but it has found that it is harder to make clear statements about the issues with which Hayek was concerned, such as the relationship between international movements of money, and changes in productivity or in the amount of investment activity (Stockman and Svensson 1987: 194–5). One must conclude then, that the basic distinction Hayek makes between the effects of real and monetary shocks in an open economy has not been verified.

What about the robustness of Hayek's policy proposals in the light of the theoretical knowledge extant in the 1980s? It is clear from Hayek's writings that he believed that money only had no real effects if the quantity of money is held constant. Persson (1982, 1984) examined this policy in the simplest possible case. Persson assumed that all of the assumptions of Helpman's (1981) cash in advance model (presented in Chapter 3) hold, except that the only money is a fixed world stock of currency which is termed gold. Countries have no power to create or destroy money. This regime, termed the 'gold standard' by Persson, therefore corresponds exactly to Hayek's proposal for neutral money. Persson, however, shows that this regime does in fact have real effects. This is because there is an opportunity cost of holding the monetary reserves which are endogenized in the country's budget constraint. This point can be easily demonstrated using the model of Chapter 3.[9] It is an interesting example of the phenomenon of recurrence that Persson should have chosen to analyse a problem treated by Hayek in a similar theoretical context. It appears that the examination of such a scheme is an interesting problem for the researcher who works with the theoretical tools of intertemporal equilibrium. There is no evidence that either the Mundell–Fleming or monetary approaches dealt with the desirability of such a scheme (judging for example by Kenen's 1985 survey).

As was shown in Chapter 3, fixed and flexible exchange rates preserve the neutrality of money and impose no real costs on the economy in the context of a simple cash in advance model. Modern theory, however, is well aware that the equivalence theorem presented in the last chapter is just a benchmark and that real allocations will be effected in different ways by violations of the various assumptions required for the neutrality result. So far, however, the sources of non-neutrality presented in *Monetary Nationalism* have not been studied.[10] Whether Hayek's scheme would have more desirable welfare properties than other exchange rate regimes in a model where, for example, changes in the money supply influence the investment decisions of profit-maximizing firms is therefore an open question.[11] We can be certain that his policy will have some real effects in such a cash in advance scenario, since we know it leads to non-neutrality in the basic case.

To conclude then, it is evident that Hayek began to build up a normative theory of international monetary arrangements based on the principle of intertemporal equilibrium. In his early article of 1928, Hayek struggled to break away from the use of money illusion in order to justify his proposal for the achievement of a regime of neutral money, but in

*Monetary Nationalism* he was able to present arguments for non-neutrality consistent with rational behaviour.

Hayek's *Monetary Nationalism* seems to strongly suggest that if governments would not use protectionism and exchange or capital controls as a means of achieving internal balance, then monetary changes would not cause temporary, but welfare-reducing, real effects, and that these real changes in turn would be free to create desirable monetary reallocations. Another theme is that of the role of the banking systems in altering the money supply and thus interfering with real reallocations. Both of these problems can be prevented by holding the world money supply constant. The focus of theory in the 1980s, however, was rather different. Government intervention is not the only cause of second-best problems; incomplete futures markets and private information also play a role, and it is not clear that an analysis based on these factors can give clear guidance as to the nature of an ideal monetary system.[12]

Nevertheless, the strong family resemblances noted between Hayek's analyses and those of Stockman (1988) and Persson (1982, 1984) are evidence for the similarity between his approach and some of the literature of the 1980s, when the modern intertemporal model was presented.

### Reynaud

Fortunately, it seems that Hayek had an interpreter who was capable of extending some of his ideas. J.L. Reynaud, in his 1937 article *Monnaie Neutre et Echanges Internationaux*, extends some of Hayek's ideas, apparently independently of *Monetary Nationalism*, which he does not cite. It is the second of two 'Essais sur la Monnaie Neutre', developing Hayek's concept of neutral money. At the beginning of the first, *Monnaie Neutre et Economie Re'elle*, which deals largely with closed economy issues, Reynaud cites an extremely precise definition of international neutral money, made by a colleague of his (all translations are mine):

> M. Oualid wrote recently: 'In order to preserve some importance in commercial relations (between nations poor and rich in gold), one must imagine an advanced technique eliminating money and its perturbing effects, such as a clearing house or the form of rights to compensation one sees in actual exchange conventions: the economy again tends to become a barter economy again. Everything takes place as if money does not exist or simply plays the role of a unit of exchange.'
>
> But one can conceive of this real economy in two ways: as being an underlying reality which can serve as a base for evaluating the general evolution of the economy, or as an economic ideal to be realized insofar as that is possible.

(Reynaud 1937a: 1175–6)

Here we have a succinct restatement of the concept of neutral international money. In his second article, Reynaud gives an even more grandiose definition of the term, which places it exactly as an exemplar made up of the explanatory ideal conditions to be found in intertemporal trade theory. This definition is in fact more remarkable in the way in which, in a grand intellectual sweep, it describes neutral money as that which is consistent with the intertemporal equilibrium of the international economy:

> Let us assume for an instant that money will be passive on the international exchanges and can do nothing but reflect the real value of commodity movements or of capital movements due to truly economic causes: we have settled on a determinate equilibrium of the exchange rate, the commercial balance, and the current account. This equilibrium will be that of the real economy; in other words we are speaking of an economic organization where money cannot modify the decisions of individuals and the price relations will be those which would permit the greatest present and future productivity of capital endowments. In effect, capital will be uniquely placed as a function of the real utility of its employment, and not for the purposes of speculation or security.
>
> (Reynaud 1937b: 1370)

This view of the international economy clearly reflects the Hayekian view of the deleterious effects of monetary fluctuations, described by Reynaud in his first article:

> Credit fluctuations join, doubtless, those of money to contribute to throwing into confusion the real relations between economic agents ... 'money illusion' prevents the optimal allocation of value between producer and consumer goods ... it prevents rational comparison between present and future utilities.
>
> (Reynaud 1937a: 1193)

Here Reynaud takes over Hayek's characteristic belief, associated with the alleged non-optimality of a money economy, that money illusion exists even though, in the context of a real economy, individuals are endowed with perfect foresight. (See Hayek 1928 [1984]: 99 for a typical example, previously quoted.) Reynaud relied on this type of money illusion for some of his results. It is apparent then that money will not be neutral in Reynaud's view, any more than it is in Hayek's, except under certain special circumstances. Neutral money, therefore, is an explanatory ideal condition which serves as a heuristic device. In certain situations this device can be used to prove the neutrality of money (as in Chapter 3), but not in all circumstances.

Reynaud also sets out, rather more explicitly than Hayek, explanatory ideal conditions. Thus, he explicitly accepts at the outset that purchasing power parity holds (1937b: 1972–3). Second, interest rate parity between countries is implied by the following statement about a closed economy, where money functions as a numeraire: 'If there is no money, equilibrium cannot be established: in particular one cannot even conceive of an equilibrium interest rate; each product will have its own rate' (Reynaud 1937a: 1973).

Clearly, if the own rates of interest which exist in intertemporal equilibrium are equated by means of money as a numeraire, by analogy one type of country-specific money can play this role across countries. Reynaud, however, fails to be any more explicit about the role of money, noting merely that it serves as a medium of exchange.

Reynaud then undertakes a series of thought experiments of the following type: Suppose there is some type of external monetary shock. Will this or will this not maintain the neutral, intertemporal monetary equilibrium of the economy? This is the essence of neutral money as a method of analysis. He examines several examples, of which I shall discuss two: a tribute paid in money, and foreign investments. In the case of the enforced transfer, he concludes that it has real effects on both the creditor and debtor countries. This is because, in the manner of Hayek's business cycle theory in *Prices and Production*, it causes overinvestment, distorts the structure of production, and causes forced saving in the creditor country (Reynaud 1937b: 1380, 1382). The situation is very different with foreign lending or borrowing which reflect higher rates of return in the debtor country. In this case, money is a 'faithful mirror of changes in the economic structure'; movements of money are neutral since they 'reflect the definitive gain of industries used more advantageously' (Reynaud 1937b: 1385, 1386).

Reynaud concludes his discussion with an interesting justification of the policy of neutral money in an open economy. In true Hayekian fashion, he states that such a policy consists of keeping the quantity of money in the world constant, where money is defined as all means of exchange (Reynaud 1937b: 1930). In individual countries, the quantity of money does change in response to changes in real output. The great advantage of such a system, he says, is that it would achieve exactly what the advocates of a system of moveable parities, under a regime where the quantity of money in each country is stabilized, set out to do but cannot achieve. Under such a regime of monetary nationalism, it is necessary to judge when to devalue by calculating purchasing power parities, and it is likely that mistakes will be made in such calculations. Under the Hayekian policy of a stable world money supply, however, variations in the price level automatically bring about the necessary adjustment:

> Movements in the price level are therefore the correction which indicates that sometimes the economy is in a process of devaluation or revaluation; sometimes it is growing faster than other countries, some-

times lower. In devaluing or revaluing money itself, one is not giving it an active role to play, but, on the contrary, one is returning it to the point of equilibrium where it must be passive.

(Reynaud 1937b: 1392)

Notice the identity between this view and Hayek's belief that maintaining the world quantity of money constant would allow movements in the price level of a particular country to reflect changes in productivity (Hayek 1928 [1984]: 108). The basis of the two are the same – a belief that some monetary flows are reallocations reflecting real changes. Such policies are, of course, the ultimate consequences of a theoretical system based on neutral money and intertemporal equilibrium. They only arise because of the idea that the neutrality of money and the optimality of intertemporal equilibrium can only coexist in one particular position – that in which the quantity of money is stabilized, the only major exception to this rule being that of real disturbances in particular countries.

Reynaud concludes with a statement which sums up his vision of desirable international monetary relations:

A 'real economy' policy based on all the profound conditions of production, in which money will be the mirror of fundamental economic relations, will be a policy of economic stability. It will help us above all to suppress the cause of the greatest disorders in the modern economy, and which, once more, is causing the most trouble in international economic relations: money illusion.

(Reynaud 1937b: 1393)

This places a stronger emphasis on money illusion than occurs in the work of Hayek. This statement is consistent with Hayek's theoretical position in 1928, but not with the more intricate analysis in *Monetary Nationalism*. The purest Hayekian model of the open economy, originally set out in 'Das Intertemporale', shorn of the refinements adapted from the theory of *Prices and Production*, depends on a curious coexistence of money illusion and intertemporal equilibrium. It seems that Reynaud was prepared to accept this inconsistency, which was the one weakness in Hayek's innovative article on intertemporal equilibrium.

### Hayek's followers: Fraser, Robbins, Lachmann

The extent to which Hayek's ideas appeared in the writings of others can serve as a measure of his influence. H.F. Fraser's *London and the Gold Standard* (1933) and Lionel Robbins's better known *The Great Depression* (1934) are relevant not because they add anything to the development of economic theory, but because of their use of Hayek's business cycle theory to criticize the abandonment of the Gold Standard. Thus Fraser states the same type of argument against 'international inflation' under flexible exchange rates which Hayek made in *Monetary Nationalism*:

> The inflationary period is certain to last too long, and to stimulate the industries making producer goods, to hold out to entrepreneurs' hopes of gain through lengthening the productive process, hopes that will certainly be disappointed when the costs of production, both capital and labor, rise, making the new methods unprofitable. In short, the inflationary process will cause a vertical maladjustment of industry which will require a new deflation to straighten it out by forcing through liquidation a new equilibrium.
>
> (Fraser 1933: 184)

Robbins uses the Austrian theory of business cycles in the same way to denounce the alleged inflationary evils of flexible exchange rates (Robbins 1934: 105–6). This is essentially a statement of Hayek's argument in *Monetary Nationalism* that any international monetary arrangement which permits expansion of the world money supply, whether through direct monetary policy or elastic bank credit, will cause business cycle fluctuations with temporary real effects.

Lachmann (1944) produced the most interesting of the contributions by those of Hayek's followers who worked in British or American universities. Lachmann was an avowed follower of van Mises and Hayek (see Lachmann 1940, where he reviews Hayek's closed economy business cycle theory). Not surprisingly then, his analysis focuses upon what he calls 'dynamic equilibrium', a concept which seems to be roughly equivalent to intertemporal equilibrium. He does this in a context of the critique of the British and American plans for a postwar international monetary order. Lachmann was strongly critical of proposals to correct 'fundamental disequilibrium' by devaluation or by restricting capital movements (Lachmann 1944: 186–7). Lachmann believed in the fundamental tenet of the intertemporal approach – that the economy can be in equilibrium when it has a current account deficit. In Lachmann's case, the focus is on such equilibria in the context of a growing economy:

> The idea suggests itself that in all cases in which the cause of international disequilibrium lies in processes connected with capital expansion the most natural remedy, and the most desirable from the point of view of world prosperity, is international lending. Where a country is importing large quantities of capital goods and raw materials and unable to pay for them with commodity exports, its resources are strained to the limit by a process of internal expansion. Is it not natural that it should redress the balance by exporting claims and titles to the new wealth it is creating?
>
> (Lachmann 1944: 189)

Thus Lachmann argues that the appropriate equilibrium conditions for the economy are 'the conditions of the dynamic equilibrium of an expanding world economy with continuous investment, not the conditions of static equilibrium' (Lachmann 1944: 189).

Lachmann also takes issue with the argument that loans cannot be used as a long run means of attaining balance of payments equilibrium because they must eventually be repaid. Current account deficits can, he argues, be 'permanent':

> Economically, bonds are alternatives to shares, and successful loans are typically not repaid but converted into holdings and thus made into the source of a permanent income stream. The economist has to formulate the dynamic equilibrium conditions for an expanding world economy in which there are permanent capital flows as well as com- modity flows. This task raises some further problems germane to risk and uncertainty which theoretically center round the distinction between dynamic equilibrium at a point of time and dynamic equilib- rium over time.
>
> (Lachmann 1944: 190)

Permanent capital flows were dealt with in the optimizing models of the 1980s, which are based upon this type of rational economic behaviour. It is easy in fact to reformulate the Fisherian framework in terms of perpetu- ities and derive permanent current account surpluses or deficits (Bruce and Purvis 1985: 848–50). Lachmann's statement can therefore be verified theoretically in a rigorous framework. Lachmann, however, has no faith that such an equilibrium could exist: 'Dynamic equilibrium over time is almost certainly quite unattainable. In a world of uncertainty and imper- fect foresight some misinvestment, i.e. the loss of some capital owing to circumstances unforeseen at the moment of investment, is inevitable' (Lachmann 1944: 190). Note the difference in emphasis from the modern literature, a difference also common to Reynaud. Dynamic equilibrium is a theoretical ideal, but individuals are never endowed with the perfect foresight which would enable it to be attained.

Lachmann's proposals for a new international monetary order could not be more different from those mooted during the run-up to Bretton Woods or from those adopted at Bretton Woods itself. Lachmann's schemes follow from the above statement that equilibrium over time is unattainable because of uncertainty. His objective is to reduce the 'risks of international lending' (Lachmann does not distinguish between risk and uncertainty). This would be done by creating two bodies, one 'like the U.S. Securities and Exchange Commission' and the other an 'International Bankruptcy Court'. The first institution, by vetting loan projects, would 'reduce the risks of international lending'; the second institution would reduce 'the loss suffered by foreign creditors' when 'readjustment of claims' become necessary. The only purpose of international economic institutions is thus to 'coordinate capital flow and commodity flow in an expanding world economy' (1944: 191).

Clearly Lachmann adopts the policy implications of intertemporal equilibrium, since his only departures from laissez-faire consist of official provision of information and the enforcement of contract. The logic of his proposals follow from the conception of a dynamic equilibrium, in which claims are traded over time by the private market, as being the optimal state for the world economy.

## Mosak

Mosak's work in the field appeared in his monograph *General Equilibrium Theory in International Trade* (1944). The relevant material is contained in the second part of the book, entitled 'Intertemporal General Equilibrium Theory and International Trade'. This consists of 63 pages, about one-third of the entire work. Here the theory of intertemporal trade takes a qualitative leap of considerable proportions. The purpose was to apply the analysis of the second and third parts of Hicks's *Value and Capital* (first edition 1939; all references are to the second edition, published in 1946), to the problems of an open economy. The treatment of money, the use of the concept of temporary equilibrium and the extensive role in the analysis played by the stability properties of a temporary equilibrium all are closely related to Hicks's work. Mosak's Chapters 6 and 7, dealing with the household and firm in intertemporal (not temporary) equilibrium are extensions of Chapters 10, 11, 16 and 17 of *Value and Capital*. The discussions of the role of money at the end of Mosak's two chapters are an attempt to develop monetary theory beyond Chapters 11 and 19 of *Value and Capital*. Mosak's chapters on the stability and comparative statics of a temporary general equilibrium in a closed and open economy are also extensions of Hicks's three chapters on the stability and what Hicks calls the 'formal rules of behavior' (Hicks 1946: 273) of a temporary general equilibrium. Hicks's treatment of temporary equilibrium is more satisfactory than Hayek's treatment of intertemporal equilibrium. This is because Hicks's system is capable of a complete formalization which is closely related to his original exposition (see for example Grandmont 1983). This is not the case with Hayek's version of a monetary intertemporal general equilibrium system, which Hicks himself found impossible to formalize (Hicks 1982: 4). In this sense then, Mosak's Hicksian treatment is clearly only a step away from recent modern mathematical models, whereas in the case of Hayek the analysis is relatively lacking in clarity so that its relation to the modern literature is unclear and the matter requires tortuous exegesis. Mosak's relatively greater success in establishing propositions which are correct in a strict theoretical sense will be seen in the following pages as resulting from his use of a firmer theoretical basis than Hayek to describe the dynamic equilibrium of a closed economy.

The exact provenance of the work is obscure. Obviously, it could not have been written before *Value and Capital*. We read in the Preface that it was submitted as a Chicago Ph.D. thesis in 1942 with Oscar Lange as the supervisor. The relationship to Lange's *Price Flexibility and Full Employment* (1944), another application and extension of Hicksian temporary equilibrium concepts, is transparent. Lange's contribution will be discussed separately.[13] Hicks (1933 [1980]) contained the germ of the notion of temporary equilibrium and suggested that this concept would solve the problem of reconciling the existence of a monetary equilibrium with optimization over time, a problem which Hayek was unable to solve satisfactorily. Nurkse (1935: 229–30) suggested that Hicks's approach in that article of 1933 might prove to be the correct method for treating fluctuations in the trade balance. He noted in particular that from Hicks's standpoint, which took explicit account of different time periods, the distinction between money and capital flows was irrelevant. Mosak, however, makes no reference to this hint of Nurske's. He in fact refers to no other international economics literature other than the Keynesian work of Metzler and Machlup. His investigation is therefore *sui generis*, with the possible exception of Lange's brief discussion of open economy issues.

The avowed purpose of Mosak's work was to replace the classical $2 \times 2 \times 2$ approach, with representative consumers, which was 'insufficient to lay bare the complexities of an economic system in which there are millions of different individuals, products and factors in hundreds of countries' (1944: 179). Thus he proposed applying the apparatus of the 'Lausanne theory' (i.e. Walrasian theory) to trade theory, something which had only recently become possible (presumably due to Hicks's work). This would include: '(1) an analysis of the characteristics of the equilibrium position under given conditions and (2) an analysis of how the equilibrium values differ for different values of the determining parameters' (1944: 180). Ultimately these operations would be applied to a 'dynamic temporary equilibrium'. Against this background, it is understandable that Mosak's heuristic for international monetary theory is quite different from that of modern theory. First, he analyses the temporary equilibrium of a closed economy, consisting of very many individual firms, in considerable detail. He then introduces international economic issues by introducing those characteristics he regards as specific to them, namely exchange rates and individual country monies (1944: 165). Having already analysed the interactions of exchange between individuals and firms for a closed economy in considerable detail, Mosak considers that: 'The market equilibrium in an international economy may be analyzed in essentially the same manner as the equilibrium in a closed economy' (Mosak 1944: 165).

The results for the open economy depend heavily on those already derived for the multi-individual closed economy. These peculiarities of method are undoubtedly confusing for anyone schooled in two-country representative consumer analysis and may account for the difficulties contemporaries had in understanding Mosak's work (of which more below). Another aspect, unique to Mosak's heuristic, is the extensive use of Hicks's style of stability analysis to derive qualitative macroeconomic propositions.[14] This is another case where I shall show that Mosak's borrowing of the methods of *Value and Capital* gives his work a different emphasis from the models which show the work of the 1980s.

Before presenting a detailed rational reconstruction of Mosak's model of the international economy, it is important to dwell briefly on the sheer immensity of scope to be found in Mosak's work. The first point is that Mosak attempts to give a complete analysis of the dynamic equilibrium of a closed economy. As Neisser (1945) remarked at the time, 'Mosak's book will prove of enormous value to economic theorists, who have hitherto had to gather the mathematical framework of Hicks's theory from the scattered notes in the mathematical appendix to Value and Capital.' This 'includes presentation of the modern microeconomic approach both to static equilibrium and intertemporal equilibrium' (Neisser 1945: 507).

Mosak presents a completely correct mathematical analysis of the intertemporal (not temporary) equilibrium of the consumer and firm under perfect foresight. This was the first time that the appropriate conditions for intertemporal utility maximization and their relationship to the concept of discounted future prices were stated fully and correctly.[15] Turning to the role of money, Mosak gives a detailed theoretical analysis of the reasons why money might be held in intertemporal general equilibrium. Here Mosak sets out most of the reasons which would be given today for money being held in conjunction with interest-bearing assets. He discusses transaction costs (134) and cash in advance (133, 147),[16] and even attempts a mathematical derivation of the demand for money under conditions of uncertainty due to default risk (131–3, 146–7). Mosak assumes that he has supplied enough reasons to justify the existence of well-defined demand functions for money and bonds, without deriving those functions directly from his first-order conditions. This clearly cannot bear the scrutiny of modern theory.[17] There is even more to Mosak's analysis, for example he clearly understands that intertemporal consumption programmes can be divided into two parts, first optimizing consumption of different commodities within a period, then maximizing aggregate consumption over time, a result much used in the literature (e.g. Razin and Svensson 1983) to simplify intertemporal problems.

More significantly, to take a completely different example, he alights on the case of unit elastic price expectation functions as being especially problematic for temporary equilibrium. He believed that in this case, unemployment of at least one factor would be likely to occur. This is formally incorrect, but the case of unit elastic (i.e. static) expectations is precisely that in which non-existence of a monetary economy has been found (e.g. Grandmont 1983: 23). The underlying basis of Mosak's argument – the lack of an equilibrating intertemporal substitution effect in consumption in response to a current price change – is the same as that of modern theory. In addition, Mosak's statement that in this case 'the level of money prices is completely indeterminate' (153) is intuitively equivalent to nonexistence. Mosak uses Hicks's stability conditions on determinants to provide a mathematical proof of this assertion. Here one sees the centrality of Hicks's stability conditions to Mosak's method.[18]

The above examples bring out the richness and complexity of Mosak's work, a feature which is inevitably lost in a rational reconstruction like that which I shall perform. It is quite evident, however, that Mosak's reach exceeded his grasp; he was simply unaware of the highly complex nature of the issues involved in the existence of a temporary equilibrium and the existence of a demand for money in an economy with interest-bearing assets. This was through no fault of his own: these subtle problems had hardly been posed at the time he was writing. In fact, if anyone was posing them at all, in embryonic form, it was Mosak himself. Mosak is no more to blame here than Hicks himself (see Weintraub 1979: 57–9 on Hicks). In fact, as has been shown, he was often more rigorous than the master.

If the canvas of Mosak's vision of the closed economy was vast, consider his treatment of the open economy. Here he treats both fixed and flexible exchange rates in a world economy where there are two traded goods and a nontraded good. The analysis is conducted for the cases of flexible prices and what Mosak calls the Keynesian case of 'rigid wage rates'. Within this compass Mosak attacks most of the problems of international economics, such as tariffs, the transfer problem, the effect of devaluation on the trade balance, the effects of technology and preference shocks and the ultimate determinants of exchange rates. This, all in the course of only 16 pages! Clearly, it was impossible for Mosak to solve most of the issues which preoccupied intertemporal international macroeconomics in the 1980s. That he should have tried is a measure of his confidence in the new temporary equilibrium theory.

The above description has given a general impression of the scope and richness of Mosak's vision and the complexity of his general equilibrium model. I shall now attempt to reconstruct the structure of Mosak's theory, using the structuralist methods employed in the last chapter, particularly in connection with the monetary cash in advance model. This makes it possible to assess the consistency of Mosak's model of the international economy and to demonstrate some of the particular propositions he put forward.

I start with the relevant presuppositions. These diverge from those of intertemporal equilibrium in that there are incomplete futures markets. There are assumed to be at the most two assets, money and 'securities' which can be traded over future dates; this is not the case with ordinary commodities. Mosak acknowledges that in the absence of uncertainty, money would not be held along with securities. He was also prepared sometimes to assume, for convenience, that there is only one asset – money, and no bonds in the economy (e.g. 175–7). As has already been mentioned, Mosak sets out standard conditions, which, by the standards of his time, represent an extremely careful formal representation of intertemporal equilibrium (115–21, 137–41). These are later modified so that they represent a Hicksian temporary equilibrium, in which, instead of having perfect foresight, individuals hold subjectively certain expectations concerning future prices, which are derived from forecasts based on current prices (124–5). The treatment of firms, however, causes severe difficulties for even the most sophisticated specifications of temporary equilibrium (Weintraub 1979: 105), and Mosak naturally fails to solve these problems.

Mosak, however, is prepared to go further and alter the standard conditions in the middle of his analysis. He does this by sometimes assuming fixed prices in order to get Keynesian results. In this context he notes, in a fashion identical to the fixprice literature of the 1980s (e.g. Benassy 1986: 36–9) that rationing schemes may be necessary: 'If wages are fixed below the equilibrium level the demand for labor will have to be rationed in some form' (161).

As in my discussion and application of the structuralist approach in the previous chapter, the analysis of a particular theory is made by describing the conditions underlying it in a sequence of steadily decreasing generality. We therefore come next to Mosak's explanatory ideal conditions. These conditions are much more specific than the standard conditions and presuppositions which I have previously discussed. Recall that these conditions constitute the additional assumptions needed to apply the general framework (in this case temporary general equilibrium theory) to a specific area of economics (in this case international monetary theory). In addition, within fully developed mathematical theories of post-Second World War vintage, for example Samuelson's version of Heckscher–Ohlin theory, these conditions do not vary across the various models which are eventually constructed. Mosak, as I shall show, does not adhere fully to this systematic method of theory construction. He often alters these conditions in the middle of his discussion, thereby substantially modifying the content of the theory in the middle of what purports to be a self-contained, theoretically closed piece of analysis.

## Government

The first aspect of Mosak's explanatory ideal conditions to be considered is the role of government. Here his analysis suffers from a serious lack of specification, since he neglects the role of government as a creator of fiat money. It is apparent that in Mosak's system there is no obvious place for outside money. Money is described as a form of interest and default-free credit between individuals (130). As is well known, and indeed obvious, the lack of an outside money prevents means that no real balance or 'Pigou' effect operates in the system. (Hicks 1946: 334 states this proposition in the way that it was understood by Mosak's contemporaries.)[19] Unfortunately, in specifying international monetary arrangements, Mosak does not take account of the complications which might arise in an 'inside money only' international economy.[20] To make his model consistent, we must assume that Mosak was implicitly assuming that each country in Mosak's international economy has a national outside money currency, since this would imply the existence of a real balance effect, a component of monetary theory which is lacking in Mosak's work. To sum up then, Mosak did not specify the fact that in each country a government exists whose role is to create outside money. This has the implication that nothing exists to tie down the absolute price level both in a closed economy and in a world divided into a number of countries, each with its own monetary system.

## Consumers

To work out issues like the real balance effect in more detail requires a much more detailed description of consumer behaviour. Enough has already been said to indicate that consumers solve a well-defined maximization problem over time (116–21). More significantly, no sooner has Mosak, like Hicks in *Value and Capital* (see Hicks 1946: 140), discovered the perfect foresight equilibrium than he abandons it in favour of 'a technique which will enable us to allow for the effects of current price changes upon future price expectations' (123). In this analysis, time is divided into a sequence of trading periods. In each trading period, individuals have an endowment of goods and a stock of money held over from the last period. In each period, each consumer must choose a one-period consumption plan and an amount of money to carry forward. Consequently, the next period's prices must be forecast in the current period in order to formulate an optimal plan. These expectations are based on 'the course of past and present prices' (124). Since the current price, $P_t$, was established by previous forecasts, expectations can be collapsed to a function of current prices $\psi/J(p_t)$, which Mosak calls an 'expectation function' (124).

As I have already mentioned several times, Mosak was no more successful than Hicks in reconciling the coexistence of money and interest-bearing assets. This is as much a problem for temporary general equilibrium theory as it is for intertemporal general equilibrium under perfect foresight or rational expectations. A temporary general equilibrium also requires a device like cash in advance to generate a demand for money and bonds (see Hool 1979). Yet even when this is done, the assumptions required are much more unrealistic and implausible than those of the usual cash in advance model.[21] As already stated, Mosak's treatment of these problems is not enough, from a rigorously formal point of view, to generate well-defined demand functions for money and bonds which represent the behaviour of consumers.

I would like to attempt to briefly formalize Mosak's approach in more detail. Consider the following two-period maximization problem for a representative consumer:

$$\text{Max } U(c_1, c_2) \tag{1}$$

$$\text{s.t. } p_1(c_1 - E_1) + m - \bar{m} \le 0 \tag{2}$$

$$\psi(p_1)(c_2 - E_2) - m \le 0 \tag{3}$$

$$c_1, c_2, m \ge 0$$

Here $c_1$ and $c_2$ are period one and two consumption. $\bar{m}$ is the consumer's initial endowment of money, $m$ is money held at the end of period 1, and $\psi(p_1)$ is the price expectation function by which the consumer forecasts second-period prices. $E_1$ and $E_2$ are endowments of the consumer good in the two periods. Particular restrictions on the expectation function are sufficient to ensure the existence of a solution to the above problem (Grandmont 1983: 16–27). In this simple case, the condition is that with more than one consumer in the economy, their expectations functions are continuous and the expectations of at least one agent are bounded in the sense that $a \le \psi(p_1) \le b$, where $a$ and $b$ are positive real numbers (Grandmont 1983: 26). Analogous conditions exist for more complicated multiperiod, multi-consumer cases. These are that for at least one consumer $\psi(p_1)/p_1$ approaches zero (infinity) as $p$ approaches infinity (zero). In other words, when $p$ is very large (small) future consumption is very cheap (expensive) relative to present consumption. An excess supply of money raises the price level, which leads agents to delay consumption, thus increasing the demand for money. An excess demand for money similarly leads to a fall in prices, reducing the demand for money as agents bring forward their consumption (Grandmont 1983: 21–3; for a formal proof, see Grandmont 1983: 166–7).

It is easy to show that the above problem is equivalent to the following problem, where the consumer maximizes an indirect utility function which depends on current consumption, endowments, money holdings and current prices. This is demonstrated in footnote 22. Grandmont (1983: 27–8) gives a proof for the multiperiod case.[22] The equivalent problem to (1)–(3) is:

$$\text{Max } V\left(c_1, E_2 + \frac{m}{\psi(p_1)}\right) \tag{4}$$

$$\text{s.t. } p_1(c_1 - E_1) + m - \bar{m} \le 0 \tag{5}$$

Clearly, this problem can be solved to yield well-defined demand functions for the consumer good and money, (6) and (7) respectively.

$$c_1 = c_1(p_1, \psi(p_1), \bar{m}, e_1, e_2) \tag{6}$$

$$m^d = m(p_1, \psi(p_1), e_1, e_2\bar{m}) \tag{7}$$

Given the dependence of prices on the expectation function, (6) is normally not homogeneous of degree zero in prices, nor is (7) homogeneous of degree one in prices (Grandmont 1983: 38–9). This will 'only be the case' if expectations are static, or in a situation in which the expectations are homogeneous of degree one in prices. This special case, however, of zero homogeneity in the goods demand function and homogeneity of degree one in the money demand function is that which was assumed in much neoclassical monetary theory (Weintraub 1979: 48). It is precisely in this case of neutral money, however, that the expectations function will not be bounded and no monetary equilibrium will exist.

There is a great degree of congruence between the solution to this problem and Mosak's treatment of consumer behaviour. He believes that the economy can be represented by a system of excess demand equations for money, bonds and commodities which will be in equilibrium when these excess demand equations are equal to zero. Just like Grandmont, Mosak stresses that in general demand functions such as (6) will not be homogeneous of degree zero. He does not treat existence by name, but recognizes that in the case of zero homogeneity the system will be 'indeterminate' (153), a situation he associates with unemployment. Instead of boundedness of expectations as a condition for the existence of an equilibrium, we have inelasticity of expectations emphasized as a condition for the stability of equilibrium. The two ideas are similar, however, in that they both require the response of expectations of future prices to current prices to be 'not too large' in some sense. Mosak's concept of stability depends on the 'intertemporal substitution effect', also emphasized greatly by Lange (1944: 20–8). Suppose the current price rises from $P_1$ to $\lambda P_1$, and that the elasticity of price expectations is less than one, so that expected prices $\psi(\lambda p_1)$ are less than $\lambda\psi(p_1)$. In this case, the intertemporal substitution effect is likely to favour a decrease of current consumption and thus reinforce the reduction in today's consumption induced by the price rise. The intertemporal substitution effect therefore reinforces, in the one-good case, the standard stability condition that the demand curve is downward sloping.[23] The converse is true if expectations are elastic. This condition, derived by Mosak initially in the context of a closed economy (closed in the sense peculiar to him, that is if there are no country-specific monies or exchange rates, see p. 61 above), is later used extensively by him to treat open economy issues such as tariffs, transfers and devaluation (170, 172,

175). Mosak also gives a rate to intertemporal income effects, which result from changes in the discounted value of future incomes and their influence on optimal future consumption: 'The behavior of a dynamic economy depends in large part upon the elasticity of the capital values of the expenditure plans with respect to a proportionate change in all current and discounted expected prices' (157).[24] These interest rate effects, however, play a much smaller rate in Mosak's treatment of the open economy than intertemporal substitution effects.

*Firms*

In general, it is the rate of intertemporal price effects which give Mosak's analysis its unique flavour in the context of the open economy economics of his time. Mosak's attempt to derive demands for securities is, as I have discussed, much less convincing. It is well known that the incorporation of firms into rigorous models of temporary equilibrium creates serious difficulties for the theory (Weintraub 1979: 105). To Mosak's credit, he shows some awareness of the difficulties involved in modelling firms' expectations with regard to future prices (145–6), but none of this is carried over into his treatment of the open economy. More important is Mosak's introduction of a 'Keynesian' labour market in which 'wages are fixed above the equilibrium level' (161). The context is in fact one of 'rigid wage rates', not rigid real wages. In modern jargon, this case is called 'classical unemployment'. (Benassy (1986), and Cuddington *et al.* (1984: Ch. 2) summarize the extensive relevant literature.) Keynesian unemployment, in this literature, results from deficient demand in the product market, not wage rigidity in the labour market. In order to treat the behaviour of the labour market in as simple a form as possible, while maintaining consistency with Mosak's framework, it must be assumed that the firm has a production function with decreasing returns to scale and production is only carried out by labour. The firm maximizes short-run profits without investing or building up inventories. If the firm were to build up inventories, it would be necessary to take its expectations into account (Benassy 1982: 137–44). Under classical unemployment the firm's demand function for labour, which is derived from profit maximization, will be less than what workers want to supply at the given wage rate:

$$L^d\left(\frac{w}{p}\right) < L^s\left(\frac{w}{p}\right).$$

Inserting labour demand in the production function $y = y(L^d)$ yields a constrained level of output

$$\bar{y} = y\left(\frac{w}{p}\right) \tag{8}$$

which would rise if the price level rises or the parametric wage rate falls.

Mosak sometimes explicitly assumes classical unemployment, and sometimes assumes that labour markets clear.

The international environment that Mosak assumes is a version of the law of one price, modified to take account of the existence of price expectations:

> For each country the prices are expressed in terms of its own currency, but each such price may be expressed in terms of the currency of some one country and the exchange rates between the currencies of the two countries, both current and expected. (The expected exchange rate may, of course, differ from individual to individual, just as the expected prices do.) This is the basic relationship which we have already considered in our static analysis of international trade. Thus we have:
>
> $$P_{rt}^{(1)} = e_{1i,t} P_{rt}^{(i)}$$
>
> where, as previously, the superscript indicates the country, and where $e_{1i,t}$ is the expected (or current) number of units of currency which one must give for one unit of currency 1 in period $t$.
>
> (Mosak 1944: 165)

Mosak does not assume interest rate parity, even though international trade in securities is sometimes treated in his analysis.

Let us now consider Mosak's assumptions about the assumed number of commodities and time periods. His closed economy analysis is one of multiple commodities and time periods. With multiple commodities, comparative static results are indeterminate (Razin and Svensson 1983). Mosak in fact usually assumes, for an open economy, that there are three commodities, 'importables', 'exportables' and 'domestic' (i.e. nontraded) commodities. As Cuddington and Vinals (1986: 109), who assume in their work that there are three commodities, remark, even in this case the influence of cross-price effects is such that 'these complications render virtually all comparative static effects indeterminate, as is well known from the earlier literature on the elasticities approach to devaluation as well as the new intertemporal optimization models'. The lack of additional assumptions on functional forms, termed special conditions in the previous chapter, is a major problem for Mosak's analysis. Thus Mosak often fails to come up with any clear-cut result when examining shocks to the system, for example, 'country Y's expenditures on all goods may also rise or decline or remain unchanged' (in response to a devaluation, p. 175) and that 'it appears normally an expansion in one country will tend to overflow into the rest of the world. It is possible, however, that it should have no effect or that it should even lead to a contraction in the rest of the world' (in the context of demand shocks under flexible exchange rates, p. 177). Similar ambiguities appear on almost every page of Mosak's open economy analysis. Specific assumptions on a limitation of the field to one good would have allowed clearer results to emerge at the expense of less generality.

Turning to the number of time periods, one notes that Mosak assumes a finite horizon. Here he neglects the so-called 'hot potato problem' – who will hold worthless money at the end of the last period (see the previous chapter). It must be assumed that the government is prepared to hold all money at the end of the last period.

Let us now put all the pieces assembled by Mosak together, and set out a model of the economy which constitutes the simplest version of his theory and is applied in part of the text (in particular pp. 175–7). I will then demonstrate three modifications of this basic model implied by the above discussion.

In the simplest version of Mosak's theory, money is the only asset in the system and all markets clear, including that for labour. Well-defined money demand functions are generated from the existence of money in the utility function, an assumption consistent with temporary equilibrium, as in equations (4) and (5). There are two countries and demand functions for goods and money are given by (6) and (7):

> If the exchange rates are fixed, it follows immediately that, given the expectation functions of future prices and interest rates, the current demand and supply functions for every country may be written as functions of the current prices expressed in terms of the currency of country 1. We may therefore sum up the total demand and supply for each commodity and for each security and for money as functions of the same variables.
>
> (Mosak 1944: 165)

I shall assume, for simplicity, that there are only two periods. Thus Mosak specifies the following conditions:

$$c^i(p_1, p_2, \bar{m}) + c^i(p_1^*, p_2^*, \bar{m}^*) = 0 \qquad (9)$$

$$p_2^i = \psi(p_1^i) \qquad (10)$$

$$p_2^{i*} = \psi(p_1^{i*}) \qquad (11)$$

$$p_t^i = e p_t^{i*} \qquad (12)$$

In (9) $c^i$ and $c^{i*}$ are the home and foreign excess demand functions for commodity $i$, derived from (6) and (7), which depend on period (1) and period 2 prices. Period 2 prices are given by the expectation functions (10) and (11), whose nature and implications are discussed at length by Mosak (124–7, 150–7). (12) is the purchasing power parity relationship for each commodity in each period, previously discussed in the context of Mosak's specification of the international environment. To these must be added the balance of payments relation in each country which is equivalent to the excess demand for money:

$$m^d(p_1, p_2, \bar{m}) - m^s = b \tag{13}$$

$$m^{d*}(p_1^*, p_2^*, \bar{m}^*) - m^{s*} = b^* \tag{14}$$

Mosak's description of these conditions (13) and (14) is particularly important and is the heart of the intertemporal approach to the balance of payments:

> In a static economy the conditions of equilibrium required that for each country the value of exports of goods and services excluding 'money' shall be equal to the value of imports. No money was supposed to move in equilibrium. These conditions were valid in our static economy because we had no true money in our system for which a demand function existed.
>
> In our dynamic economy, however, we have introduced a true money for which demand and supply functions exist just as for any other security. Here, money is no longer a counter which bears a fixed relationship to the value of one's 'income', but a store of value very much like a security for which the demand and supply vary according as prices and interest rates vary. It is obvious, therefore, that the equilibrium for any given period do not require that no transfers of money shall take place. The volume of exports or imports of money for each country may very well differ from zero in the equilibrium for any given period.
>
> (Mosak 1944: 166)

Mosak therefore constructed a model of international economic equilibrium based on individual optimization and showed how such an equilibrium implied that the current account was not usually in balance. He also showed how such an equilibrium resulted from the intertemporal choice problems of individuals. Mosak thus showed how the Hicksian theory of temporary equilibrium, within a choice-theoretic framework, dictated that the appropriate equilibrium conditions implied current account imbalance. This was his major achievement and it involved the application of a theoretical apparatus infinitely more sophisticated than the Keynesian multiplier models of that time. More generally, Mosak in the above passage clearly draws the dividing line between static and intertemporal international monetary economics.

There exist three other versions of the model defined by (9)–(14). The first of these has a flexible as opposed to a fixed exchange rate regime.

Here Mosak correctly states (pp. 167, 174) that the appropriate equilibrium condition, instead of (14)–(15), is that the money market must clear and that, in the absence of trade in 'securities', the current account must be balanced in equilibrium (p. 174). The second variant is the case of classical unemployment, 'rigid wages' in Mosak's terminology. We must add a condition such as (8) to the system and a further condition such as $w = \bar{w}$ determine the wage rate. The case where wages are set below the market clearing level and the excess labor demands are rationed (called today 'repressed inflation') was known to Mosak (p. 161), but not applied by him to the open economy. For consistency the excess demand function formulation of (9) should also be written as:

$$c_t^i(p_1, p_2, y + \bar{m}) + c_t^{i*}(p_1, p_2, y* + m*) - y\left(\frac{w}{p}\right) - y\left(\frac{w*}{p*}\right) = 0 \tag{9'}$$

Here the first two expressions are total demand functions, not excess demand functions. (9') takes account of the complications that parametric changes in wage rates may have on incomes and outputs. Mosak, however, did not explicitly set out these necessary modifications. Notice that the classical unemployment regime is implicitly assumed to prevail in all future periods as well.

The third variant of the basic model is the case where bonds are held as well as money, a situation of course not fully explained by Mosak's analytical apparatus. At least some of Mosak's open economy analysis, however, treats comparative static problems with no reference to money, but only to the implications for the balance of payments of movements of securities (pp. 168–9). Implicitly then, Mosak also has a temporary equilibrium model where there is an interest-bearing asset for which a futures market exists, but no money.[25] Mosak's text contains various comparative static exercises which alternate between these various cases.

Mosak's system (9)–(14) closely resembles that of Anderson and Takayama (1977) and Dixit and Norman (1980: Ch. 7 and Ch. 8). There is a major difference, however, in that they assume that the expectations functions are homogeneous of degree one in current prices. As noted by Mosak, this assumption is analytically equivalent to static expectations and rules out all intertemporal substitution effects (p. 153). Dixit and Norman (1980: Ch. 7, Sec. 1 and 2) replicate the results of the monetary approach to the balance of payments in a choice-theoretic framework. Mosak's use of intertemporal substitution effects has quite different implications. An example of this is Mosak's insistence that exchange rate changes have real effects (p. 175). Assume that we have only one good and substitute (11) and (12) in (14):

$$b* = m^{a*}(ep_1^*, \psi(ep_1^*), \bar{m}*) - m^{s*} \tag{15}$$

In Dixit and Norman's case (1980: 207), where demand is homogeneous of degree zero in prices and incomes and expectations are linearly homogeneous in prices, we can divide through by $e$ to find that the effect of a devaluation will be equivalent to a reduction in the country's money supply.

$$b^* = m^a(p_1^*, \psi(p_1^*), \bar{m}^*/e) - m^{s^*}/e \qquad (15')$$

Equivalent operations could obviously be carried out for the home country. This is obviously not the case in Mosak's system, where linear homogeneity is treated, as we have seen, as a pathological case somewhat akin to that of the nonexistence of a monetary economy. In Mosak's case, these homogeneity properties do not hold and devaluation must induce intertemporal substitution effects through the effect of expectations on the demand for money. In the well-behaved stable case of inelastic expectations, this intertemporal substitution effect will reinforce the real balance effect, shifting planned holdings of money balances from the future to the present, shifting planned consumption from the present to the future, and reducing the current demand for the consumption good. Therefore, in Mosak's system devaluation improves the current account, provided that expectations are inelastic.

As I have noted in the context of Mosak's failure to restrict the field of commodities in his model (see p. 76), clear-cut results often do not emerge from his analysis. This is not at variance with his vision, given his declared purpose which was to 'lay bare' the complexity of the general equilibrium system (pp. 179–80). Nevertheless, he does come up with some rather characteristic propositions, which can be verified in the context of his model. The first interesting proposition follows from the previous discussion on the role of intertemporal substitution effects in a devaluation, and states that: 'After a fall in the exchange rate on the assumption that the elasticity of exchange rate expectations is not greater than unity, country X's demand for foreign exchange will decline, namely its demand for imports will go down' (p. 175). (By (11) and (12), exchange rate expectations can equally well be expressed as price expectations.) Characteristically, Mosak then qualifies this result out of existence by examining the complications caused by the existence of cross-price elasticities in a multi-good world. (He explicitly refers to 'importables', 'exportables' and 'domestic commodities', i. e. nontraded goods (p. 175).)

Many of Mosak's other results must be seen in the context of his research programme, which was 'designed to close the gap between the theory of international value and the theory of value in the closed economy' (p. 180). As pointed out previously, Mosak regarded 'dynamic temporary equilibrium' theory as being an extension of static micro-theory. Mosak therefore tests whether he has supplied a microeconomic foundation for various well-known propositions in international macro-economics. He tests both the characteristic results of the classical and Keynesian approaches.

Such a result of Mosak's is that in the rigid nominal wage case, where there is unemployment, import tariffs can be expansionary (p. 172). Under the hypothesis of 'classical unemployment' embodied in equation (9') it can easily be shown that this claim is correct (Cuddington *et al.* 1984: 154–6). They present a formal analysis in the case where a country is 'small in the world market for an import good', and 'large' in the market for its export good. The reason for this result is easy to grasp intuitively: the import tariff will lower the real product wage paid by import-competing firms and they will hire more labour and produce more output. Mosak appears to accept the standard Keynesian view of tariffs, but gives this story a characteristic twist by bringing in expectations. Thus, he claims that if the exports of foreign countries 'constitute an important fraction of their income, the secondary repercussions may aggravate the contraction to such an extent as to lead to a general world depression which spreads to the first country as well. This is particularly likely under elastic price expectations' (pp. 172–3). In effect, this is a claim that the instability of a temporary equilibrium under elastic price expectations, as previously demonstrated by Mosak (p. 154), will cause a world business depression if one country initiates a 'beggar my neighbour' policy.

Mosak also emphasized the implications which his treatment of international macroeconomics on the basis of 'value theory' had for the analysis of the transfer problem:

> In our static analysis the payment of reparations implied a decrease in the paying country's demand function for commodities by the full amount of the reparations and a corresponding increase for the receiving country. The reason for this correspondence lay in the fact that our system really contained only commodities; there were no securities or real money in the system. It is conceivable therefore that the payment of reparations should leave the demand functions for commodities in one or both countries unaltered. Thus in the paying country the government may finance its payment of reparations through the flotation of a loan. The reparations payments would therefore be offset by an increased demand function for securities rather than by a decreased demand function for commodities.
>
> (Mosak 1944: 170)

Under perfect foresight, this argument is not correct; reparations, being a permanent shock, require adjustment in the first period. It is possible, however, that under Mosak's assumptions about expectations where foresight is imperfect, that some adjustment might be postponed in the first period. Mosak's statement is therefore consistent with his usual assumptions about the nature of foresight. Mosak' s next claim is that: 'If the reparations payments are made through the flotation of a loan and the

receipts are used to repay the debt, then the primary effects of the reparations will be in movements of interest rates in the two countries' (p. 170).

Frenkel and Razin (1987: 162–5) analyse this problem in the simplest
one-good, two-period case. They demonstrate that if the country making
the transfer has a higher (lower) rate of time preference than the receiving
country, the world rate of interest will fall (rise). The intuition behind this
result is that if a transfer is made to the country who has a low rate of time
preference and is thus the larger saver, the world rate of interest must fall
in order to eliminate excess savings in the world economy. Mosak's intuition is therefore correct. It is the case, however, that under perfect foresight the Ricardian equivalence theorem holds, and it is irrelevant whether
the payment is financed by debt or taxes; both measures will put upward
pressure on interest rates under the above conditions on rates of time preference. Mosak then discusses various combinations of debt and taxes
which could be used to make a reparations payment, and various
responses by the foreign government such as using the receipts to reduce
taxes or to reduce the internal debt. In all of these cases, Mosak stresses
the real effects of such policies. Real effects of government tax and expenditure policies, other than terms of trade changes, will not occur under
perfect foresight because the Ricardian equivalence theorem holds. To
determine whether they are consistent with Mosak's version of temporary
equilibrium with price expectation functions would require a much more
detailed treatment than he gives. Mosak deserves credit, however, for
raising these issues in the proper theoretical context of intertemporal equilibrium and Hicksian temporary equilibrium. It was Dornbusch (1977)
who initially pointed out to modern economists that the intertemporal
approach was the natural way to model fiscal policy in the open economy.
Mosak anticipated him by 35 years, even if he failed to make a rigorous
analysis of the problem.

It would be impossible to deal in detail with all of the comparative static
exercises carried out by Mosak, since he performs 17 of these under the
assumption of flexible wages and prices, and seven under the assumption
of rigid nominal wages. The results are often straightforward consequences of temporary equilibrium. For example, Mosak claims that a
decision to borrow more abroad will worsen the current account (p. 169)
and raise the domestic price level. This confirms the traditional account
given in the classical literature, for example in Taussig's *International
Trade* (1927: Ch. XI). The difference is that in Mosak's account, this result
depends on the existence of inelastic expectations which are necessary for
the stability of the economy. In addition, the context of Mosak's result is
completely different from that in which the classical results were derived.
Mosak's temporary equilibrium does not require the classical result that a
new equilibrium will be attained with improved terms of trade and current
account balance. Mosak's comparative statics therefore allows outcomes
where the current account is not in balance.

### Lange

Lange's contribution consists of the six pages of his *Price Flexibility and Full Employment* (1944) which deal with the open economy. His work is so closely related to that of Mosak that it can be treated as an addition to Mosak's analysis, one which Mosak could easily have added himself. The theoretical framework is fundamentally the same, although much less rich than that of Mosak. There is a temporary equilibrium in which the intertemporal substitution effects induced by expectations play a key role (Lange 1944: 20–6). Money is the only asset treated in the discussion of the open economy, and for half of the analysis two countries are assumed, so Lange's system can also be summarized by equations (9)–(13).

Lange, however, is concerned with one issue only in this book – can price flexibility restore full employment? This is thus also the only matter treated in his discussion of international money flows. *Price Flexibility and Full Employment* is concerned with discovering under what conditions, in a general equilibrium model, further price flexibility might induce multi-market repercussions which would not ameliorate involuntary unemployment. In this context, Lange introduced the notion of a 'positive monetary effect', which reduces unemployment as individuals substitute goods for money as the price level falls and their real balance holdings rise. As in Mosak, it is intertemporal substitution which causes the complications and may prevent unemployment from being reduced in the unstable case where the elasticities of price expectations are greater than unity (Lange 1944: 22–3; Weintraub 1979: 60). In such a case, when prices fall today, people wish to shift consumption to the future, when prices will be even lower. In such a situation, the real quantity of money must increase even more than the current demand for cash balances if unemployment is to be reduced. In Lange's terminology, 'elastic price expectations require a responsive monetary system whereas inelastic expectations require an unresponsive monetary system' (1944: 23). Against this background, Lange asks the question as to how the stability of the economy will be modified if the economy is opened to international trade.

In the case of a small ('atomistic') country trade enhances stability. The reason for this is simply that, if factor prices are flexible, unemployment cannot occur in the traded goods sector of a small country. A fall in the price of an underemployed factor will always generate a rise in its employment, a fall in the price of the final good and an increase in foreign demand for exports. These effects are stronger 'the greater the proportion of the underemployed factor engaged in the production of export goods' (1944: 48). Thus, in an open economy, 'since an intratemporal substitution effect and expansion effect are much more likely to exist and are also stronger than in the absence of international trade, the adverse intertemporal substitution resulting from elastic price expectations is also less likely to prevail over them' (Lange 1944: 47).

In a large country trade is also stabilizing, provided that the reduction in the price of an unemployed factor leads to a trade surplus. (This surplus may not occur because income may also increase when unemployment falls, thus increasing the demand for imports.) In this case, the inflow of money under trade plays a stabilizing role:

> If in the new equilibrium exports are greater and imports are smaller than they were before the reduction of the price of the underemployed factor, the real quantity of money in the country is greater than would have been the case were the country not involved in international trade. According to the General Rule this always reinforces a positive monetary effect, weakens a negative monetary effect, or turns an absent monetary effect into a positive one. For, if the effective elasticities of (discounted) price expectations are prevailingly less than unity, a proportional fall of all factor and product prices leads to a diminution of the real demand for cash balances, while the real quantity of money in the country increases. If, instead, the effective price elasticities of (discounted) price expectations are prevailingly greater than unity, the real demand for cash balances increases, but the real quantity of money is greater than it would have been in the absence of international trade. Finally, if elasticities of expectation are unity, the real demand for cash balances is constant, but the real quantity of money increases. Thus, the influence of international trade upon the economy of a country with flexible factor prices acts here in a stabilizing direction.
>
> (Lange 1944: 50)

The converse of course is claimed by Lange to be true if the fall in the price of an 'underemployed factor' induces a trade deficit, because the income effect increases imports. Lange shows that, in the theoretical framework used by him and Mosak, the real balance effect is stronger in an open than in a closed economy, even in the case of elastic price expectations. An important aspect of Lange's treatment here, insufficiently emphasized by Mosak, is the way in which intertemporal substitution under inelastic expectations, in conjunction with international monetary flows, reinforces the real balance effect, which acts as an automatic stabilizer for the economy.

### The reception of Mosak's work

The formalization and rigorous proof of Mosak's many propositions would have constituted a complete alternative programme of research in international monetary problems. Mosak set out a correct framework in which to analyse shocks to the current account and exchange rates, in a context where there was a clear micro-theoretic justification for holding financial assets which are a claim against the future. He attempted to answer all the questions which could be asked of a theory of this type. The logical next stage would have been for other researchers to specify more exact special conditions under which exact comparative static results on the current account or the exchange rates could be obtained. Let me briefly set out a relevant analogy. Ohlin's *Interregional and International Trade* (1933) also set out an extremely broad general equilibrium model and attempted the same type of informal and inconclusive comparative static exercises as Mosak carried out in his temporary equilibrium model. Ohlin was also unable to offer formal proofs of his central propositions – factor price equalization and the Heckscher–Ohlin theorem. Even so, Ohlin's model, his central propositions and his claim that they were approximately true under very general propositions was sufficient to set the research agenda in real trade theory for over 40 years.[26] The formal weakness and lack of clarity in Mosak's theory, exemplified by his failure to clearly prove many interesting propositions, can also be found in Ohlin's work. Indeed, it is only to be expected that a theory, if it is to spawn a successful research tradition, must present new recruits with a large number of interesting problems to work on. I have shown that Mosak produced a coherent framework for analysing the open macroeconomy and showed that his framework had a considerable potential for supplying economists with useful Kuhnian puzzle-solving activity. Mosak's work also marked the evolution of the intertemporal approach into a coherent theory with a logical structure, as opposed to the string of striking insights produced by writers such as Fetter, Iversen or Lachmann. It is therefore important, from a historical point of view, to explain why Mosak's work was not accepted by the discipline of economics as a whole.

One explanation for the disappearance of the intertemporal theory is that the leaders of the economics profession rejected it. Samuelson (1945) reviewed Mosak's work. He treated Part One, on real trade theory, favourably. Part Two – 'Intertemporal General Equilibrium Theory and International Trade' – pointedly received no mention whatsoever, apart from Mosak's treatment of unemployment in a closed economy. This omission indicates that Samuelson found nothing of serious interest in the open economy section of Part Two. Hicks's review article (1945) referred to Part Two at length, but was only concerned with the implications of Mosak's discussion of stability for the temporary equilibrium of the closed economy. Mosak's findings on the open economy were dismissed in one line as uninteresting (Hicks 1945: 235). A favourable review was given by Hans Neisser in *Social Research* (1945), although Neisser, while he may have been a leader of the economics profession in Weimar Germany, was much less well placed in postwar America.[27] Anyway, Neisser misunderstood Mosak's analysis, describing it as being 'as far as I can judge, on macroeconomic lines rather than in the direction of extending the apparatus developed in the preceding chapters'. He then goes on to praise

Mosak for succinctly developing the theory of the foreign trade multiplier (Neisser 1945: 507). This is a curious judgement, given how careful Mosak is to distinguish between the fixprice and flexprice assumptions, and the relatively greater weight he gives to the latter case in his exposition. Later, Neisser joined with a leading figure of the younger generation to produce a pioneering piece of open economy econometrics (Neisser and Modigliani 1953). Here, more understanding is shown of the nature of Mosak's analysis. Neisser and Modigliani discussed Mosak's work respectfully, understanding that it was trying to give a microeconomic foundation 'in a manner analogous to that in which Pareto and Ohlin approached the problem of long-run equilibrium', to what they called the 'short-run equilibrium of an open economy' (Neisser and Modigliani 1953: 32). They regarded the generality of Mosak's system as being its main drawback. They stated that 'the effect exerted by changes in important economic variables (prices, consumption, output, imports, exports) can be represented only by extremely complicated formulas' (Neisser and Modigliani 1953: 32). Such formulas, they state, could:

> give no answer to the crucial question concerning the level of income, employment and real wages at which a short-run equilibrium in both the domestic economy and balance of payments will be altered. To discover this level it would be necessary to solve the equation system for these variables and to measure all relations statistically, a task which is in practice impossible.
>
> (Neisser and Modligiani 1953: 33)

Here then, Mosak's work is rejected because of its lack of congruence with what was then advanced macroeconometrics. It must be said that Mosak himself undermined the empirical applicability of his own approach by his explicit rejection of representative consumer theorizing (in his conclusion, p. 179). General equilibrium econometrics usually requires representative consumer assumptions. It is clear, therefore, from the record, that neither Samuelson, Hicks nor Modigliani favoured Mosak's theory. One is particularly surprised by Hicks's failure to grasp that Mosak had hit on the profound implications of the dynamic theorizing of *Value and Capital* for the interpretation of the balance of payments.

Another reason for the failure of Mosak's work to generate interest lies in his thoroughgoing adoption of the temporary equilibrium method. This in itself would have made the work incomprehensible to many of his contemporaries. As Weintraub (1979: 58) remarks, 'perusal of the post-Hicksian literature, particularly modern work on temporary equilibrium, suggests that Hicks was thirty years too early for the economics profession'.

The fate of Mosak could not have been much different from that of Hicks himself. There is, however, a basic difference in that Hicks's work on temporary equilibrium was not irretrievably lost in a Kuhnian sense, as was Mosak's work. I would advance, as a tentative explanation for this loss, the fact that the leaders of the economics profession did not share Mosak's interests. They were either not concerned with trade theory, like Hicks, or were not concerned with temporary general equilibrium theory, like Samuelson. The conceptual difficulties resulting from the excessive breadth of Mosak's general equilibrium method, while presenting difficulties for applied work, was not in itself sufficient to make his work incomprehensible to his audience, but coupled with the subtleties of temporary equilibrium, the barriers to understanding were considerable, even to central figures in the development of modern economics.

### New versus old theories of intertemporal international macroeconomics

The fact that the older theories understood the behaviour of the balance of payments to be a consequence of individuals' optimal decisions with respect to time is decisive in establishing that we are dealing with a case of theory recurrence. This is because both the literature of the 1980s and that which I have unearthed are in full agreement as to the correct starting point for explaining the behaviour of the current account. In spite of this similarity, there exist substantial differences between the two sets of analyses. These differences concern:

1   the equilibrium concepts employed;
2   the neutrality of money in an international environment; and
3   the prominence of the time preference motive.

1. First and probably most important, much of the earlier literature uses equilibrium with perfect foresight (or its stochastic counterpart, rational expectations equilibrium) only in an attenuated and qualified form. I have thus shown that Reynaud maintained that money illusion would mean that intertemporal equilibrium could not be secured in the face of external monetary shocks. In the work of Lange and Mosak, intertemporal equilibrium is abandoned completely in favour of Hicksian temporary equilibrium. If their work were to be translated into modern terms it would resemble, not so much the models of cash in advance or overlapping generations which were common in the 1980s, as the type of theory exemplified by Grandmont (1983), extended to an open economy. In such a theory, individuals can be systematically wrong in their estimates of future prices, despite the fact that they practise maximizing behaviour. The closest analogue to this approach to be found in the work is Persson and Svensson (1983), who treat the case of incorrect expectations about the future, although they assume that these errors concern quantities, not prices. In their version of temporary equilibrium (which was originated by

Neary and Stiglitz 1983), individuals are able to forecast correctly future market clearing prices, even if they do not know quantities. Nevertheless, the resemblance between this concept and that of Mosak is very strong: in both cases, expectations about the future which may well be incorrect have a strong influence on the behaviour of the current account today.[28] Despite this one case, where a parallel can be drawn, it is clear that the most sophisticated early piece of work – that of Mosak – differs from the vast majority of the models of the 1980s, which employ unambiguously perfect foresight or rational expectations.

2. I have turned up no theorems similar to the equivalence of fixed and floating exchange rates or the irrelevance of exchange rates. This finding is clearly related to the relatively low weight some of the earlier literature gave to assumptions of total perfect foresight. Recall how, for example, Mosak shows that the characteristics of price expectation functions cause all kinds of real effects under flexible exchange rates. Another case where the type of exchange rate regime selected was regarded as having real effects is in the work of Hayek and Reynaud. Here money is only neutral if the quantity of money in the whole world is held constant, fractional reserve banking abolished, and governments prevented from altering exchange rates. It has, however, been shown by Persson (1982 and 1984) that money is not neutral under such a scheme when individuals have perfect foresight. Of course, Hayek was concerned with more complex frameworks than that used by Persson, frameworks in which international monetary flows have real effects because of noisy price signals. One can, however, be sure that if the Hayekian policy has real effects in a simple model, it will also have real effects in a more elaborate version of the same model. It is, of course, possible that Hayek's scheme has desirable properties in the type of model where incomplete markets or imperfect information mean that money has real effects. The results are, however, so sensitive to the type of imperfection assumed that modern theory can give no clear-cut guidance as to the desirability of a particular exchange rate regime (Stockman 1988: 353). The modern intertemporal approach therefore asserts that under the special assumptions set out in Chapter 3, money is neutral under fixed and perfectly flexible exchange rates, but it is not neutral if the quantity of money in the world is held constant. If these special assumptions are dropped, then 'anything goes'. Hayek and Reynaud's condition for 'neutral money' has not been upheld by modern theory of the 1980s, at least.

3. The last major point of difference concerns the role of the time preference motive for running a current account surplus or deficit. I have shown that Fetter and Iversen produced a discussion of this effect, but it does not figure in the work of other writers. In Mosak and Lange, different expectations of future prices, which exist in one country as opposed to another, play the role that differing preferences for current and future consumption play in much of the modern literature.

Formally, there is some similarity between their approach and the time preference motive.[29] The emphasis is different, however, for in the Fisherian style model of current account determination the ratio of present to future prices does not differ across countries because of differences in the elasticities of expectation functions.

Hayek and his followers only make explicit statements about the consumption-smoothing motive. The time preference motive is thus not very prevalent in the earlier literature. The trade theoretic content of this body of work is thus relatively small, since, unlike much modern work, it makes less reference to the role of international differences in intertemporal prices. In modern theory, the time preference motive creates an analogy between real and intertemporal trade theories, as demonstrated originally by Norman Miller (1968). (These results were surveyed in Chapter 3.) This analogy is lacking in the earlier literature.

### Can the recurrence of the research tradition in intertemporal trade be explained?

The last subject of concern is that of the applicability of Laudan's methodological approach to explaining the disappearance and reappearance of the research tradition in intertemporal trade. I have shown, in detail, that the theories of Fetter, Iversen, Hayek, Lachmann, Mosak and Lange – developed over the interwar period – belong to the same research tradition as the dominant intertemporal approach to international macroeconomics of the 1980s. This is because what marks out a research tradition is, to use a phrase of Laudan's, the fact that 'there are significant family resemblances between certain theories which mark them off as a group from others' (Laudan *et al.* 1986: 111).

In this chapter, numerous 'family resemblances' between the literature of the 1980s and the interwar literature have been detected, despite the differences highlighted in the last section. As was discussed in Chapter 2, Laudan states that a research tradition must have a set of metaphysical and methodological commitments ('ontology' and 'heuristic') which individuate it. I have argued that both groups of writers share the same metaphysical commitment in that they view current account 'disequilibrium' as in effect consistent with an equilibrium state of the economy. They share the same methodological commitment in that they both believe that intertemporal equilibrium, or a variant of it with incomplete markets, like Hicksian temporary equilibrium, should be used to explain why such international payments imbalances exist. The question we now have to ask is why did this approach die and why was it later revived?

In order to explain this, recall that Laudan regards the purpose of a science to be the solution of problems. To solve a problem means to resolve ambiguity and 'to show that what happens is somehow intelligible and predictable' (Laudan 1977: 13). An empirical problem is 'anything about the world which strikes us as odd or otherwise in need of explanation', whereas conceptual problems are 'higher order questions about the wellfoundedness of the conceptual structures (e.g. theories) that have been designed to answer the first order questions (empirical problems)' (Laudan 1977: 15). The success of a research tradition is judged by the number of problems it solves and also by its rate of progress in solving them.

I believe that Laudan's problem-solving criterion provides a convincing explanation for the long break in the development of the intertemporal research tradition. First, consider the ability of the earlier theory to solve empirical problems. I have shown above that Neisser and Modigliani (1953) regarded the theory as being too complex for the easy examination of real world problems. There do exist modern counterparts to Mosak's system 'consisting of thousands of equations'. These are the computable intertemporal general equilibrium models of the open economy such as that of Feltenstein (1986). In effect, Mosak's method required the computational techniques used to solve models of this type, but, of course, these were not then available. Given the urge to generalize characteristics of the early intertemporal literature, he could only bring out a 'verbal' large-scale general equilibrium model whose results were often inconclusive. Thus I have shown that Mosak often left problems unresolved within a knot of ambiguity. The alternative research tradition, which was broadly Keynesian at that time (see the account in Metzler 1948: 215–20, 225–7), offered a plethora of solutions, expressed by formulae and diagrams and was applicable econometrically, as Neisser and Modigliani were able to show. Another point is that the main external empirical problem which the intertemporal approach was well adapted to solve – movements of capital where these consist of goods and securities, was not very pressing in the 1950s. As Kenen (1985) shows, the dominant theory of the early Bretton Woods era was designed for the analysis of a world with no financial capital movements. The intertemporal approach therefore demanded great theoretical refinement but offered little in return by way of solving relevant empirical problems.

Second, consider the area of conceptual problems. Here the earlier writers had to contend with all the deep conceptual problems associated with intertemporal macroeconomics. Why is money held in intertemporal equilibrium? How much knowledge do individuals have about the future? What type of expectations make such an economy stable? In the open economy these problems are even harder to solve. In international economics we must explain why different monies are held and what happens if individuals in different countries have different expectations about the future. Attempts such as those of Hayek and Mosak to resolve these problems naturally failed and led to theoretical unclarities such as Reynaud's use of money illusion in intertemporal equilibrium. I have shown that the more formal and rigorous the analysis became, the more acute became these various contradictions – Fetter's account is, on the surface, less problematic than Mosak's but this is only because the deeper conceptual problems of intertemporal economics were unknown at that time. Lange and Mosak showed that the most developed relevant theoretical apparatus of the time, Hicks's temporary equilibrium theory, was well adapted to answer questions about the influence of expectations about the future on the stability of the open economy. This, however, only allowed a limited number of problems to be solved. It was obviously of no use in solving problems concerning the comparative static effects of changes in a stable economy.

To conclude then, Laudan's problem-solving approach points out the inadequacy of the earlier intertemporal literature from a pragmatic point of view. What Laudan's concepts cannot explain directly is why these works were totally forgotten. Here the fact that Samuelson and Hicks damned Mosak with faint praise is particularly important. This is an example of Kuhn's conception that unsuccessful ideas are literally written out of the scientific world and may well be lost. I do not have enough information to be able to assess the reasons for their reaction. I would conjecture though, that the leaders of a profession will try to warn others off a false trail which does not lead to theories of a high problem-solving effectiveness. The fact that Hicks, Samuelson, Neisser and Modigliani all admired Mosak's technical sophistication, but still did not adopt his concepts, demonstrates how success in problem solving was considered, in this case, to be more important than mere technique.

## Summary and conclusion

This chapter has provided both a historical and a rational reconstruction of the research tradition in intertemporal open economy macroeconomics. The historical reconstruction has uncovered a number of writers who belonged to this tradition, while the rational reconstruction has attempted to explain their contribution in modern terms and locate it in relation to the various strands of the literature of the 1980s.

The historical reconstruction has discovered the following contributions:

1    The prehistory of the intertemporal approach, represented by Cairnes and Wieser. They formulated some of the building blocks of the theory without stipulating it explicitly.
2    Fetter, who discovered the time preference and consumption-augmenting motives for running a balance of payments deficit in an intertemporal framework, and Iversen, who also was aware of the time preference motive.
3    Hayek, who developed an original theory concerning the nature of monetary movements, in response to real shocks, within the context of an

economy in intertemporal equilibrium. Hayek's theory suffered from the problem that it was not completely consistent with his own assumptions of rationality and perfect foresight. His followers, Reynaud, Fraser, Robbins and Lachmann all applied Hayek's insights to policy problems. A typically Hayekian policy, treated by Reynaud, is that the quantity of money in the world should be kept constant but that international money must be allowed to move freely from country to country.

4   Mosak brought this literature to fruition with a thoroughgoing application of Hicks's theory of temporary equilibrium to the open economy. Lange made a small contribution with identical methods.

5   Three leading economists of the day, Samuelson, Hicks and Modigliani, all openly ignored the potential of Mosak's approach. Thus, it was not adopted by the profession as a whole.

The rational reconstruction reveals the following:

1   Fetter's approach is close to the modern literature, which assumes endogenous rates of time preference.

2   Hayek's approach has requirements for the neutrality of money which are different from those of modern theory.

3   Mosak's theory is different from much modern work, in that it involves a temporary equilibrium in which future prices are not forecast correctly. The existence of nonhomogeneous price expectations introduces the non-neutrality of money, the nonequivalence of exchange rate arrangements and the non-neutrality of government policy into his analysis. Mosak, however, did produce a completely theoretically consistent model of an economy in which intertemporal choice by individuals generates current account imbalances. The main drawback of Mosak's work lay in the fact that the very general nature of his assumptions prevented the discovery of many clear-cut theorems. Despite this drawback, Mosak also presented a correct but partial statement of the modern fixprice approach to the open economy, and applied it to several problems.

4   The earlier intertemporal approach was not accepted by the economics profession. This can be explained by Laudan's concept that a successful theory must be able to solve a large number of empirical and conceptual problems.

# Notes

## 1 Introduction

1  Stockman (1988: 356) states that: 'Large swings in the current account and exchange rates can occur in a competitive equilibrium without any distortion or externalities that might rationalize corrective government policies.'

2  This definition is adapted from Watkins (1953). Hodgson (1988) has emphasized the role that methodological individualism has come to play in macroeconomics since the advent of the rational expectations school. Kyun (1988: 86–7) argues that Hayek's concept of methodological individualism is at variance with the practice of equilibrium business cycle theorists such as Lucas and Sargent. It is, however, the case that Watkins, invoking the authority of Hayek and Popper, attacks Keynes for failing to base his theory of the consumption function on rational behaviour by the individual (Watkins 1953: 95–6). This is precisely the methodological position that equilibrium business cycle theory adopts.

3  Reynaud, Mosak and Iversen do not appear in the *New Palgrave*.

4  Fogel (1964) gives a complete statement of the epistemological position of the New Economic History, emphasizing the fact that it sets out clear assumptions and testable implications which follow from them. Elster (1983: 38–9) describes Fogel's work as a particularly all-embracing attempt to apply causal explanations in economics, and Nelson and Winter's work as a pioneering attempt to apply functional models in economics.

5  The term has also been given a different meaning by the German Marxist philosopher Jurgen Habermas, who defines a rational reconstruction as being a means of explicating general rules of human competence in areas such as linguistics or cognitive psychology (Habermas 1975: 303–4).

   The Popperian concept of a problem situation has been extensively applied to studying the development of an economic theory by Wong (1978). My description of the rational reconstruction of a problem situation is based on Wong (1972: 9–12).

6  S. Horsley Palmer (1779–1858) was Governor of the Bank of England in 1830–1833 and a significant figure in nineteenth-century controversies concerning the Bank's proper management. Oliver W. Sprague (1882–1938) was a professor at the Graduate School of Business Administration at Harvard, an expert on the finance of the American war effort during the First World War, and an adviser to the Bank of England in the late 1920s and early 1930s who testified before the Macmillan Committee on the Bank's behalf. Karl Helfrerich (1872–1924), originally an academic economist, held a number of important university, banking and governmental posts in Wilhelmine Germany, including that of Secretary of State in the Treasury office in 1915–1916. After

the war, he was both an important nationalist politician and the originator of a plan to stabilize the hyperinflation. Many of the essential details of his plan were ultimately included in the stabilization scheme which was actually adopted by the Weimar government.

7 Croce's arguments appear in his *Essays on Historiography* (1924) and are similar to those of Oakeshott. They both seem to have taken an interest in economics. In particular, Croce argued that the historian's highly contingent view of human activity also constituted a criticism of Pareto's view that one could develop a science of economics based on certain constant features of human behaviour (Croce 1900 [1953]). Oakeshott regarded his ideas as being consistent with Henry Simon's views on economic policy (Oakeshott 1962). The presence of these two philosophers is thus not as incongruous here as it appears at first sight.

## 2 The problem of recurring doctrines in economics

1 Hacking (1981: 1–2) presents nine points which characterize the received view. The most relevant of his points for us is 'science is cumulative. Science by and large builds on what is already known.' The new historical philosophy is summarized by Laudan *et al.* (1986: 141–54), an indispensable layman's guide which has naturally influenced my thinking on these subjects.

2 Of these, only Stegmuller's ideas have been applied extensively to economics, so they have influenced my treatment of Chapter 2. His approach, however, is static and has little to say about theory transitions (see Stegmuller *et al.* 1982, a work I shall use in the next chapter of this book).

3 They are both discussed further below.

4 See Coats's article (1984) on the sociology of knowledge cited in the Bibliography.

5 Nickles (1986: 256) is a useful critique of large-scale philosophical theories of scientific change, and I have followed him on this point.

6 One has to be careful even with one's use of 'ideas'. For example, we are told that this word is an 'antique term of art', not used in modern philosophy (see Hacking 1975: 11–12, 163–70).

7 This is what the Lakatosian case studies in the second part of Blaug's *Methodology of Economics* (1980) are all about. Blaug, as a result of his scientific enquiries, finds the scientific practice of economics lacking by Popperian standards. I have no such normative aims. I am interested only in historical explanation.

8 The strong role of relative price changes in the canonical classical price–specie–flow mechanism makes this a rather dubious case of recurrence at first blush, and Frenkel and Johnson were rightly criticized for this by Samuelson (1971), who sorted out the theoretical problems. Perlman (1986) has produced an excellent account of Ricardo and Thornton's emphasis on relative price changes which reinforces, in my view, the inappropriateness of Frenkel and Johnson's claim. Bordo (1984) regarded James W. Angell (of whom more much later in the thesis) to be an appropriate originator of the monetary approach in the 1920s.

9 Patinkin (1976: 79). I am thinking of Robert Bryce's lecture notes reproduced by Patinkin. Another version of Keynes's equations, which appears in his notes for the drafts of the General Theory, is reproduced in his *Collected Writings*, vol. XIII. For a more comprehensive treatment of Keynes's lectures, see Rymes 1989.

10 Hausman (1981: 44–52) sorts out the different uses of the terms and concepts 'models' and 'theories' in philosophy and economics.

11  Grandmont (1983), Jones (1976), Lindahl (1919), Sargent and Wallace (1982) and Steedman (1979), reworked originally by Samuelson (1969).

12  However, if Hacking's (1983: Ch. 5) definitions of incommensurability are applied to economics, it is hard to detect cases of incommensurability in the history of the subject.

13  See also Pigou (1921: Ch. 17, 210–11). Buchanan (1958), in an otherwise erudite account, neglects the way the issue arose during the First World War.

14  Baumol and Goldfeld (1968) reproduced some of Remak's work, but not enough to do him full justice, judging by Wittman's demonstration of his worth.

15  Backhouse (1985: 134), Hicks (1939: 19). Since Johnson published in English in the *Economic Journal*, their neglect of him is more surprising than the more well-known case of Slutsky, who published in an Italian journal in Italian.

16  Hutchison (1978: 65–6) comments on this. To be fair, Jevons attacked the 'Ricardo–Mill' theory, but Ricardo's reputation survived. See also Walras's (1874) extensive references to Mill in his chapter on 'English Theories of Rent'.

17  Lakatos's great work, *Proofs and Refutations* (1976), was of course about the history of mathematics. Here he used a method of rational reconstruction which seems to me to be much more static than the *Methodology of Scientific Research Programmes*. Something similar has been brilliantly done by Wong (1978) for revealed preference theory in economics. The MSRP, however, has always been applied to experimental research programmes in science (see the case studies collected in Howson 1976), not to theoretical programmes.

18  Blaug (1980: 72) complains that there seems to be no connection between Mill's *System of Logic*, the work which interests Laudan, and his *Principles of Political Economy*. He, however, has neglected the references to political economy in Mill's '*Logic*' discussed by Whitaker (1975: 1039–43).

19  Margaret Schabas (1987) has argued that the prominent role played by Mill and Jevons in the nineteenth-century philosophy of science undermines Laudan's methodological position. This is because their position as practising social scientists means that they were not concerned with the conceptual problems which had arisen in contemporary mid-nineteenth-century science, but rather were concerned with the implications of the philosophy of science for the social economics. For example, Jevons used his sceptical image of science to justify the scientific merits of economics: 'Since Jevons's work showed that Newtonian mechanics was not as exact and certain as had once been thought, economists did not have as far to go in emulating the more revered branches of knowledge' (Schabas 1987: 50). The case of Keynes strengthens Schabas's argument. Anna Carabelli (1985) has found that a 'mixture of anti-empiricism and antirationalism constitutes the core of Keynes's methodological position' (Carabelli 1985: 205) and that this constitutes a link between the *Treatise on Probability*, the *General Theory* and Keynes's *Quarterly Journal of Economics* article of 1937 which emphasized the importance of uncertainty (in the Knightian sense). Schabas may be correct to claim that all this evidence for the relationship between the epistemology of science and statistics and the development of economics may weaken Laudan's philosophy of science, but it suggests that Laudan's view of the relationship between the growth of knowledge and philosophy is relevant to the history of economic thought.

20  The fundamentally sociological basis of the concept of normal science, and its centrality in Kuhn's thought, is emphasized by Barnes (1985: 87–9).

21  See the discussion in Barnes (1977) of the late nineteenth-century Eugenics Movement in Britain.

22  Barnes (1977: Ch. 3) attacks even sophisticated Marxists like Lukacs, since for them a true knowledge resides in the revolutionary consciousness of the proletariat. This potential for a true understanding of reality will be realized when

revolution destroys false consciousness. For Barnes, on the other hand, the impossibility of evaluating competing knowledge claims is true for all time, including the future. In so far as the Strong Programme has a declared ideology, it is conservative (Barnes 1985: 84).

23 In his foreword to the translation of Fleck's work (1935: x).

24 There was at one time a revisionist fashion, exemplified by Robbins (1952), which emphasized that classical policy prescriptions were guided more by expediency than by ideology. This view is also reflected, if moderated, in Coats (1971). I have relied on the painstaking research of Fetter (1975), Hilton (1977) and Gordon (1979). Fetter has shown, by analysing the voting pattern of British MoP's who were classical economists, just how very homogeneous their social and political weltanschaung really was. Hilton has demonstrated exactly how the classical economists operated to promote free trade legislation, a mechanism which historians at first seemed not to find (e.g. Gordon 1971: 198–9, and the references he cites). Gordon (1971: Ch. 2) demonstrates the strong influence of Ricardian attitudes in the later 1820s.

25 Hilton (1977: 140–5) gives a detailed account of Huskisson's policies. Gordon (1979: 201–11) describes Huskisson's approach to applying political economy. See Thompson (1963: 845–6) on James Mill and Bentham's influence on Place, a significant source, since Thompson would doubtless have ignored the role of the economists if he possibly could.

26 Gilmour's analysis of *The Gradgrind School* (1967) is most revealing in this respect. One can perhaps go further and note the permeation of political economy into religious tracts. The evangelical slogan 'take out a saving interest in the Blood of Jesus', was originated by the Clapham Sect, of whom Thornton was a member. According to Spring (1961: 38–41), the discourse of the Clapham Sect was permeated by the phraseology of Political Economy.

27 Coats (1971: 21) summarizes some conflicting views on Bentham. A radical politician like Sir Francis Burdett, unlike Bentham, can be regarded as belonging to the philosophic radicals' thought collective, but not to that of the Political Economists.

28 Of course, the Classical Economists were perfectly aware of the limits to Laissez-Faire, as the last chapter of J.S. Mill's '*Principles*' makes clear, with the seven 'large exceptions' to the principle. The value of an account like Fleck's lies precisely in the fact that we would expect to find crude doctrinaire accounts in the exoteric circle, not among the sophisticates of the esoteric circle.

29 I have in mind work produced by the Strong Programme, such as Collins' (1985) study of how a group of scientists decided when a type of laser had reached an appropriate stage of development, and the network of relations which developed between them during this project.

## 4 The research tradition in intertemporal international trade theories

1 See Bordo's summary of this literature in Bordo and Schwartz (1984).

2 Hicks (1983: Ch. 2) gives an account of how the article of 1933 emerged from his failure to write down a system of equations which could describe Hayek's system.

3 Kyun (1988: 88–9) argues that this is close to, but not exactly identical with, the modern treatment of rational expectations in the context of intertemporal equilibrium.

4 What Ellis in effect points out is that Hayek's use of intertemporal equilibrium implies some form of perfect foresight or rational expectations. He notes that Hayek actually stated such a concept in passing, but did not grasp its implications:

What Hayek apparently misses is that any announced and persisting policy with regard to the price level of consumers' goods would, upon the assumptions he makes, be appropriately discounted into the present and give no grounds for a distortion of resources. Hayek himself admits in one passage that if the producer repeatedly went through the experience of losses occasioned by stabilizing the price level in the teeth of falling costs, he would 'need in his own interest to increase his current output through more intensive exploitation ... at the outset'. In other words, anticipating the glut in the future, he will immediately increase current production enough to secure equal returns on investment at all points of time. If the content of the improvement is known in advance, if price level policy is known and consistent, if there is no resistance of prices because of contracts and tradition – Hayek apparently assumes as much – it would make no difference to a rational community of entrepreneurs whether prices rose, fell, or remained constant. Upon the same assumptions, relative and not absolute price changes are the important thing, a fact which Hayek himself often reiterates in criticizing the older monetary theories of cycles. This signalizes the collapse of the case for a 'constant effective volume of money', so far as it turns upon Hayek's hypothetical situations involving calculations of future prices.

(Ellis 1934: 352)

This is the first ever clear statement I have seen to the effect that intertemporal equilibrium and perfect foresight imply the ineffectiveness of monetary policy.

5 Ellis emphasizes that 'to appreciate the unique character of Hayek's vision one must begin with the concept of intertemporal equilibrium' (Ellis 1934: 340). If Ellis's penetrating commentary on Hayek had been remembered, much recent Hayekian exegesis which has seized on the importance of Hayek's 1928 article would be redundant. The case of Ellis and Milgate can be regarded as a case of recurrence in the history of economic thought itself.

6 Fischer (1979) demonstrates such a result in an optimizing model where investment takes place and real balances appear in the utility function.

7 It is not in fact clear from Hayek's model whether short-run nonneutrality of money occurs because of some kind of Tobin effect – increasing the capital stock in response to inflation – or whether the source is noisy price signals which cause confusion between relative and nominal magnitudes, as in Lucas (1972). The latter explanation does not require any reference to capital accumulation. As Lucas (1977) explains, new classical models usually derive such real effects because noisy price signals cause individuals to supply more labour temporarily.

8 Stockman and Svensson's model (1987) is the closest that the recent intertemporal general equilibrium models have come to presenting a formal fully mathematized version of Hayek's vision. In particular, the model treats output as depending both on random disturbances and on the investment decisions of firms. The strong neutrality theorems surveyed in Chapter 3 do not hold because households only receive information about the state of the world after they have made their decisions concerning their asset holdings. Stockman and Svensson are thus able to study the relationships between changes in the growth of the money supply, productivity shocks, investment and the current account, in both the home and the foreign country. At the time of writing this is the only model which features uncertainty, endogenous investment and production, all features which are important in *Monetary Nationalism*.

9 In Persson's set-up the money stocks in the home and foreign country evolve according to:

$$M_t = M_{t-1} + D_t + \Delta G_t$$

$$M_t^* = M_{t-1}^* + D_t^* + \Delta G_t^*$$

(where the star denotes the foreign country and $\Delta G_t$ denotes the change in one of the gold stocks in a one-time period.)

Since $G_t + G_t^* = G^w$ – the fixed world stock of gold – we must have $\Delta G_t^* = -\Delta G_t$. If, as Hayek would prescribe, there is no credit creation, $D_t = 0$ and the world money supply given by adding the two equations must be constant. Given this set-up, it is very easy to show, in a two-period model, the Hayekian policy effects of the level of wealth in the two countries which make up the world, using equations (24) and (25) of Chapter 3, which now becomes:

$$M_1 = M_0 + \Delta G_1 = p_1 y_1$$

$$M_2 = M_1 + \Delta G_2 = p_2 y_2$$

where $\Delta G_1 = \bar{G} = G_1$, where $\bar{G}$ is the initial stock of gold and $G_1$ is the gold held in the first period.

Substituting this in the budget constraint (equation (9) of Chapter 3) and bearing in mind that $D_2$, second-period credit creation is equal to zero, gives us an expression for the wealth of the home country:

$$W = y_1 + \frac{y_2}{1+r} + \left( \bar{G} - \frac{r_1 G_1}{1+r_1} / P_1 \right).$$

The second term constitutes the interest costs of carrying these reserves from the first to the second period. (Persson assumes that there is some international monetary authority which is willing to take back all reserves at the end of period 2, so from the country's point of view $G_2 = 0$.)

One can derive an analogous equation for the foreign country. As Persson (1982: Ch. 5, 14) points out, such a system involves a real transfer from one country to another, the size and direction of which depends on the intercountry gold flows and changes in the price level. The country that loses gold has its wealth reduced, while the country that gains gold has its wealth increased. This will not occur under a flexible exchange rate or the fixed exchange rate regime devised by Helpman (1981). In this model, therefore, Hayek's scheme implies that the need to hold 'gold' reserves alters the level of wealth. In addition, note from the above expression for wealth that changes in the price level affect the value of the real gold stock and thus alter the level of wealth. Persson also deals with the more complicated case where the world stock of outside money is fixed, but each country can create credit. In this case he derives identical results. Holding the world money supply constant is therefore no more desirable than holding the world stock of outside money constant.

Persson points out that the Hayekian monetary regime gives countries an incentive to indulge in strategic behaviour, since one can raise its wealth, at the expense of the other, by increasing its gold stock and thus establishing a claim over the other's future output.

10 Svensson (1989) and Persson and Svensson (1989) assume incomplete asset markets. Greenwood and Williamson (1989) introduce endogenous financial intermediation, which results from transactions costs and the costs of monitoring the characteristics of heterogeneous borrowers.

11 If firms face a cash in advance constraint on the purchase of goods for investment purposes, there will be a direct link between changes in the money supply and the capital stock, as in Abel (1985). Stockman and Svensson (1987: note 11), note that this channel for non-neutrality could be introduced into their

model. Such a modification would bring it much closer to the overinvestment theory which plays an important role in *Monetary Nationalism*.

12 Both Greenwood and Williamson (1989: 429), and Persson and Svensson (1989: 506) doubt whether it is possible to Pareto rank exchange rate regimes in the presence of incomplete markets. They both find, however, that a flexible exchange rate regime reduces real output volatility, so a government that wished to stabilize output should adopt flexible rates. Helpman and Razin (1982), who introduced uncertainty only in the first period of a two-period cash in advance model, found fixed rates to be Pareto superior to flexible rates.

13 Weintraub (1979: 55–69) gives a useful summary of the development of the dynamic general equilibrium literature from Hicks through Lange to Patinkin; Mosak is not mentioned.

14 As is well known, Hicks's stability conditions for static general equilibrium are formally equivalent, under certain restrictive conditions, to the local stability conditions developed by Samuelson (see Takayama 1985: 316–17). Whether this is also the case for a temporary equilibrium is unclear to me. There seems to be no discussion of stability in the modern mathematical literature (Grandmont 1983) on the temporary equilibrium.

15 Compare Mosak (pp. 118–21) and Henderson and Quandt (1971: 295–305). Apart from their development of second-order conditions, Henderson and Quandt's treatment of optimization over time is identical to that of Mosak. They give no reference to the early literature apart from *Value and Capital*. Hicks did not treat optimization over time by consumers rigorously; he did so for firms but rather sketchily. Here, as elsewhere, Mosak's original contributions have gone unnoticed.

16 A firm 'holds money within any given period for purchases within the same period' (p. 147). An individual holds money 'temporarily in any given period for consumption in the same period' (p. 133). This is not a direct statement of a cash in advance constraint, but since IOUs are ruled out as a means of payment, Mosak's restrictions are equivalent to that idea.

17 Helpman and Razin (1982) and Svensson (1989) appear to be close to Mosak's approach, in that they combine cash in advance constraints with incomplete futures markets to derive a demand for money which depends on risk and returns on other assets, and transcends the crude quantity equation derived in Chapter 3 above. No well-defined demand for money function similar to a commodity demand function emerges, however, and the existence of such a function is what Mosak assumes. Marschak (1938) derived a completely rigorous, watertight demand for money under intertemporal utility maximization. He did this by assuming a transactions technology into which money is the least expensive input. An almost identical approach, in an open economy context, was taken by Greenwood (1984). Mosak could simply have applied Marschak's work, which he cites. He chose not to do so and went instead for Hicksian temporary equilibrium.

Mosak's own analysis of the demand for money in the context of perfect foresight, being an attempt to combine uncertainty and incomplete markets which predates the use of von Neumann–Morgenstern utility functions, is clearly formally incorrect.

18 Lange (1944: 16–18) talks about the failure 'to restore full employment' under static expectations, but makes no statement as emphatic as that of Mosak.

19 In 'a pure credit economy' money 'merely registers a debt from one of the "individuals" (who may be a bank) in the economy to another. In this case the positive and negative holdings of money must have been initially equal ... In this case the positive and negative holdings of bonds must certainly have been equal. A rise in the price level must consequently make some "individuals"

better off to exactly the same extent as it makes others worse off. If the income effects set up by these two movements are symmetric, the net income effect will be zero. The system is in neutral equilibrium' (Hicks 1946: 334).

20 Indeterminacy of the world price level being one example, as occurs in Fama's (1980) free banking system.

21 In Grandmont (1983: Ch. 2) there is a credit market, but individuals are allowed to borrow only from the government, so money is the only asset they hold. In Chapter 4 he introduces perpetuities which are demanded because their coupon is offset by expected capital losses. But here the expectations are extremely irrational. In order for any individual to hold money he must expect, with positive probability, a capital loss greater than the coupon. But then for consistency he must expect that, again with positive probability, the price of bonds will be negative in finite time. Gale (1985) remarks: 'Even the most weakly rational agent cannot be expected to hold such beliefs.'

22 Consider the individual's maximization problem in period 2, on the assumption that the period 1 problem has been solved:

Max $u(c_2)$

s.t. $\psi(p_1)(c_2 - e_2) - m \leq 0$

$$c_1 > 0, m > 0$$

Clearly, given period 1's choice, period 2's choice is given by the budget constraint:

$$c_2 = e_2 + \frac{m}{\psi(p_1)}$$

Substituting for $c_2$ in the original problem yields the maximization problems (3) and (4).

23 Mosak never explains how this would carry over to the multi-good case.

24 Henderson and Quandt (1971: 307–8), formalize this point in a set-up identical to that of Mosak.

25 Standard existence theorems are known today for this case; see for example Bliss (1983).

26 See de Marchi (1976) on the Heckscher–Ohlin 'Research Programme' (de Marchi's approach is Lakatosian, but nevertheless succeeds in showing how the Heckscher–Ohlin theory generated almost unlimited employment for theoretical economists. Hamminga (1982) carries out a similar exercise from a structuralist point of view).

27 Krohn (1983) gives a history of the Kiel School of German economists which included Neisser.

28 Persson and Svensson (1983) show that in a two-period model with Keynesian unemployment in the first period, optimistic expectations concerning output in the second period will cause an initial current account deficit. This deficit will not occur if individuals are endowed with perfect foresight concerning future quantities.

29 Svensson (1988, 1989) developed a trade-theoretic treatment of consumption-smoothing behaviour. A country whose expected future output is less variable than another's will wish to lend by selling sure bonds if it is risk averse. These exports of capital take place because the autarky prices of safe assets are higher in a high-risk country than a low-risk country, and the differences in autarky prices can be used to predict the pattern of asset trade, in a manner completely analogous to that of real trade theory (see Svensson 1988: 380–1, 383–4). Such an interpretation does not occur in the earlier literature.

# Bibliography

Abel, A. (1985) 'Dynamic Behavior of Capital Accumulation in a Cash-in-Advance Model', *Journal of Monetary Economics* 16: 55–71.

Alesina, A. and Tabellini, G. (1988) 'Credibility and Politics', *European Economic Review* 32: 542–50.

Allais, M. (1947) *Capital et Interet*, Paris: Imprimerie Nationale.

Anderson, R.K. and Takayama, A. (1977) 'Devaluation, the Specie Flow Mechanism and the Steady State', *Review of Economic Studies* 44: 347–61.

Angell, J.W. (1926) *The Theory of International Prices*, Cambridge, Massachusetts: Harvard University Press.

Arrow, K. and Hahn, F. (1971) *General Competitive Analysis*, San Francisco: Holden-Day.

Ault, R.E. and Ekelund, R.B. (1987) 'The Problem of Unnecessary Originality in Economics', *Southern Economic Journal* 53: 650–61.

Aupetit, A. (1901) *Essai sur la Théorie Générale de la Monnaie*, Paris: Guillaumin.

Bachelard, G. (1951) 'Les recurrences historiques: epistemologie et histoire des sciences', in *L'Activite rationaliste de la Physique contemporaine*, Paris: Presses Universitaires de France.

Backhouse, R. (1985) *A History of Modern Economic Analysis*, Oxford: Basil Blackwell.

Backus, D. and Kehoe, P. (1987) 'Trade and Exchange-rate Dynamics in a Dynamic Competitive Economy', Discussion Paper #684, Queens University.

Bagehot, W. (1876) *Lombard Street: A Description of the Money Market*, London: Henry S. King and Company.

Baldwin, R.E. (1948) 'Equilibrium in International Trade: A Diagrammatic Analysis', *Quarterly Journal of Economics* 62: 748–62.

—— (1966) 'The Role of Capital Goods Trade in the Theory of International Trade', *American Economic Review* 56: 841–8.

Barber, W.J. (1985) *From New Era to New Deal*, Cambridge: Cambridge University Press.

Bardhan, P. (1966) 'Optimal Foreign Borrowing', in K. Shell (ed.) *Essays on the Theory of Economic Growth*, Cambridge, Massachusetts: MIT Press.

Barkai, H. (1986) 'Ricardo's Volte-face on Machinery', *Journal of Political Economy* 94: 595–613.

Barnes, B. (1977) *Interests and the Growth of Knowledge*, London: Routledge.

—— (1982) *T.S. Kuhn and Social Science*, London: Wheatsheaf Books.

—— (1985) 'Thomas Kuhn', in Q. Skinner (ed.) *The Return of Grand Theory in the Social Sciences*, Cambridge, UK: Cambridge University Press.

Barro, R. (1974) 'Ace Government Bonds Net Wealth', *Journal of Political Economy* 82: 1095–1117.

Baumol, W.J. and Goldfeld, S.M. (eds) (1968) *Precursors in Mathematical Economics*, London: LSE Reprints #19.

Bazdarich, M.J. (1978) 'Optimal Growth and Stages in the Balance of Payments', *Journal of International Economics* 8: 425–43.

Becker, R.A. (1981) 'The Duality of a Dynamic Model of Equilibrium and an Optimal Growth Model', *Quarterly Journal of Economics* 96: 271–300.

Benassy, J.-P. (1982) 'Developments in Non-Walrasian Economics and the Microeconomic Foundations of Macroeconomics', in W. Hildenbrand (ed.) *Advances in Economic Theory*, 2nd edn, London and New York: Cambridge University Press.

—— (1986) *Macroeconomics: An Introduction to the Non-Walrasian Approach*, Orlando, Florida: Academic Press.

Ben-David, J. (1984) *The Scientist's Role in Society*, Chicago: University of Chicago Press.

Bensusan-Butt, D.M. (1954) 'A Model of Trade and Accumulation', *American Economic Review* 44: 511–29.

Berg, M. (1980) *The Machinery Question and the Making of Political Economy, 1815–1848*, Cambridge: Cambridge University Press.

Bernanke, B. and Gertler, M. (1989) [1986] 'Agency Costs, Collateral and Business Fluctuations', *American Economic Review* 79: 14–31; originally appeared as NBER Working Paper #2015.

Blaug, M. (1980) *The Methodology of Economics: Or, How Economists Explain*, 1st edn, Cambridge, UK: Cambridge University Press.

—— (1998) 'Disturbing Currents in Modern Economics', *Challenge*, May–June.

Bliss, C. (1975) *Capital Theory and the Distribution of Income*, Amsterdam and London: North-Holland.

—— (1983) 'Consistent Temporary Equilibrium', in J.-P. Fitoussi (ed.) *Modern Macroeconomic Theory*, Oxford: Basil Blackwell.

Boland, L.A. (1982) *The Foundations of Economic Method*, London: George Allen and Unwin.

Bordo, M. (1984) 'The Gold Standard: The Traditional Approach', in M. Bordo and A. Schwartz (eds) *A Retrospective on the Classical Gold Standard, 1821–1931*, Chicago and London: University of Chicago Press.

Brown, H.G. (1914) 'The Discount Versus the Cost of Production Theory of Capital Valuation', *American Economic Review* 4: 340–9.

Bruce, N. and Purvis, D.D. (1985) 'The Specification of Goods and Factor Markets in Open Economy Macroeconomic Models', in R.W. Jones and P.B. Kenen (eds) *Handbook of International Economics*, vol. II, Amsterdam and New York: North-Holland.

Bruno, M. (1982) 'Adjustment and Structural Change under Supply Shocks', *Scandinavian Journal of Economics* 84: 199–221.

Buchanan, J.M. (1958) *Public Principles of Public Debt*, Homewood, Illinois: Richard D. Irwin.

—— (1976) 'Barro on the Ricardian Equivalence Theorem', *Journal of Political Economy* 84: 337–42.

Butts, R.E. (1979) 'Scientific Progress: The Laudan Manifesto', *Philosophy of the Social Sciences* 9: 420–4.

Cairnes, J.E. (1874) [1967] *Some Leading Principles of Political Economy*, New York: Augustus M. Kelley.

Carabelli, A.M. (1985) 'Keynes on Probability and Induction', in T. Lawson and M.H. Pesaran (eds) *Keynes's Economics: Methodological Issues*, London: Croom Helm.

Champernowne, D. (1954) 'On the Uses and Misuses of Mathematics in Presenting Economic Theory', *The Review of Economics and Statistics* 36: 369–72.

—— (1961) 'A Dynamic Model Involving a Production Function', in F.A. Lutz and D.C. Hague (eds) *The Theory of Capital*, London: Macmillan.

Chandrasekhar, S. (1987) *Truth and Beauty: Aesthetics and Motivations in Science*, Chicago: University of Chicago Press.

Chipman, J. (1954) 'Empirical Testing and Mathematical Models', *The Review of Economics and Statistics* 36: 363–5.

—— (1965a) 'A Survey of the Theory of International Trade: Part 1, the Classical Theory', *Econometrica* 33: 477–519.

—— (1965b) 'A Survey of the Theory of International Trade: Part 2, the Neo-classical Theory', *Econometrica* 33: 685–760.

Clapham, J.H. (1922) 'Of Empty Economic Boxes', *Economic Journal* 32: 305–14.

Coats, A.W. (ed.) (1971) *The Classical Economists and Economic Policy*, London: Methuen and Co.

—— (1984) 'The Sociology of Knowledge and the History of Economics', *Research in the History of Economic Thought and Methodology* 2: 211–34.

Colander, D.C. and Klamer, A. (1987) 'The Making of an Economist', *Journal of Economic Perspectives* 1: 95–113.

Collard, D.A. (1983) 'Pigou on Expectations and the Cycle', *Economic Journal* 93: 411–14.

Collins, H.M. (1985) *Changing Order: Replication and Induction in Scientific Practice*, London: Sage Publications.

Cooter, R. and Rappaport, P. (1984) 'Were the Ordinalists Wrong about Welfare Economics?', *Journal of Economic Literature* 22: 507–30.

Cowen, T. and Kroszner, R. (1987) 'The Development of the New Monetary Economics', *Journal of Political Economy* 95: 567–90.

Crawford, V.P. (1987) *International Lending, Long-Term Credit Relationships, and Dynamic Contract Theory*, Princeton Studies in International Finance #59, Princeton, New Jersey: Princeton University Press.

Croce, B. (1900) 'On the Economic Principle: A Letter to Professor V. Pareto', trans. in A.T. Peacock, R. Turvey and E. Henderson (eds) (1953) *International Economic Association Papers*, vol. II, no. 3, London: Macmillan.

—— (1921) *History: Its Theory and Practice*, trans. D. Ainslie, London: George G. Harrap & Co.

Cross, R. (1982) 'The Duhem–Quine Thesis, Lakatos and the Appraisal of Theories in Macroeconomics', *Economic Journal* 92: 320–40.

Cuddington, J.T., Johansson, P.O. and Lofgren, F.G. (1984) *Disequilibrium Macroeconomics in Open Economies*, Oxford: Basil Blackwell.

—— and Vinals, J.M. (1986) 'Budget Deficits and the Current Account in the Presence of Classical Unemployment', *Economic Journal* 96: 101–19.

Deardoff, A. (1994) 'Overview of the Stolper–Samuelson Theorem', in A. Deardorff and R. Stern (eds) *The Stolper–Samuelson Theorem: A Golden Jubilee*, Ann Arbor: University of Michigan Press.

Debreu, G. (1959) *Theory of Value*, New Haven: Yale University Press.

—— (1986) 'Theoretic Models: Mathematical Form and Economic Content', *Econometrica* 1986: 1259–70.

—— (1991) 'The Mathematization of Economic Theory', *American Economic Review* 81: 1–7.

De Marchi, N. (1976) 'Anomaly and the Development of Economics: The Case of the Leontief Paradox', in S.J. Latsis (ed.) *Method and Appraisal in Economics*, Cambridge: Cambridge University Press.

Dixit, A.K. and Norman, V. (1980) *Theory of International Trade*, Cambridge: Cambridge University Press.

Doppelt, G. (1981) 'Laudan's Pragmatic Alternative', *Inquiry* 42: 253–71.

Dorfman, R. (1954) 'A Catechism: Mathematics in Social Science', *The Review of Economics and Statistics* 36: 374–7.

Dornbusch, R. (1973) 'Devaluation, Money and Nontraded Goods', *American Economic Review* 63: 871–80.

—— (1977) 'Capital Mobility and Portfolio Balance', in R. Aliber (ed.) *The Political Economy of Monetary Reform*, London: Macmillan.

—— (1980) *Open Economy Macroeconomics*, New York: Basic Books.

—— (1983) 'Real Interest Rates, Home Goods and Optimal External Borrowing', *Journal of Political Economy* 91: 141–53.

—— (1985) 'External Debt, Budget Deficits, and Disequilibrium Exchange Rates', in G.W. Smith and J.T. Cuddington (eds) *International Debt and the Developing Countries*, Washington, DC: The World Bank.

Dow, S. (1985) *Macroeconomic Thought: A Methodological Approach*, Oxford: Basil Blackwell.

Duesenberry, J. (1954) 'The Methodological Basis of Economic Theory', *The Review of Economics and Statistics* 36: 361–3.

Eatwell, J. (1982) 'Competition', in M. Howard and I.G. Bradley (eds) *Classical and Marxian Political Economy*, London: Macmillan.

Ellis, H. (1934) *German Monetary Theory: 1905–1933*, Cambridge, MA: Harvard University Press.

Elster, J. (1983) *Explaining Technical Change: A Case Study in the Philosophy of Science*, Cambridge: Cambridge University Press.

Fama, E.F. (1980) 'Banking in the Theory of Finance', *Journal of Monetary Economics* 6: 39–57.

Feltenstein, A. (1986) 'Financial Crowding Out: Theory with an Application to Australia', *IMF Staff Papers* 33: 60–89.

Fetter, F.A. (1914) 'Interest Theories, Old and New', *American Economic Review* 4: 68–92.

—— (1914) 'Capitalization versus Productivity: A Rejoinder', *American Economic Review* 4: 856–9.

—— (1927) 'Interest Theory and Price Movements', *American Economic Review* 17 (Supplement): 62–105.

Fetter, F.W. (1965) *The Development of British Monetary Orthodoxy*, Cambridge, Massachusetts: Harvard University Press.

—— (1975) 'The Influence of Economists in Parliament on British Legislation from Ricardo to John Stuart Mill', *Journal of Political Economy* 83: 1051–64.

Feyerabend, P.K. (1975) *Against Method*, London: Verso Books.

—— (1981) 'More Clothes from the Emperor's Bargain Basement', *British Journal for the Philosophy of Science* 32: 57–71.

Findlay, R. (1987) 'Free Trade and Protection', in J. Eatwell *et al.* (eds) *The New Palgrave Dictionary of Economics*, vol. II, London: Macmillan.

Fischer, S. (1979) 'Capital Accumulation on the Transition Path in a Monetary Optimizing Model', *Econometrica* 47: 1433–40.

Fisher, I. (1930) *The Theory of Interest*, New York: Macmillan.

Flanders, M.J. (1989) *International Monetary Economics 1870–1960: Between the Classical and the New Classical*, Cambridge: Cambridge University Press.

Fleck, L. (1935) *Genesis and Development of a Scientific Fact*, trans. F. Bradley and T.J. Trenn (1976) Chicago and London: University of Chicago Press.

Fogel, R. (1964) *Railroads and American Economic Growth*, Baltimore: Johns Hopkins University Press.

Foss, N. (1997) 'The New Growth Theory: Some Intellectual Growth Accounting', Working Paper 1997-02, Copenhagen Business School.

Fraser, H.F. (1933) *Great Britain and the Gold Standard: A Study of the Present World Depression*, London: Macmillan.

Frenkel, J.A. (1976) 'A Dynamic Analysis of the Balance of Payments in a Model of Accumulation', in J.A. Frenkel and H.G. Johnson (eds) *The Monetary Approach to the Balance of Payments*, London: George Allen and Unwin.

—— and Johnson, H.G. (1976) 'The Monetary Approach to the Balance of Payments: Essential Concepts and Historical Origins', in J.A. Frenkel and H.G. Johnson (eds) *The Monetary Approach to the Balance of Payments*, London: George Allen and Unwin.

—— and Mussa, M.L. (1985) 'Asset Markets, Exchange Rates and the Balance of Payments', in R.W. Jones and P.B. Kenen (eds) *Handbook of International Economics*, Amsterdam and New York: North-Holland.

—— and Razin, A. (1985) 'Government Spending, Debt and International Economic Interdependence', *Economic Journal* 95: 619–39.

—— (1987) *Fiscal Policies and the World Economy*, Massachusetts: MIT Press.

Frenkel, J.A. and Rodriguez, C. (1975) 'Portfolio Equilibrium and the Balance of Payments: A Monetary Approach', *American Economic Review* 65: 674–88.

Friedman, M. (1957) *A Theory of the Consumption Function*, Princeton: Princeton University Press.

Fulton, G. (1984) 'Research Programmes in Economics', *History of Political Economy* 16: 187–205.

Gale, D. (1985) 'Review of Grandmont, Money and Value', *Journal of Political Economy* 93: 430–3.

Gareganani, P. (1983) 'The Classical Theory of Wages and the Role of Demand Schedules in the Determination of Relative Prices', *American Economic Review, Papers and Proceedings* 73: 309–13.

Gilmour, R. (1967) 'The Gradgrind School: Political Economy in the Classroom', *Victorian Studies* 2: 207–24.

Goodwin, C.D. (1980) 'Toward a Theory of the History of Economics', *History of Political Economy* 12: 610–19.

Gordon, B.J. (1979) *Economic Doctrine and Tory Liberalism, 1824–30*, London: Macmillan.

Gordon, H.S. (1971) 'The Ideology of Laissez-Faire', in A.W. Coats (ed.) *The Classical Economists and Economic Policy*, London: Methuen and Co.

Grandmont, J.-M. (1983) *Money and Value*, London and New York: Cambridge University Press.

Greenwood, J. (1984) 'Non-Traded Goods, the Trade Balance and the Balance of Payments', *Canadian Journal of Economics* 17: 806–24.

—— and Williamson, S.D. (1989) 'International Financial Intermediation and Aggregate Fluctuations under Alternative Exchange-rate Regimes', *Journal of Monetary Economics* 23: 401–33.

Gunnison Brown, H. (1914) 'Interest and Productivity: A Comment', *American Economic Review* 4: 340–9.

Haberler, G. (1936) *The Theory of International Trade*, trans. F. Bentham, London.

Habermas, J. (1975) 'A Postscript to Knowledge and Human Interests', *Philosophy of the Social Sciences* 3: 111–41.

Hacking, I. (1975) *Why Does Language Matter to Philosophy?* Cambridge: Cambridge University Press.

—— (1981) 'Lakatos's Philosophy of Science', in I. Hacking (ed.) *Scientific Revolutions*, Oxford: Oxford University Press.

—— (1983) *Representing and Intervening: Introductory Topics in the Philosophy of Science*, Cambridge: Cambridge University Press.

Hahn, F.A. (1973) *On the Notion of Equilibrium in Economics*, Cambridge: Cambridge University Press.

Hamada, K. (1966) 'Economic Growth and Long-term International Capital Movements', *Yale Economic Essays* 6: 48–96.

Hamminga, B. (1982) 'Neoclassical Theory Structure and Theory Development: The Ohlin–Samuelson Programme in the Theory of International Trade', in W. Stegmueller, W. Balzer and W. Spohn, *Philosophy of Economics*, Berlin: Springer.

Hands, D.W. (1985) 'Second Thoughts on Lakatos', *History of Political Economy* 17: 1–16.

—— (1996) 'Economics and Laudan's Normative Naturalism', *Social Epistemology* 10: 137–52.

Hausman, D. (1981) *Capital, Profits and Prices: An Essay in the Philosophy of Economics*, New York: Columbia University Press.

Hawtrey, R. (1928) *Trade and Credit*, London: Longmans, Green and Co.

Hayek, F.A. (1928) 'Intertemporal Price Equilibrium and Movement in the Value of Money' (in German) *Weltwirtschaftliches Archiv*, translated and reprinted in R. McCloughry (ed.) (1984) *Money, Capital and Fluctuations: Early Essays*, London: Routledge and Kegan Paul.

—— (1933) 'On Neutral Money' (in German) *Zeitschrift fur Nationalokonomie*, 4, 659–61, translated and reprinted in R. McCloughry (ed.) (1984) *Money, Capital and Fluctuations: Early Essays*, London, Routledge and Kegan Paul.

—— (1933) *Monetary Theory and the Trade Cycle*, London: Jonathan Cape.

—— (1935) *Prices and Production*, 2nd edn, London: Routledge and Kegan Paul.

—— (1937) *Monetary Nationalism and International Stability*, London: Longmans, Green and Co.

—— (1939) *Price Expectations. Monetary Disturbances and Malinvestments in Profits, Interest and Prices*, London: Routledge.

—— (1941) *The Pure Theory of Capital*, London: Routledge.

Hegel, F. (1912) *Hegel's Doctrine of Formal Logic*: translation of *Subjective Logic*, with introduction and notes by H. Macran, Oxford: Oxford University Press.

Helpman, E. (1981) 'An Exploration in the Theory of Exchange Rate Regimes', *Journal of Political Economy* 89: 865–90.

—— and Razin, A. (1979) 'Towards a Consistent Comparison of Alternative Exchange Rate Systems', *Canadian Journal of Economics* 12: 394–409.

—— (1982) 'A Comparison of Exchange Rate Regimes in the Presence of Imperfect Capital Markets', *International Economic Review* 23: 365–88.

—— (1984) 'The Role of Saving and Investment in Exchange Rate Determination under Alternate Monetary Mechanisms', *Journal of Monetary Economics* 13: 307–25.

—— (1987) 'Exchange Rate Management: Intertemporal Tradeoffs', *American Economic Review* 77: 107–23.

Hempel, C.G. (1959) 'The Empiricist Criteria of Meaning', in A.J. Ayer, *Logical Positivism*, Glencoe: Free Press.

Henderson, J.M. and Quandt, R.E. (1971) *Microeconomic Theory: A Mathematical Approach*, 2nd edn, Kogakusha, Tokyo, London: McGraw-Hill.

Hicks, J.R. (1933) 'Equilibrium and the Trade Cycle', *Zeitschrift fur Nationalokonomie* 4: 441–55 (in German), reprinted (1980) in *Economic Inquiry* 18: 523–34.

—— (1939) *Value and Capital*, 2nd edn, Oxford: Oxford University Press.

—— (1945) 'Recent Contributions to General Equilibrium Economics', *Economica* 12: 235–42.

—— (1982) *Money, Interest and Wages*, Oxford: Basil Blackwell.

—— (1983) *Classics and Moderns: Collected Essays in Economic Theory*, Oxford: Basil Blackwell.

—— and Allen, R.G.D. (1934) 'A Reconsideration of the Theory of Value: Part I' and 'A Reconsideration of the Theory of Value: Part II. A Mathematical Theory of Individual Demand Functions', *Economica* 1: 52–76, 196–219.

Hilton, B. (1977) *Cash, Corn and Commerce: The Economic Policy of the Tory Governments, 1815–30*, Oxford: Oxford University Press.

Hodgson, G. (1988) *Economics and Institutions*, Cambridge: Polity Press.

Hollis, M. and Nell, E.J. (1975) *Rational Economic Man: A Philosophical Critique of Neo-Classical Economics*, Cambridge: Cambridge University Press.

Hool, B. (1979) 'Liquidity, Speculation and the Demand for Money', *Journal of Economic Theory* 21: 73–87.

Hoover, K. (1988) *The New Classical Macroeconomics*, Oxford: Blackwell.

Howson, C. (1976) *Method and Appraisal in the Physical Sciences*, Cambridge: Cambridge University Press.

Hutchison, T.W. (1953) *A Review of Economic Doctrines, 1870–1929*, Oxford: Clarendon Press.

—— (1978) *On Revolutions and Progress in Economic Knowledge*, Cambridge: Cambridge University Press.

Iversen, C. (1935) *Aspects of the Theory of International Capital Movements*, Copenhagen: Levin and Munksgaard.

Jarvie, I. (1979) 'Laudan's Problematic Progress', *Philosophy of Social Sciences* 17: 425–37.

Johnson, H.G. (1971) 'Trade and Growth: A Geometrical Exposition', *Journal of International Economics* 1: 83–101.

Johnson, W.E. (1913) 'The Pure Theory of Utility Curves', *Economic Journal* 23: 483–513, reprinted in W.J. Baumol and S.M. Goldfeld (eds) (1968) *Precursors in Mathematical Economics*, London: LSE Reprints #19.

Jones, R.A. (1976) 'The Origin and Development of Media of Exchange', *Journal of Political Economy* 84: 757–76.

Jones, R.W. (1956) 'Factor Proportions and the Heckscher–Ohlin Theorem', *Review of Economic Studies* 24: 1–10.

Kalecki, M. (1943) 'Political Aspects of Full Employment', *Political Quarterly* 7: 322–31.

Kantor, B. (1979) 'Rational Expectations and Economic Thought', *Journal of Economic Literature* 17: 1422–41.

Kenen, P.B. (1985) 'Macroeconomic Theory and Policy: How the Closed Economy was Opened', in R.W. Jones and P.B. Kenen (eds) *Handbook of International Economics*, Amsterdam and New York: North-Holland.

Keynes, J.M. (1973) *The General Theory and After: Collected Writings*, vol. XIV, London: Macmillan (for the Royal Economic Society).

Kiker, B.F. (1966) 'The Historical Roots of the Concept of Human Capital', *Journal of Political Economy* 74: 481–99.

Kindleberger, C.P. (1986) *The World in Depression* (2nd edn), London: Penguin.

Klein, L. (1954) 'The Contributions of Mathematics in Economics', *The Review of Economics and Statistics* 36: 359–61.

Kohn, M. (1981) 'A Loanable Funds Theory of Unemployment and Monetary Disequilibrium', *American Economic Review* 71: 859–79.

Koopmans, T. (1954) 'On the Use of Mathematics in Economics', *The Review of Economics and Statistics* 36: 377–9.

Kotter, R. (1982) 'General Equilibrium Theory – An Empirical Theory?', in W. Stegmueller, W. Balzer and W. Spohn (eds) *Philosophy of Economics*, Berlin: Springer.

Krips. H. (1980) 'Some Problems for "Progress and its Problems"', *Philosophy of Science* 47: 601–16.

Krohn, C.D. (1983) 'An Overlooked Chapter of Economic Thought: The New School's Effort to Salvage Weimar's Economy', *Social Research* 50: 452–68.

Krueger, A. (1983) *Exchange Rate Determination*, Cambridge: Cambridge University Press.

Krugman, P. (1980) 'Scale Economies, Product Differentiation and the Pattern of Trade', *American Economic Review* 70: 950–9.

Kuhn, T. (1970) *The Structure of Scientific Revolutions* (2nd edn), Chicago: University of Chicago Press.

—— (1977) *The Essential Tension*, Cambridge, Massachusetts: MIT Press.

Kunin, L. and Weaver, F. (1971) 'On the Structure of Scientific Revolutions in Economics', *History of Political Economy* 3: 391–7.

Kyun, K. (1988) *Equilibrium Business Cycle Theory in Historical Perspective*, Cambridge: Cambridge University Press.

Lachmann, L. (1940) 'A Reconsideration of the Austrian Theory of Industrial Fluctuation', *Economica (n.s.)* 7: 179–96.

—— (1944) 'Notes on the Proposals for International Currency Stabilization', *Review of Economics and Statistics* 26: 184–91.

Laidler, D. (1982) *Monetarist Perspectives*, Cambridge, Massachusetts: Harvard University Press.

Lakatos, I. (1970) 'Falsification and the Methodology of Scientific Research Programmes', in I. Lakatos and A. Musgrave (eds) *Criticism and the Growth of
Knowledge*, Cambridge: Cambridge University Press.
—— (1976) *Proofs and Refutations: The Logic of Mathematical Discovery* (ed. J.
Worall and E. Zahar), Cambridge: Cambridge University Press.
—— (1978) *The Methodology of Scientific Research Programmes* (*Philosophical
Papers Vol. 1*) (ed. J. Worrall and G. Currie), Cambridge: Cambridge University
Press.
—— (1981) 'History of Science and its Rational Reconstructions', in I. Hacking
(ed.) *Scientific Revolutions*, Oxford: Oxford University Press.
Lange, O. (1943) 'The Theory of the Multiplier', *Econometrica* 11: 227–45.
—— (1944) *Price Flexibility and Full Employment*, Cowles Commission Monograph #8, Bloomington, Indiana: Principia Press.
Latsis, S.J. (ed.) (1976) *Method and Appraisal in Economics*, Cambridge: Cambridge University Press.
Laudan, L. (1977) *Progress and its Problems*, Berkeley: University of California
Press.
—— (1981a) 'A Problem-Solving Approach to Scientific Progress', in I. Hacking
(ed.) *Scientific Revolutions*, Oxford: Oxford University Press.
—— (1981b) *Science and Hypothesis: Historical Essays on Scientific Methodology*,
Dordrecht: Reidel.
—— (1984) *Science and Values: The Aims of Science and Their Role in Scientific
Debate*, Berkeley: University of California Press.
—— *et al.* (1986) 'Scientific Change: Philosophical Models and Historical
Research', *Synthese* 69: 141–223.
Lee, C. and Lloyd, P. (2002) 'Beauty and the Economist: The Role of Aesthetics in
Economic Theory', Working Paper 2002-4, University of Melbourne.
Leontief, W. (1958) 'Theoretical Note on Time-Preference, Productivity of
Capital, Stagnation and Economic Growth', *American Economic Review* 48:
105–11.
Lerner, A.P. (1932) 'The Diagrammatical Representation of Cost Conditions in
International Trade', *Economica* No. 37 (Old Series): 346–56.
Leshan, L. and Margenau, H. (1982) *Einstein's Space and Van Gogh's Sky: Phys-
ical Reality and Beyond*, New York: Macmillan.
Liebowitz, S.J. and Palmer, J.P. (1984) 'Assessing the Relative Impacts of Eco-
nomics Journals', *Journal of Economic Literature* 22: 77–88.
Lindahl, E. (1919) *Just Taxation – A Positive Solution*, trans. in R.A. Musgrave and
A.T. Peacock (eds) (1958) *Classics in the Theory of Public Finance*, London:
Macmillan.
Lucas, R. (1972) 'Expectations and the Neutrality of Money', *Journal of Economic
Theory* 4: 103–24.
—— (1977) 'Understanding Business Cycles', *Journal of Monetary Economics* 5:
7–29.
—— (1981) *Studies in Business Cycle Theory*, Cambridge, Massachusetts: MIT
Press.
—— and Stokey, N.L. (1984) 'Optimal Growth with Many Consumers', *Journal of
Economic Theory* 32: 139–71.
——, Prescott, E.C. and Stokey, N.L. (1989) *Recursive Methods in Economic
Dynamics*, Cambridge, Massachusetts: Harvard University Press.

McAlister, J. (1996) *Beauty and Revolution in Science*, Ithaca: Cornell University Press.

McCloskey, D.N. (1983) 'The Rhetoric of Economics', *Journal of Economic Literature* 21: 481–517.

—— (1988) 'Thick and Thin Methodologies in the History of Economic Thought', in N. de Marchi (ed.) *The Popperian Legacy in Economics*, Cambridge: Cambridge University Press.

McMullin, E. (1979) 'Discussion Review: Laudan's Progress and its Problems', *Philosophy of the Social Sciences* 46: 623–44.

Mahr, A. (1951) 'Die wesentliche bedingung des gleichgewichts der zahlungsbilanz', *Economia Internazionale* 4: 350–69.

Malinvaud, E. (1953) 'Capital Accumulation and Efficient Allocation of Resources', *Econometrica* 21: 233–68.

—— (1987) 'The Overlapping Generations Model in 1947', *Journal of Economic Literature* 25: 103–5.

Marion, N.P. and Svensson, L.E.O. (1984) 'World Equilibrium with Oil Price Increases: An Intertemporal Analysis', *Oxford Economic Papers* 36: 86–102.

Marschak, J. (1938) 'Money and the Theory of Assets', *Econometrica* 6: 311–25.

Masterman, M. (1970) 'The Nature of a Paradigm', in I. Lakatos and A. Musgrave (eds) *Criticism and the Growth of Knowledge*, Cambridge: Cambridge University Press.

Mays, W. (1962) 'Jevons's Conception of Scientific Method', *Manchester School* 30: 223–49.

Metzler, L.A. (1948) 'The Theory of International Trade', in H.S. Ellis (ed.) *A Survey of Contemporary Economics*, vol. 1, Homewood, Illinois: Richard D. Irwin.

Meyen, J. (1770) *Wie kommt es, das die Oekonomie bisher so wenig Vortheile von der Physik und Mathematik gewonnen hat...?* Berlin: Haude & Spener.

Milgate, M. (1979) 'On the Origin of the Notion of "Intertemporal Equilibrium"', *Economica* 46: 1–10.

Mill, J.S. (1848) *Principles of Political Economy*, W.J .Ashley (ed.) (1926) London: Longmans, Green & Co.

—— (1963) *Earlier Letters, Collected Works, Vol. VII*, F.E. Mineka (ed.) Toronto: University of Toronto Press.

Miller, A. (1996) *Insights of Genius: Imagery and Creativity in Science and Art*, New York: Copernicus Press.

Miller, N.C. (1968) 'A General Equilibrium Theory of International Capital Flows', *Economic Journal* 78: 312–20.

Mirowski, P. (1982) 'Adam Smith, Empiricism and the Rate of Profit in Eighteenth-Century England', *History of Political Economy* 14: 178–98.

—— (1984) 'Macroeconomic Instability and the "Natural" Processes in Early Neoclassical Economics', *Journal of Economic History* 44: 345–54.

Mitchell, W.C. (1912) 'The Backward Art of Spending Money', *American Economic Review* 2: 269–81.

Mosak, J.L. (1944) *General Equilibrium Theory in International Trade*, Cowles Commission Monograph #7, Bloomington, Indiana: Principia Press.

Mundell, R.A. (1962) 'The Appropriate Use of Monetary and Fiscal Policy for Internal and External Stability', *IMF Staff Papers* 9: 70–9.

Musgrave, A. (1979) 'Problems with Progress', *Synthese* 42: 443–64.

Myrdal, G. (1939 [1933]) *Monetary Equilibrium*, London: William Hodge.

Neary, J.P. and Stiglitz, J. (1983) 'Toward a Reconstruction of Keynesian Economics: Expectations and Constrained Equilibria', *Quarterly Journal of Economics* 98: 199–228.

Negishi, T. (1985) *Economic Theories in a Non-Walrasian Tradition*, Cambridge: Cambridge University Press.

Neisser, H. (1936) *Some International Aspects of the Business Cycle*, Philadelphia: University of Pennsylvania Press.

—— (1945) 'Review of Mosak, *General Equilibrium Theory in International Trade*', *Social Research* 12: 506–9.

—— and Modigliani, F. (1953) *National Incomes and International Trade: A Quantitative Analysis*, Urbana, Illinois: University of Illinois Press.

Newman, P. (1962) 'Production of Commodities by Means of Commodities', *Schweizeriche Zeitschrift fur Volkswirtschaft und Statistik* 98: 58–75.

Newton-Smith, W. (1981) *The Rationality of Science*, London: Routledge and Kegan Paul.

Nickles, T. (1986) 'Remarks on the Use of History as Evidence', *Synthese* 69: 253–66.

Nordhaus, W.D. (1975) 'The Political Business Cycle', *Review of Economic Studies* 42: 169–90.

Novick, D. (1954) 'Mathematics: Logic, Quantity and Method', *The Review of Economics and Statistics* 36: 357–8.

Nurkse, R. (1935) *Internationale Kapitalbewegungen*, Vienna: Institut fur Konjunkturforschung.

Oakeshott, M. (1933) *Experience and its Modes*, Cambridge: Cambridge University Press.

—— (1962) 'The Political Economy of Freedom', in *Rationalism in Politics and Other Essays*, London: Methuen.

Obstfeld, M. (1981) 'Macroeconomic Policy, Exchange Rate Dynamics and Optimal Asset Accumulation', *Journal of Political Economy* 89: 1142–61.

—— (1982) 'Aggregate Spending and the Terms of Trade: Is there a Laursen–Metzler Effect?', *Quarterly Journal of Economics* 97: 251–70.

—— (1987) 'International Finance: The Interwar Period', in J. Eatwell, M. Milgate and P. Newman (eds) *The New Palgrave Dictionary of Economics*, London: Palgrave.

—— and Rogoff, K. (1996) *Foundations of International Macroeconomics*, Cambridge, Massachusetts: MIT Press.

—— and Stockman, A.C. (1985) 'Exchange Rate Dynamics', in R.W. Jones and P.B. Kenen (eds) *Handbook of International Economics*, Amsterdam and New York: North-Holland.

O'Driscoll, G.P. (1977) *Economics as a Coordination Problem: The Contributions of Friedrich A. Hayek*, Kansas City: Sheed, Andrews and McMeel.

—— (1980) 'Frank A. Fetter and "Austrian" Business Cycle Theory', *History of Political Economy* 12: 542–57.

Ohlin, B. (1933) *Interregional and International Trade*, Cambridge, Massachusetts: Harvard University Press.

Pasinetti, L. (1977) *Lectures on the Theory of Production*, London: Macmillan.

Patinkin, D. (1976) *Keynes's Monetary Thought: A Study of its Development*, Durham, North Carolina: Duke University Press.

Perlman, M. (1986) 'The Bullionist Controversy Revisited', *Journal of Political Economy* 94: 745–62.

Persson, T. (1982) *Studies of Alternative Exchange Rate Systems: An Intertemporal General Equilibrium Approach*, Monograph #13, Stockholm: Institute for International Economics Studies: Stockholm.

—— (1984) 'Real Transfers in Fixed Exchange Rate Systems and the International Adjustment Mechanism', *Journal of Monetary Economics* 13: 349–69.

—— and Svensson, L.E.O. (1983) 'Is Optimism Good in a Keynesian Economy?', *Economica* 50: 291–300.

—— (1989) 'Exchange Rate Variability and Asset Trade', *Journal of Monetary Economics* 23: 485–509.

Pigou, A.C. (1919) 'The Burden of War and Future Generations', *Quarterly Journal of Economics* 33: 242–55.

—— (1921) *The Political Economy of War*, London: Macmillan.

Razin, A. (1982) 'Comment on T. Persson, *Global Effects of National Stabilization Policies under Fixed and Floating Exchange Rates*', *Scandinavian Journal of Economics* 84: 193–7.

—— and Svensson, L.E.O. (1982) 'The Current Account and Productivity Changes: A Diagrammatic Note', Working Paper #21-82, Foerder Institute for Economic Research, Tel Aviv University.

—— (1983) 'The Current Account and the Optimal Government Debt', *Journal of International Money and Finance* 2: 215–24.

Reid, M.G. (1934) *Economics of Household Production*, New York: John Wiley & Sons.

Reinert, E. (2000) 'Full Circle: Economics from Scholasticism Through Innovation and back into Mathematical Scholasticism', *Journal of Economic Studies* 27: 364–76.

Remak, R. (1929) 'Kann die volkswirtschaftslehre eine exakte wissenschaft werden? *Jahrbucher fur Nationalokonomie und Statistik* 98: 58–75.

Remenyi, J. (1979) 'Core Demi-core Interaction: Toward a General Theory of Disciplinary and Subdisciplinary Growth', *History of Political Economy* 11: 30–63.

Reynaud, J.P. (1937a) 'Monnaie neutre et economie reale', *Revue d'Economie Politique* 51: 1192–1216.

—— (1937b) 'Monnaie neutre et echanges internationaux', *Revue d'Economie Politique* 51: 1367–93.

Ricardo, D. (1810; corrected, 1810; enlarged, 1810; enlarged again, 1811) *The High Price of Bullion, A Proof of the Depreciation of Bank Notes*, London: John Murray.

Robbins, L.C. (1934) *The Great Depression*, London: Macmillan.

—— (1952) *The Theory of Economic Policy in English Classical Political Economy*, London: Macmillan.

Robinson, J. (1933) *The Economics of Imperfect Competition*, London: Macmillan.

—— (1936) 'Disguised Unemployment', *Economic Journal* 46: 225–37.

—— (1962) *Economic Philosophy: An Essay on the Progress of Economic Thought*, Harmondsworth: Penguin.

—— (1971) *Economic Heresies: Some Old-fashioned Questions in Economic Theory*, London: Macmillan.

Rorty, R. (1984) 'The History of Philosophy: Four Genres', in R. Rorty, Q. Skinner and J. Schneewind (eds) *Philosophy in History*, Cambridge: Cambridge University Press.

Rothbard, M.N. (1977) 'Introduction' to F.A. Fetter, *Capital, Interest and Rent: Essays in the Theory of Distribution* (M. Rothbard (ed.)), Kansas City: Sheed, Andrews and McMeel.

Rymes, T. (1989) *Keynes' Lectures 1932–35: Notes of a Representative Student*, London: Macmillan.

Sachs, J.D. (1981) 'The Current Account and Macroeconomic Adjustment in the 1970s', *Brookings Papers on Economic Activity*, 201–68 (excludes discussants).

Samuelson, P.A. (1945) 'Review of J.L. Mosak, *General Equilibrium Theory in International Trade*', *American Economic Review* 35: 943–5.

—— (1954a) 'Introduction: Mathematics in Economics – No, No or Yes, Yes, Yes?, *The Review of Economics and Statistics* 36: 359.

—— (1954b) 'Some Psychological Aspects of Mathematics and Economics', *The Review of Economics and Statistics* 36: 380–6.

—— (1969) 'Pure Theory of Public Expenditure and Taxation', in J. Margolis and H. Guitton (eds) *Public Economics*, London: Macmillan.

—— (1971) 'An Exact Ricardo–Hume–Marshall Model of International Trade', *Journal of International Economics* 1: 1–18.

Sargent, T.J. and Wallace, N. (1981) 'The Real Bills Doctrine vs. the Quantity Theory: A Reconsideration', *Journal of Political Economy* 90: 1212–36.

Schabas, M. (1987) 'An Anomaly for Laudan's Pragmatic Model', *Studies In History and Philosophy of Science*, Part A, 18: 43–52.

Schaffer, S. (1986) 'Scientific Discoveries and the End of Natural Philosophy', *Social Studies of Science* 16: 387–420.

Schlesinger, K. (1914) *Theorie der Geld und Kreditwirtschaft*, Munich and Leipzig:.

—— (1931) 'Felix Somary's Bankpolitik', *Archiv fur Sozialwissenschaft und Sozialpolitik* 66.

Schumpeter, J.A. (1954) *History of Economic Analysis*, Oxford: Oxford University Press.

Shackle, G.L.S. (1967) *The Years of High Theory: Invention and Tradition in Economic Thought, 1926–1939*, Cambridge: Cambridge University Press.

Shapere, D. (1981) 'Meaning and Scientific Change', in I. Hacking (ed.) *Scientific Revolutions*, Oxford: Oxford University Press.

Skinner, Q. (1969) 'Meaning and Understanding in the History of Ideas', *History and Theory* 8: 3–53.

Slutsky, E. (1915) 'On the Theory of the Budget of the Consumer', trans. in W.J. Baumol and S.M. Goldfeld (eds) (1968) *Precursors in Mathematical Economics*, London: LSE Reprints #19.

Smith, A. (1776) *An Inquiry into the Nature and Causes of the Wealth of Nations*, Cannan edn (1961), London: Methuen.

Solow, R. (1954) 'The Survival of Mathematical Economics', *The Review of Economics and Statistics* 36: 372–4.

Spring. D. (1961) 'The Clapham Sect: Some Social and Political Aspects', *Victorian Studies* 5: 35–48.

Sraffa, P. (1960) *Production of Commodities by Means of Commodities: Prelude to a Critique of Economic Theory*, Cambridge: Cambridge University Press.

Steedman, I. (1979) *Trade Amongst Growing Economies*, Cambridge: Cambridge University Press.

—— (1984) 'Natural Prices, Differential Profit Rates and the Classical Competitive Process', *Manchester School* 52: 123–40.

Stegmueller, W., Balzer, W. and Spohn, W. (1982) *Philosophy of Economics*, Berlin: Springer.

Steiner, P. (1957) 'Peak Loads and Efficient Pricing', *Quarterly Journal of Economics* 71: 585–610.

Stigler, G. (1955) 'Mathematics in Economics: Further Comment', *The Review of Economics and Statistics* 37: 299–300.

—— (1965) *Essays in the History of Economics*, Chicago: University of Chicago Press.

—— (1983) 'Nobel Lecture: The Process and Progress of Economies', *Journal of Political Economy* 91: 529–45.

Stigler, S.M. (1980) 'Stigler's Law of Eponymy', *Transactions of the New York Academy of Sciences*, 2nd series, 39: 147–58.

Stockman, A.C. (1980) 'A Theory of Exchange Rate Determination', *Journal of Political Economy* 88: 673–98.

—— (1988) 'On the Roles of International Financial Markets and their Relevance for Economic Policy', *Journal of Money, Credit and Banking* 20: 531–49.

—— and Svensson, L.E.O. (1987) 'Capital Flows, Investment and Exchange Rates', *Journal of Monetary Economics* 19: 171–201.

Svensson, L.E.O. (1985) 'Currency Prices, Terms of Trade and Interest Rates: A General Equilibrium Asset-Pricing Cash-in-Advance Approach', *Journal of International Economics* 18: 17–41.

—— (1988) 'Trade in Risky Assets', *American Economic Review* 78: 375–94.

—— (1989) 'Trade in Nominal Assets: Monetary Policy and Price Level and Exchange Rate Risk', *Journal of International Economics* 26: 1–28.

Takayama, A. (1985) *Mathematical Economics* (2nd edn), Cambridge: Cambridge University Press.

Taussig, F.W. (1927) *International Trade*, New York: Macmillan.

Teigen, R.L. (1965) 'The Demand for and Supply of Money', in W.L. Smith and R.L. Teigen (eds) *Readings in Money, National Income and Stabilization*, Homewood, Illinois: Richard D. Irwin.

Thompson, E.P. (1963) *The Making of the English Working Class*, Harmondsworth: Penguin.

Tiles, M. (1984) *Bachelard: Science and Objectivity*, Cambridge: Cambridge University Press.

Tinbergen, J. (1954) 'The Functions of Mathematical Treatment', *The Review of Economics and Statistics* 36: 365–9.

van Wijnbergen, S. (1987) 'Government Deficits, Private Investment and the Current Account: An Intertemporal Disequilibrium Analysis', *Economic Journal* 97: 596–615.

Vickrey, W.S. (1973) 'Risk, Utility, and Social Policy', in E.S. Phelps (ed.) *Economic Justice*, Harmondsworth: Penguin.

Viner, J. (1937) *Studies in the Theory of International Trade*, New York: Harper.

Walras, L. (1874) *Elements of Pure Economics*, trans. W. Jaffe (1954), London: George Allen and Unwin.

Watkins, J.W.N. (1953) 'Ideal Types and Historical Explanation', in H. Feigl and M. Brodbeck (eds) *Readings in the Philosophy of Science*, New York: Appleton–Century–Crofts.

Webb, L.R. (1970) 'The Role of International Capital Movements in Trade and

Growth: The Fisherian Approach', in I.A. McDougall and R.H. Snape (eds) *Studies in International Economics*, Amsterdam: North Holland.

Weintraub, E.R. (1979) *Microfoundations: The Compatibility of Microeconomics and Macroeconomics*, Cambridge: Cambridge University Press.

—— (1985) *General Equilibrium Analysis: Studies in Appraisal*, Cambridge: Cambridge University Press.

—— (2002) *How Economics became a Mathematical Science*, Durham: Duke University Press.

West, E.G. (1983) 'Marx's Hypotheses on the Length of the Working Day', *Journal of Political Economy* 91: 266–81.

Whitaker, J.K. (1975) 'John Stuart Mill's Methodology', *Journal of Political Economy* 83: 1033–50.

—— (1982) 'A Neglected Classic in the Theory of Distribution', *Journal of Political Economy* 90: 333–55.

White, L.H. (1984) *Free Banking in Britain: Theory, Experience, and Debate, 1800–1845*, Cambridge: Cambridge University Press.

Wieser, F.V. (1927) *Social Economics*, New York: Adelphi, reprinted (1967) New York: August M. Kelley, originally published (1914) as *Theoriesder gesellschaftlichen Wirtschaft Tubingen*.

Williamson, O. (1966) 'Peak Load Pricing and Optimal Capacity under Indivisibility Constraints', *American Economic Review* 56: 810–27.

Wilson, E. (1955) 'Mathematics in Economics: Further Comment', *The Review of Economics and Statistics* 37: 297–8.

Wittmann, W. (1967) 'Die extremale wirtschaft Robert Remak – ein vorlaufer der aktivitatsanalyse', *Jahrbucher fur Nationalokonomie und Statistik* 180: 397–404.

Wong, S. (1978) *The Foundations of Paul Samuelson's Revealed Preference Theory*, London: Routledge and Kegan Paul.

Young, W., Leeson, R. and Darity, W. (2004) *Economics, Economists, and Expectations: Microfoundations to Macroapplications*, London: Routledge.

Zahar, E. (1976) 'Why did Einstein's Research Programme Supersede Lorentz's', in C. Howson (ed.) *Method and Appraisal in the Physical Sciences: The Critical Background to Science, 1850–1900*, Cambridge: Cambridge University Press.

Zylberberg, A. (1987) 'The First French Disciples of Leon Walras', paper presented at the annual meeting of the History of Economics Society.

# Index

affinity theory 17
Alesina, A. 22
Allais, Maurice 23, 25
Anderson, R.K. 124
Angell, James W. 81, 139n
Arrow, K. xv, 18
Arrow–Debreu model 43, 79
Ault, R.E. 24
Aupetit, A. 26
Austrian business cycle theory 110
Austrian capital theory 80
Austrian interest theory 83
Austrian school 83

Bachelard, G. xvi, 11, 13, 29–30
Backus, D. 59
balance of payments: adjustment
    mechanism x, 39; intertemporal
    approach 77–8; monetary approach
    xii, 3, 4–5, 18; 'new' approach 2–3;
    older theories 132
balance of payments equilibrium 12,
    42–3, 72, 80–1
Baldwin, R.E. 71
Baldwin envelope 56
Bank of England 87
bank rate policy 87
Barber, W.J. 9
Bardhan, P. 71
Barkai, H. 6
Barnes, Barry 35, 141n
Barone, E. 24
Barro, R. 22
basic vision 46–7, 73
'bastard' Keynesian paradigm 79
Bazdarich, M.J. 81
Bensusan-Butt, D. 23
Bentham, Jeremy 37
Bernanke, B. 26

Berg, M. 6
Bing, F. 23
Blake, William 3
Blaug, M. xiv, 139n, 140n
Bliss, C. 79
Bloor, David 35
Bohm-Bawerk, Eugen von 88
Boland, L.A. 32
Bordo, M. 139n
borrowing: international ix–x
Bretton Woods agreement 111
Brown, Harry Gunnison 88–9
Bruno, M. 55, 74
Buchanan, J.M. 22
business cycle theory 100, 102, 108, 109,
    110
Bye, R.T. 24

Cairnes, J.E. 78, 80–1, 82
capital accumulation: theory of 79
capital movements x–xi, 103–4, 135
cardinal utility 18
cash in advance approach 60, 61–70,
    114, 117, 144n
central banks 87
Chamberlin, Edwin H. 26
Champernowne, D. 23
Chipman, J. 24
Clapham, J.H. 32
Clapham Sect 141n
Clark, J.B. 23
Classical Economics 36
classical economists 4
classical models: competitive process 18
classical theories of value 18
classical unemployment 120–1, 126
Coats, A.W. 35, 141n
Cohen, B. 14
commodities: Mosak's theory 121–2

comparative advantage 51–2, 74
competitive process: classical models 18
conceptual problems 32–3, 34
consumer behaviour: Mosak's theory 117–20
consumption augmenting motive 86
consumption function 33, 45, 46
consumption smoothing motive 102–3, 145n
conventialism 32
Cooter, R. 18
'counterfactual' methods: New Economic History 7
Cournot, A. 26
Cowen, T. 22
credit market 145n
Croce, B. 9–10
Cunliffe Committee Report 87
currency xi
Currency School 4
currency system 4
current account balance 3, 5, 12, 51, 54–5, 72, 98, 123
current account deficits 111

Debreu, G. xiv, xv–xvi, 83
demand theory: Hicks–Allen 24
Descartes 34
devaluation 108–9
discount rates 87
discretionary policy 4
Dixit, A.K. 124
doctrines: as a term 15
dollars xi
Dornbusch, R. 47, 127
Dow, S. 18
'dynamic equilibrium' 110–12, 113
dynamic general equilibrium literature 144n
'dynamic temporary equilibrium' theory 113, 124
dynamic trade theory 81

economics: history of xi, 1; as social mathematics xiv
economic theory: structure of 43–4
economic thought: history of 7, 13; study of 1
Edgeworth box 55
education 19–20
Ekeland, R.B. 24
Ellis, H.S. 95, 96, 99
Elster, J. 138n
empirical problems 32, 135

employment: full 128–9; government intervention 4
equilibrium: concept of 5
equilibrium business cycle theory 138n
evolutionary theory of the firm 7
*ex ante/ex post* method 90
exchange rate effects 47, 60, 133
exchange rate equivalence 70–1
exchange rate regimes 144n
exchange rate theory 39, 42
exegesis: of economic thought 6–9
explanation: of economic thought 7
explanatory ideal conditions 43, 75

factor-price equalization 74
Fama, E.F. 22–3, 145n
Feltenstein, A. 135
Fetter, Frank A. 5–6, 83–9, 133, 136
Fetter, F.W. 4, 141n
Feyerabend, P.K. 8, 14, 21
'field' condition 43
finance constraint 23
financial capital movements 135
firms: Mosak's theory 120
Fischer, S. 142n
Fisher, I. 41, 45, 83
Fisherian interest theory 83
Fisherian model 49–52, 55, 73, 74, 134
Flanders, M.J. 3, 41
Fleck, Ludwig xvi, 11, 36, 37
Fogel, R. 138n
foreign debt: rationality of x
foreign investment ix–x
foreign trade multiplier 131
Fraser, H.F. 109–10
Free Banking 22
free banking system 145n
Frenkel, J.A. 4, 41, 42, 47, 48, 50, 74, 86, 127
Friedman, Milton 45
Fulton, G. 43, 47

Gale, D. 145n
*geisgeschichte* 8
general equilibrium model 130
*General Equilibrium Theory and International Trade* 12, 112
General Theory 41
Gervaise, Isaac xi
Gilmour, R. 141n
gold standard 87, 101, 105, 109
Goodwin, C.D. 16, 27
Gordon, B.J. 141n
Gordon, H.S. 141n

Gossen, H.H. 24
government intervention 4, 5, 106
government role: Mosak's theory
   116–17
'The Gradgrind School' 141n
Grandmont, J.-M. 118, 119, 132, 145n
Greenwood, J. 144n
growing economies 110
guiding assumptions 17, 28, 32, 38

Haberler, G. 24
Habermas, Jurgen 138n
Hacking, Ian 14, 140n
Hahn, F. 18
Hamada, K. 71
Hamminga, B. 40, 145n
Hausman, D. 139n
Hawking, Stephen xi
Hayek, F.A. 5, 6, 26, 79, 80, 93–106,
   133, 135
Hecksher–Ohlin theory 24, 130
Hegel, F. 6
Helferich, Karl 9
Helpman, E. 39, 48, 60, 74, 144n
Helpman's cash in advance model
   60–70, 105
Henderson, J.M. 144n, 145n
Hesse, Mary B. 14
Hicks, J.R. 18, 26, 30, 79, 94, 112, 113,
   115, 130, 131–2, 136, 144–5n, 144n
Hicks–Allen: demand theory 24
Hicksian temporary equilibrium theory
   20, 80, 112, 113, 116, 123, 131, 132
Hick's stability conditions 115
Hilton, B. 141n
historical reconstructions 8
'historical turn': philosophy of science 14
history: of economics xi, 1; theses 27–38
Hobson, J.A. 23
Hodgson, G. 138n
Hollis, M. 32
Holton, Gerald 14
household production: theory of 18
human capital: theory of 18
Hume, David xi
Huskisson, William 36, 141n
Hutchison, T.W. 19, 23, 82
hypothetico–deductive method 34

ideal conditions 43
ideas: as a term 139n
imperfect competition xvii
imperfect competition doctrines 26
incommensurability: of theories 21–2

inductive method 34
infinite-horizon models 48, 71
intellectual history 8–9
interest rates 83, 87
international borrowing ix, 50, 86
international capital markets 77–8
international capital mobility 89
international capital movements x–xi
*International Capital Movements* 89
international economy models:
   characteristics 41–2
'International Finance' (New Palgrave
   entry) 5
international lending 81
international macroeconomics 39
international monetary theory 41–3, 48,
   74, 77–8, 113, 116
international payments problems 39
international trade theory 24
*Interregional and International Trade* 130
intertemporal equilibrium 79, 93, 95,
   100, 109, 132
intertemporal general equilibrium
   approach: advantages 39; Austrian
   capital theory 80; balance of
   payments 72; Baldwin 71; basic vision
   73; and Feltenstein 135; and Fetter
   84–5, 88; framework 49; and Hayek
   104, 112; Lucas and Stokey 84;
   methodology 41, 72; presuppositions
   47, 48; and received theory 41–3;
   structuralist approach 40, 43–5; tools
   of 74; *Value and Capital* 79
intertemporal international economics:
   development ix; new and old theories
   132–4
*Intertemporal Price Equilibrium and
   Movements in the Value of Money* 93
intertemporal theory: origins of 79–80
intertemporal trade 39–40, 56
intertemporal trade theory: basic vision
   46–7, 73; characteristics of 73–6;
   Fetter 85; Fisherian model 49–52, 55,
   73; monetary models 59–71, 75;
   overview 45–6; presuppositions 47–8,
   73–4; structuralist approach 43–4;
   trade theoretic approach 55–9, 74;
   two-period models 48–55
Iversen, Carl 6, 77, 89–93, 133

Jevons, W.S. 24, 25, 30, 34–5
Johannsen, N. 23, 27
Johnson, H.G. 4, 41
Johnson, W.E. 24

Kahn, R.F. 27
Kalecki, M. 22
Kehoe, P. 59
Kenen, P.B. 5, 135
Keynes, John Maynard x, 23, 25, 35, 39, 41
Keynesian multiplier 23
Keynesian unemployment 120
Kiker, B.F. 18
Koopmans, T. 18
Kotter, R. 40
Krohn, C.D. 145n
Kroszner, R. 22
Krueger, A. 41
Kuhn, T. 10, 14, 16, 19, 21, 35
Kuhnian losses 18–20
Kunin, L. 19
Kyun, K. 138n, 141n

labour market 120
Lachmann, L. 110–12
Lakatos, I. 8, 14, 15, 27–9, 40, 43, 47
Lakatosian approach 27–9
Lakatos' research programmes 17
Lange, Oscar 6, 113, 119, 128–9, 132, 133, 136, 144n
language barrier argument 25
Laudan, L. xvi, 7, 11, 14, 15, 16, 17, 19, 30–5, 134
Lavoisier's affinity theory 17
law of one price 121
Law of Supply and Demand 25
Leijonhufuud, Axel 8
Leontief, W. 55, 71
Leontief Fisher diagrams 55, 71
Lerner, A.P. 24
loanable funds theory 23
Lucas, R. 17–18, 39, 84, 142n

McCloskey, D.N. 14, 21
McCulloch, J.R. 36
McKenzie, Lionel xv, 24
macroeconomics: recurring theories 22–3
Malinvaud, E. 23, 79, 83
Mangoldt, Hans von 24
Mareet, Jane 37
Marion, N.P. 90
Marschak, J. 144n
Marshall, Alfred 79
Marshall–Lerner conditions 70, 74
Martineau, Harriet 37
Marxism 35
mathematics: use in economics xiii–xiv, 26–7, 33

Mays, W. 35
Meade technique 55, 71
mechanism of adjustment 4
Menger, Karl 20, 24, 26, 88
methodological individualism 5
*Methodology of Scientific Research Programmes* 27
microtheories: recurring 24
Milgate, M. 79, 93
Mill, James 36
Mill, J.S. 1, 24–5, 35, 80
Miller, Norman 55, 71, 134
Mitchell, Wesley C. 18, 23, 83
models: concept of 20; overlapping generations 23; of scientific change 16; Fisherian model; monetary models; Mundell-Fleming model; Nelson–Winter model; Stockman and Svensson's model; two-period models; *see also* Arrow–Debreu model
modern theory 12
Modigliani, F. 131, 135, 136
monetary approach: balance of payments xii, 3, 4–5, 18; resource allocation effects 39
monetary models: intertemporal trade theory 59–71, 73, 75
*Monetary Nationalism and International Stability* 93, 96, 97, 100–6
monetary shocks 96–7, 99–101
monetary theory: development xvi
money illusion 96, 100, 105, 107, 109, 132, 135
Mosak, Jacob x, 6, 12, 78, 112–27, 129–32, 132, 133, 135, 136
Mosak's theory 115–27
Mundell–Fleming model xvii, 5, 39, 70–1, 105
Mussa, M.L. 42
Myrdal, G. 25, 90

Neary, J.P. 133
Negishi, T. 23
Neisser, H. 114, 130–1, 135, 136
Nell, E.J. 32
Nelson–Winter model 7
neoclassical economics 32, 73
'Neo-Keynsian' era 4
neutral money 70, 94–5, 100, 104, 105, 106–7, 108, 133
New Classical economics 17–18
New Economic History 7
new intertemporal international macroeconomics 2–5

Newman, P. 23
*New Palgrave* 5, 138n
new philosophy of science 14
New View 22–3
Nickles, T. 15
noisy price signals 142n
noncompeting groups 25, 81
Non-Substitution theorem 18
Norhaus, W.D. 22
Norman, V. 124
Nurske, Ragnar 6, 113

Oakeshott, M. 10
Obstfeld, M. xvii, 42, 55, 60, 77–8, 84, 85
O'Driscoll, G.P. 85
Ohlin, B. 130
oligopoly 26
optimization over time 144n
overlapping generations: model of 23

Palmer, Horsley 9
paradigms 10, 16–20, 26
Patinkin, D. 8, 20
peak load pricing 24
Peel's Act 4
perfect competition 18, 30
perfect foresight 3, 42, 63, 87, 94, 99–100, 132, 133, 142n
permanent disturbances 52–4
Persson, T. 42, 48, 60, 105, 106, 132, 133
Petersen, Julius 23
Philips Curve 33
philosophy of science: 'historical turn' 14; as a phrase 15; 'received view' 14
Pigou, A.C. 22, 91
Place, Francis 36
political business cycle 22
Political Economy Club 36
Popper, K. 5, 8, 40
Porter, Ted xiii
Port-Royallogicians 34
positive monetary effect 128
precursor: idea of xiii
presuppositions: intertemporal trade theory 47–8, 73–4; of thought style 43
price expectations 121
price flexibility 128–9
*Price Flexibility and Full Employment* 113, 128
*Prices and Production* 93, 95, 96
price-specie mechanism xi
*Principles of Political Economy* 80–1
problem solving effectiveness 31–3, 134–5

*Progress and its Problems* 6–7
progressive mathematization argument 26–7
*Pure Theory of Capital* 80

Quandt, R.E. 144n, 145n

Rappaport, P. 18
rate of time preference 84
rational expectations 100, 133, 141n
rational reconstructions 8, 11
rationing schemes 116
Razin, A. 3, 39, 47, 48, 50, 55, 59, 60, 74, 86, 127, 144n
real shocks 96–7, 100–1, 102
real trade theory 44, 55–9
received approach: international monetary theory 41–3
received research tradition 39–40
'received view': philosophy of science 14
recurrence: of doctrines 10–11, 132; examples xiii–xiv; explanation xi–xii, 134–6; phenomenon 1–2, 13–15; problem 9–11; of theories 20–1, 38
recurring microtheories 24
recurring theories: definition of 20–1; hypotheses for 38
reductionist research programme 3–4
Reid, Margaret 18
Reinert, E. xiii
Remak, Robert 23, 25
Remenyi, J. 16
repressed inflation 124
research practice 75–6
research programmes: Lakatos' 17
research traditions 33–5, 39–40
Reynaud, Jean Pierre 95, 106–9, 132, 133, 135
Reynaud, Pierre-Loius 6
'rhetoric' 14
Ricardian equivalence proposition 22
Ricardo, D. 6, 35, 36, 41
Robbins, Lionel 109–10, 141n
Robertson, D.H. 23, 30
Robinson, Joan 4, 26, 30, 32, 79
Rodriguez, C. 48
Rogoff, K. xvii
Rorty, Richard 7–8
Rothbard, M.N. 85
'roundaboutness' 91–2
Rymes, T. 20

Sachs, J.D. 49, 51
Samuelson, P.A. 18, 23, 130, 136, 144n

Schabas, Margaret 140n
Schlesinger, Karl 26
Schumpeter, J.A. xvi, 1, 10, 26, 37–8, 43, 78, 81–2
scientific change: model of 27–9
scientific explanation: as a term 43
scientific revolutions 18–19
Senior, N.W. 36
Shackle, G.L.S. 30
Shapere, D. 14, 21
Simon, Henry 139n
Skinner, Quentin 8
Slutsky, E. 24
Smith, Adam 79
*Social Economics* 82
sociology of knowledge 35–8
special conditions 43–4
Sprague, Oliver 9
Sraffa, P. 23
Sraffa version: price system 23; theory of value (Ricardo) 18
stability analysis 114
Stegmueller, Wolfgang 11, 14, 40
Steiner, P. 24
Stigler, G. xiv, 24–5
Stigler's Law of Eponymy 13
Stiglitz, J. 133
Stockman, A.C. 39, 42, 60, 106, 138n
Stockman and Svensson's model 142n
Stokey, N.L. 84
Stolper–Samuelson theorem 44, 74
Strong Programme 35–6, 38
structuralist approach 11–12, 40, 43–5
Svensson, L.E.O. 42, 55, 59, 90, 132, 144n, 145n

Tabellini, G. 22
Takayama, A. 124
Taussig, Frank ix, 90, 91
temporary disturbances 52–4
temporary equilibrium method 94, 112, 113, 116, 123, 127, 130, 131, 132–3
'textbook history' 19
theories: definition 20; recurring 20–1
theory of capital accumulation 79
theory of general economic equilibrium: reformulation xv
theory of household production 18
theory of human capital 18
theory of time valuation 83, 85
theory transition 27
Thompson, E.P. 141n
Thornton, Henry 141n
Thought Collective 36, 37

Thought Style 36, 37–8
thought styles 43
time periods: Mosak's theory 122
time preference motive 84, 86, 91–2, 133–4
time-valuation theory 83, 85
Tobin effect 142n
trade: and stability 128–9
trade theoretic approach 55–9, 71, 73, 74, 113
traditional research 39–40, 78
transaction costs 114
transfer problem criteria 74
two-period models: intertemporal trade theory 48–55, 92–3

unemployment x, 120, 128–9
unit elastic expectations 114
unity: of theories xiv, 15
USA (United States of America): outflow of resources x–xi
utility: definition of 22

*Value and Capital* 18, 79, 112, 114, 131
Vickrey, W.S. 22
Viner, J. 5, 24, 41
vision 37–8, 43

wages rates 120
Wald, A. xv
Wallace, N. 23
Walras, L. 24, 25, 26, 79
Walrasian concept of equilibrium 93
Walrasian theory xiv–xv, 60, 113
Walras' Law 25
war expenditure 86
Watkins, J.W.N. 138n
Weaver, F. 19
Webb, L.R. 49, 71
Weintraub, Roy xiii, 131, 144n
welfare analysis 39
Whewell, William 32–3
Whitaker, John 23
White, L.H. 22
Wicksell, J.G.K. 79
Wieser, F. von 80, 81–3
Williamson, O. 24
Wittman, W. 23
world economy 96–9, 115
Wulff, Julius 23

Young, W. 17, 94

Zahar, E. 43, 47